Applied Psy

Applied Psychology

K.C. Shukla
Tara Chand

Commonwealth

Applied Psychology

Edition : 2026

ISBN 81-7169-904-9

Published by :

COMMONWEALTH PUBLISHERS
4831/24, Prahlad Street,
Ansari Road, Darya Ganj,
New Delhi - 110002
Ph. : 23275511, 23257835
Fax : 91- 011- 23257835
e-mail : commonwealthbooks@gmail.com

Typesetting by :

Rishu Computers
Delhi

Printed at :
Roshan Offset Printers
Delhi

PREFACE

Applied psychology is the functional side of the discipline of psychology. The knowledge gained in the field of psychology as to how people learn and how human behaviour can be modified is applied to practical side of life in the classroom, in the factory and in the army.

The first decade of the twentieth century marked the culmination of a shift in the subject-matter of psychology from mind to behaviour. The shift was not sudden nor was it solely the product of the Behaviourist movement. The latter movement was rather the climax to changes which began during the last two decades of the nineteenth century. Behaviour manifestations of mind had become more and more the objects of study until they acquired an interest status of their own and finally mind or mental reactions came to be treated as instances of behaviour. One of the remarkable consequences of this shift of emphasis and of the broadening of the concept of behaviour has been that the behaviour of people the world over and not some highly abstract behaviour in the laboratory became the subject-matter of psychology.

The author is grateful to American psychological association for its various research findings in this area which have been extensively utilized in this book.

K.C. Shukla
Tara Chand

CONTENTS

1
THE SUBJECT OF APPLIED PSYCHOLOGY

Psychology and Everyday Life

The first decade of the twentieth century marked the culmination of a shift in the subject-matter of psychology from mind to behaviour. The shift was not sudden nor was it solely the product of the Behaviourist movement. The latter movement was rather the climax to changes which began during the last two decades of the nineteenth century. Behaviour manifestations of mind had become more and more the objects of study until they acquired an interest status of their own and finally mind or mental reactions came to be treated as instances of behaviour. One of the remarkable consequences of this shift of emphasis and of the broadening of the concept of behaviour has been that the behaviour of people the world over and not some highly abstract behaviour in the laboratory became the subject-matter of psychology.

This evolution in the concepts of psychology was taking place against an historical background in which social changes were occurring at a terrifying pace. The first third of the present century is thus characterised in *Recent Social Trends in the United States* (*510, xi*):

> The first third of the twentieth century has been filled with epoch-making events and crowded with problems of great variety and complexity. The World War, the inflation and deflation of agriculture and business, our emergence as a creditor nation, the spectacular increase in efficiency and productivity and the tragic spread of unemployment and business distress, the experiment of prohibition,

> birth control, race riots, stoppage of immigration, women's suffrages, the struggles of the Progressive and Farm Labour parites, governmental corruption, crime and racketeering, the sprawl of great cities, the decadence of rural government, the birth of the League of Nations, the expansion of education, the rise and weakeninng of organised labour, the growth of spectacular fortunes, the advance of medical science, the emphasis on sports and recreation, the renewed interest in child welfare—these are a few of the many happenings, which have marked one of the most eventful periods of our history.

It should not be surprising that the problems of our rapidly changing social and economic structures have been so generally recognised to be psychological problems. The psychological implications in the following questions may be readily seen (*234*):

1. To what extent does the success of a democracy depend upon the distribution of intelligence among its citizens and to what extent is this intelligence distribution modifiable through education ?
2. Are certain races of man inherently superior to others in intelligence ?
3. Is war the consequence of deeply rooted human instincts and therefore inevitable ?
4. Must a successful society depend for its motivation upon native aggression and competitive tendencies within individuals ?
5. Are criminals born so or are they the products of unfortunate training ? If the latter, what are the factors that contribute to the making of a criminal career ?
6. What are the problems that are peculiar to the adjustments in old age ?
7. What can be done to soften the effects of technological changes upon health and satisfaction ?

Kelley (*336*), in analysing the problems of democracy, asks whether it is possible for a democracy to preserve such individual values and benefits that the citizen will fight and sacrifice to keep them.

> The writer believes that it is possible, and that an essential key to its accomplishment is through self-expression so rich as to be utterly desirable to the individual and so efficient as to be completely

> contributive to state welfare.... The democratic problem that we set is so to utilize the talents of our differentially endowed and trained citizens as to maximize their satisfactions and their social productivity. That is to say, we seek a mode of individual functioning which gives the dual return of satisfaction and welfare to the individual and goods and attitudes of value to society.

In this statement of the key to a successful democracy one finds the essence of applied psychology, namely *the recognition of individual differences in endowment and in training, and the need for the adjustment of each individual in life so as to furnish to him the maximum of satisfaction and to society the maximum of desirable goods.* The practical problem of adjustment arises out of the fact of individual differences, since it is obvious that if all people were alike, adjusting the one and only type would be a simple matter indeed.

One important aspect of adjustment that is not explicitly indicated in the statement of Kelley it that is implies a fitting of the environment to the individual as well as of the individual to the environment.

Psychology and Psychotechnology

The question has frequently been raised whether applied psychology is really sufficiently different from pure psychology to warrant giving it an independent status. Certainly it is not just another system of psychology to be added to the list of Structural, Dynamic, Behaviour, Gestalt, and others. It cannot be a systematically organised body of material, but at any moment will consist of the sum total of applications that have been made, are being made, or that can be made. For that reason one might better speak of Applications of Psychology rather than of Applied Psychology for that designation would be less misleading in its implications.

Applied psychology can be characterised as a technology resting upon the science of psychology. Münsterberg (*444*), in his *Psychotechnik*, made a distinction between theoretical psychology, applied psychology, and psychotechnics. The first is what is known as pure or general psychology. The second consists in the explanation by psychological laws of past events and the facts of other sciences. For example, the explanation of certain historical movements or historical characters by appeal to psychology, and the application of the laws of psychology to the physics of colour would be called applied psychology. Likewise, the application of the laws of mathematics to astronomy or the laws of chemistry to physiology would be applied science. Technics, on the other hand, would be represented by the application of the laws of mathematics to the construction of electrical machines for lighting purposes, or by the application of the laws of chemistry to the making of dyestuffs or medicines. In a similar manner Münsterberg would define psychotechnics as the application of psychology to the solution of practical problems.

Such a distinction is a limited one, since every scientific discovery has the possibility of leading to some practical application, so that sooner or later it will determine a future course of events for practical life. The scientific construction of medicines demands that the science of chemistry shall first have been applied to physiological processes. When this has been done, in a given concrete situation, examination will show what is lacking in the human organism, or what mechanism is functioning improperly, and medicines may be administered accordingly. Likewise, the proper blending of colour dyes in the dyeing and printing of cloth and in the construction of aesthetic colour patterns requires that the psychological laws of colour contrast shall first have been applied to the physics of light mixture and the chemistry of dyes. Applied psychology and psychotechnics thus become coextensive and even these two differ from psychology proper largely in the immediacy or remoteness of applicability.

More recently Gundlach (*233*) made somewhat the same distinction between psychology and psychotechnology. He says that the scientific man is typically not concerned with particular workaday problems but with general principles and knowledge. He is disinterested and impersonal, and is willing to follow the data of his problem no matter where they may lead. His aim is to describe and understand nature. The technologist, on the other hand, has a specific interest in the outcome. His problem is to get certain results such as building a bridge or curing a patient. He must not be distracted into following interesting leads as they arise because such diversions might interfere with the attainment of his practical ends.

Gundlach introduces an additional note into the concept of a technology by placing upon it a certain ethical responsibility for the goodness of the recommendations that it makes. It is not enough for the technologist to say that *if you want to build a bridge* this is the way to do it, but he should consider the advisability of building it at all. Such ethical responsibility has always been inherent in the profession of medicine. It is clearly expressed in the Hippocratic oath administered to every graduate in medicine. It is growing in the profession of engineering as indicated by the introduction of Philosophy, Social Science, and humanistic subjects into the engineering curriculum with the intention that they shall become the foundation for professional ideals and professional ethics (*308*). It is equally important that the psychotechnologist should build upon such a sound professional basis and there is evidence that he is doing so. The functioning of psychotechnology would then be, according to Gundlach, "to determine the conditions of living necessary for a complete and satisfactory life, and to elaborate the methods for such attainment."

To the beginning student of psychology, the two fields of pure and applied psychology are not sharply distinguished. This is due in part to the fact that the teacher draws his illustrative materials in pure psychology largely from the researches of the applied psychologist because these are closer to the everyday experiences of the student and are likely to be the more interesting on that account. In the minds of the textbook writers, moreover, the pure and the applied fields are not always sharply distinguished. Thus, William McDougall (*411*), who wold hardly be labelled as an applied psychologist, defined the aim of psychology thus : "To render our knowledge of human nature more exact and more systematic, in order that we may control ourselves more wisely and influence our fellowmen more effectively." The second clause in this statement is a fair expression of the aim of applied psychology.

For the prospective psychotechnologist, there is a very real difference between the two fields. In solving a practical problem it is seldom enough to take from the psychological laboratory either a finding and consider it the answer, or a method and consider that an adequate means for finding an answer. At the least, a high degree of flexibility and ingenuity is required to fit these into the needs of the practical situation. Two simple instances will illustrate the difference. What is the most appropriate colour to use in advertising a certain commodity to be sold to women ? An answer could be obtained immediately from the laboratory data on sex differences in colour preferences, or if such facts were not at hand, one of the stock preference measuring methods could be used under laboratory conditions. A proper applied technique would be to prepare a series of advertisements in different colours or colour combinations and to measure the preferences of a sampling of the prospective consumers of the commodity. The outcome might be identical with that of the laboratory experiment but on the other hand it might be entirely different.

What is the significance of the reaction time of the driver in automobile accidents? One could go to the laboratory records and find the distribution curves for reactions of various sorts, the simple, the discrimination, and the choice reactions. Having decided that the driver employs choice reactions, he could compute what percentage of the distribution curve would have reactions too slow to avoid accidents when the car is travelling at given speeds. Then he could measure the reaction times of drivers under the customary laboratory conditions and classify them into the fit and the unfit. The psychotechnician on the other hand would ask himself whether the process of discriminating among objects on the highway, the process of choosing an appropriate set of motions, and the process of consummating the reaction would have time values similar to those in the laboratory. Not being able to answer this question he would set up a reaction-time road test for his practical purpose (*439*).

The Growth of Applied Psychology

The history of applied psychology may be divided roughly into epochs or stages. One cannot mark off any definite period when it came into existence. In some crude from or other it has probably existed as long as men were able to formulate any laws of the mind, whether these laws were correct or not. But one can mark off four periods more or less clearly up to the present.

1. Long before the time of experimental psychology, persons were accustomed to make use of very vague notions of the workings of the mind in the problems of daily life. The mind was supposed to be subject to the influence of all kinds of outside forces, those of inanimate and animate objects, and consequently people's behaviour was influenced by superstitions and myths. Breaking mirrors, spilling salt, putting up an umbrella in the house, getting married on Friday, being a member of a party of thirteen, and the like were unlucky factors in one's experience, and in fact are still considered so by many persons.

That one cannot work so well when tired as when rested, that the memory of one person is better than that of others, that some persons are stupid and others bright, are notions that were applied to daily life before they were subjected to scientific test in the laboratory.

2. After experimental psychology had developed and a mass of standard experiments had accumulated, there was a tendency to apply these experiments directly to other fields, just as physiological and physical experiments were carried over directly into the psychological laboratory at its beginning. This tendency was perhaps most noticeable in education and medicine. For instance, education took over directly the experiments in memory, imagination, and attention and tried to use them in solving educational problems. In the attempts to measure any form of complex activity, the procedure consisted in applying a large number of the standard laboratory tests to persons of varying ability in the particular activity. Then those tests that were well done by the experts and poorly done by those known to be poor in the work, were considered good tests of that kind of ability. This procedure is still of much value and is used where it has been impossible to analyse a complex form of activity into its elements. In such cases the best that can be done is to proceed in a random fashion in the hope that a few tests will be discovered which will serve as indices of particular ability. The

relationships thus disclosed do not necessarily means that the function tested is a vital part of the process, but for some reason it serves as a symptom, in much the same manner that rose-coloured spots on the skin once served as a symptom in the diagnosis of typhoid fever.

3. In the third period the practical problems themselves are studied and the actual life situations form the material of the experiment. This is the present stage, and might with much justification be considered the beginning of a real applied psychology. In fact, Paterson (*484*), in reviewing its history, says exactly that. He divides the life-cycle of applied psychology into four periods. The first he calls the prenatal period, in which the first sign of life appeared, extending from the last two decades of the nineteenth century until America's entrance in the World War in 1917. The second he calls the birth period, which ended with the Armistice in November 1918. The third be dramatises at the period of childhood and adolescence, which extended through the boom and depression years and closed with 1937, the date of the creation of a national organisation devoted to its interests, The American Association for Applied Psychology. This date, likewise, marks the entrance of applied psychology into its fourth period in which it attained the full stature of adulthood.

This portrayal of the development of applied psychology emphasises its really remarkable growth since 1917, a growth resulting in large measure from the success of the psychological testing programme and the programme of personnel classification in the army. In addition to these specific factors, Paterson (*484*) points out a more pervasive influence:

> We must not leave the topic of Military Psychology without mentioning the fact that psychologists in the Army learned for the first time how to pool their efforts and how to coöperate with physicians, psychiatrists, line officers and practical men of affairs. They discovered that coöperation is not only possible but indispensable for carrying out large-scale operations. It is not surprising, therefore, to note that the post-war development of applied psychology was characterised by the rise of organised psychological service. This trend is so pronounced that we can sketch the history of applied psychology during the past twenty-one years without mentioning individuals at all but simply by mentioning well-known services.

Among such psychological services are those in business and industrial personnel; in education; in child guidance clinics and institutes for child welfare; in federal and state employment offices; in youth and adult guidance clinics; in hospitals; in courts; in federal, state, and local prisons; in advertising agencies and market research bureaus; in federal departments such as the Department of Labour and the Department of Agriculture; and in Federal Bureaus, including the United States Civil Service and the Social Security Board.

One of the most unique of the institutions devoted to applied psychology is the Psychological Corporation, a non-profit institution incorporated in the State of New York, whose objects, as stated in its constitution, are:

> ....the advancement of psychology and the promotion of the useful applications of psychology. It is organised as a business corporation but not for the individual profit of the incorporation, stockholders, or directors, beyond reasonable compensation for services rendered....It will promote the advancement of psychology by research, the more effective organisation of psychological work, and the diffusion of knowledge concerning psychology.

Its board of directors is composed of past presidents of the American Psychological Association, and its officers serve without compensation. It offers service in market research, personnel and employment research, vocational counselling, test construction and distribution, industrial research, and psychological testing of candidates for nurses' training. Its work is done in a central office in New York City coöperating with several hundred psychologists in various parts of the United States. It is the joint publisher and editor of the *Journal of Applied Psychology* in which its researches are frequently reported.

Another unique institution is the American Association for Applied Psychology which was organised in 1937, a professional society devoted to the promotion of work in applied psychology and with a membership of about 600. In addition to the national organisation there are many state and city branches which concern themselves with the more local problems. Of the approximately 3,000 members of the American Psychological Association, from one third to one half are engaged in some form of non-academic work which in most instances would be labelled as applied psychology.

The growth in the applications of psychology is not peculiar to the United State alone. Before the great social upheaval of the 1930 - 1940 decade there were known to be organisations similar to one or the other just described in many foreign countries, notably, England, Germany, France, Switzerland, Spain, Russia, Japan and Australia. The National Institute of Industrial Psychology in England has been outstanding in its contributions to research and service. Its journal, at present called *Occupational Psychology*, is one of the most important sources of material on applied psychology.

Applied Psychology and Individual Differences

The problems of applied psychology are problems of adjustment of individuals and groups of individuals to life situations, whether the adjustment be in the nature of fitting a given individual to a given particular environment or vice versa, or whether it be in the nature of modifying each one to fit the other. The magnitude of this adjustment programme rests upon the fact that individuals differ one from another in every respect in which they have been measured. If all individuals were alike and only their environment varied or could be varied, the adjustment problem could be solved more or less completely by fitting any one individual, as a sample of all others, to the varying environment. But one's common sense observation tells him that people are not all alike, and told him so long before there were any standardised devices for measuring differences. Hull (*297*, 5) reminds the psychologist that Plato in his *Republic* noted that no two persons are born exactly alike, one being suited to one occupation and another to another, and that an attempt should be made to put each person into the niche where he would fit best. Common sense would also suggest that these differences are of a magnitude sufficiently great to demand consideration in dealing with people.

When one passes beyond common-sense observations, it becomes extremely difficult to give acceptable estimates of the degree of the differences (*204*). The most serious obstacle to doing this is the absence of an absolute zero point from which to measure the amount of a trait. Certain anatomical, physiological, and motor functions can be measured in accepted physical units, but this is not the case with most human performances. The absence of such a zero point is particularly disturbing in estimating range of proficiency. Anastasi (*9, 54–55*) has demonstrated the difficulty clearly in supposing the measurement of height with a device where the "working zero" was not absolute zero height but was some arbitrary point such as two feet. Then a six-foot person would measure four feet on this scale, a four-foot person would measure two feet, and the former would appear to be twice as tall as the latter. Actually, he would be only one and one-half times as tall. This and other difficulties have led Anastasi to conclude that in the present stage of mental testing the question of the extent of individual differences in various traits cannot be answered at all.

Answers have been given, nevertheless, and in spite of the errors inherent in them, probably represent fairly well the ranges for different functions. Hull (*297, 36*), for instance, has collected from the literature a set of ratios of best to poorest in a variety of functions. For a group of thirteen scholastic achievement tests, such as reading, writing, arithmetic, and spelling, administered to eighth-grade children, the average ratio of best to poorest is 3.5 to 1. For a group of thirty-four psychological tests administered to ninth-grade children, the average ratio of best to poorest is 5.2 to 1. For a series of nine gainful occupations such as loom operation, shoe-making, and office work the average ratio of best to poorest is 2 to 1. He concludes from these cases that: "Among individuals ordinarily regarded as normal, in the average vocation the most gifted will be between three and four times as capable as the poorest."

Wechsler (685, 50), on the other hand, considers these estimates too high. He chooses as an expression of the range of proficiency the ratio of the 999th to the second individual in a thousand, and after taking certain precautions as to homogeneity of populations and the elimination of the obviously abnormal deviates, he finds that the majority of the total range ratios fall within the limits of 1.3 to 1 and 2.5 to 1. The more strictly mental functions listed by him such as the perceptual and intellectual abilities, show the largest range of all, namely between 2.30 to 1 and 2.85 to 1. His general estimate would be a range of about 2 to 1. Even this small figure would fully justify the consideration of individual differences as factors in successful performance and in personal satisfaction. A more recent compilation by Thorndike *(626, 257-264)* of the range within each of a great variety of human traits rightly emphasises the differences in range among the traits, but does not lessen the significance to be attached to the differences.

In addition to the range of proficiency among individuals with respect to any one task, there needs to be considered the range of abilities within any one person. Adequate adjustment would mean the opportunity to express oneself in that function which is possessed to the maximal degree. The common-sense view would be that a person is not uniformly endowed in all respects but that he can do some things distinctly better than others. Such observations do not in any sense imply the notion of compensatory development, by which a person low in one respect will be necessarily high in others.

The calculation of the range of capacities within the individual is subject to all the difficulties previously mentioned, with the added one that the measures of the many abilities would have to be made comparable one with another. Various techniques have been devised for this purpose, Hull, after taking the many complicating factors into account, ventures the estimate that trait differences within the individual average approximately 80 per cent as great as individual differences, which would make the average range between best and the poorest ability from about 2.5 or 3 to 1.

There is still another type of variation which plays a part in adjustment, namely the variation within an individual in any given ability at different times and under different circumstances. A question might be stated thus; How uniform is a person's performance from time to time? Any individual knows that level of achievement varies considerably with changes in health, with intoxication, with fatigue, with practice, with changes in incentive to performance, with the presence or absence of distractions, and under many other circumstances. When adequate adjustment is the goal such factors as these may not be excluded from the picture. Influences such as those just mentioned might well reduce performance from a high level to zero so that there is little sense in attempting to make estimates of their effects. But it is pertinent to mention the findings of Hollingworth (*268, 194–195*) concerning the extent of variation within an individual when all such conditions as are listed above are carefully controlled and when the effects of practice have been eliminated by long training. According to him:

> The magnitude of the deviations in the performance of an individual need not be expected to be so great as that for a group of subjects chosen entirely at random. But there is no present reason, for supposing that even this magnitude will not closely resemble that in the case of a group of individuals of the same general class.

And Further

> Individuals seem to very from their own average in quite the same way that they differ from the central tendency of their group. The degree to which this is the case may vary with the nature of the process.

Causes of Individual Differences

One cannot accept the existence of Individual differences and note their magnitude without inquiring as to their causes. Are they inevitable in the make-up of the human population or could they be changed in magnitude or eliminated entirely if that should seem to be desirable? This is not a merely academic question. To be sure, the present generation is what it is and little or nothing can be done about the differences that exist among its members except to make adjustments for them. But if the magnitude of human abilities is only a matter of adequate control, a few generations would be enough to modify them into a more satisfactory pattern Unfortunately the causes of individual differences cannot yet be entirely unraveled. There is insufficient basis for saying that they are due solely to the native endowment of the individual or that they are due solely to environmental influences, although proponents could be found for either point of view. Somewhere between these extremes the answer will be found. Just now controversy is most acute concerning the causes of differences in intelligence and the crucial experiment to settle the question has not yet been devised. It is the old nature-nurture controversy. If settled once and for all for intelligence the way will be open for a more speedy attack upon other differences which are equally great and equally important in successful living.

The Recognition of Individual Differences

One further question has to do with the extent to which such differences are recognised and allowed for in modern society. To the student of psychology, the existence of the differences is so obvious and the need to take them into account so equally obvious that he may be inclined to think that every one else is alive to their significance. Although differences in the make-up of people were clearly recognised by Plato and Aristotle, in succeeding centuries they were for one reason or another ignored and only came to have an influence upon practical life in the latter part of the eighteenth and the beginning of the nineteenth centuries, with the educational theories of Rousseau, Froebel, and others. In the latter part of the nineteenth century Francis Galton, aroused by Charles Darwin's studies of physical differences, sought for and found individual differences in mental functions. Since that time the continuing development of mental tests in the greatest variety has shown individual differences to exist in every measured function.

In spite of such evidence that all people are not alike, there was the inevitable lag of twenty-five to fifty years in the acceptance of this fact into the thinking and action of everyday life. The slogan that all men are born free and equal was taken literally to mean that all people are fundamentally alike, and overshadowed the findings of the scientific laboratories to the contrary. With the twentieth century, progressive educators began to apply the concept of individuality in the teaching process and the progressive efficiency engineers made a start toward introducing the same concept into business and industry. In the more enlightened public schools the influence of this movement may be seen in the introduction of technical and vocational programmer along with the more classical courses, and of classes for retarded and for advanced children. In the college one may find freedom of election of courses of study, the division of classes according to capacity level, placement examinations, and a definite trend toward individual instruction at least in the last two college years with tutors or advisors to confer with the individual students. The clearest evidence of the movement in business and industry appears in the rise of the personnel officer whose business it is to select employees, to train them, to adjust them to working conditions, to follow their records, and to shift them about if adjustment can be improved thereby. But both in education and in business and industry the concept of individuality has been relatively slow in gaining a foothold, and its influence is still local rather than widespread.

The routine of everyday living seems to conform to the notion that all people are alike and many of the forces that constitute the social environment would tend to make them so. The standardisation and universality of radio and motion-picture programms, and the huge circulation of certain newspapers and magazines provide a uniform diet. If these media of communication were to be used for propaganda purposes they might regiment a whole population into a standardised pattern of thought and action (*382*). Even aesthetic appreciation may be on the road toward standardisation, with the growth of literary guilds, book of the month clubs, music of the month clubs, and pictures of the month clubs.

A Definition of Applied Psychology

The preceding observations provide a background for the delimitation of the field of applied psychology and for the formulation of a tentative plan of organisation of its subject-matter. It will be necessary to satisfy the requirements for human planning which, according to Doob (*143*, 6), are to acquire :

1. A knowledge of the people who will be affected.
2. A knowledge of the physical and social environments confronting these people.
3. A knowledge of the goal to be achieved.

Kelley's statement (*336*) that the problem of democracy is "so to utilise the talents of our differentially endowed and trained citizens as to maximise their satisfactions and their social productivity," can be modified thus: *The problem of applied psychology is so to adjust differentially endowed individuals by training them, by selection of their environment, and by the control of this environment that they may attain the maximum of social productivity and the maximum of personal satisfaction.* This definition recognises that individuals differ by native constitution in respect to what they can do and enjoy doing, that their patterns of behaviour may be developed through training, that manifold environmental forces influence their performance, that many of these can and should be controlled; and further that it is the proper destiny of every individual to be productive for the welfare of society and that in return he is entitled to the maximum of satisfaction which this society can provide.

Any plan for dealing with such an extensive subject-matter will necessarily be arbitrary and incomplete and will have to be flexible enough to change as knowledge increases. However, it seems entirely feasible to set down certain principles which will apply in attaining the goal of adequate adjustment. Thus, the consequence of having a certain remote and family ancestry, of being of a certain age and sex, of having to acquire habits and ideas according to the laws of learning will be specified. The probable effects of certain environmental conditions such as illumination, ventilation, and noise will be listed as well as the effects of modifying them. The influence of work, rest, and sleep, and of drugs and stimulants upon the human economy will be disclosed and allowed for. The means by which one can be directed into the vocation where he will fit best, and the conditions necessary for his efficient performance there will be described in so far as they are known. Certain maladjustments such as make one unfit for productive service or bring him into conflict with the law will be interpreted and methods of dealing with them will be examined. Finally, certain general observations upon the educational process as a means of making the most out of each and every unique individual will be made in the light of all the other topics previously discussed. This programme will leave any specialised problems of adjustment untouched, but should give some useful hints even in these cases as to the methods which might be found useful in their solution.

2

LEARNING AND SKILL

The range and variety of specific adjustments that the human organism is natively equipped to make are unknown and may always remain so. The age at which modification of behaviour first occurs has been pushed back beyond the date of birth with the discovery of the possibility of prenatal conditioning of behaviour. With the birth date no longer accepted as the dividing line between the unlearned and the learned, no form of reaction is immune from the suspicion on the part of some investigators that it may have been acquired. Many of the "instincts" have long ago been transferred from the native to the acquired category. At last the native reflexes such as the grasping reflex are being explained away in terms of the conditioning process. Whatever the doubts and disagreements upon the question of nature and nurture, there is universal agreement that the human being cannot possibly long survive in the world on his unlearned reaction mechanism alone. How then do the necessary and desirable adjustments come about, whether they be the adjustments of the food-taking reactions or the adjustments requisite for success in a highly complicated social environment? This is a problem in psychology. It is the applied psychologist's task to discover how the individual can make his adjustments most profitable and satisfying to himself and to society.

The processes of behaviour modification have a variety of names, among them being learning, habit formation, acquisition of skill, thinking and, possibly also, suggestion and imitation. All of them have so much in common that they can be discussed economically in two groups, the first, learning and the requisition of skill, and the second, thinking and suggestion.

Theories of Learning

Many theories have been proposed for the explanation of the learning process. The applied psychologist need endorse no one of them. On the contrary, he may pick and choose among them, taking only those aspects of each that have the most substantial factual support and that seem to have the greatest practical value, discarding the remainder. Three of these theories have something to contribute and therefore deserve his attention. They are the conditioned-response theory, the trial-and-error theory, and the insight theory.

The conditioned-response theory is an association theory in which contiguity appears to be the potent factor in making a connection between a stimulus and a response. It may be stated in a variety of ways. Guthrie (*235*, *26*) expressed it thus: "A combination of stimuli which has accompanied a movement will on its recurrence tend to be followed by that movement." A more conventional statement would be that if a stimulus leading to a response is accompanied by another stimulus, the occurrence of this latter alone will tend to be followed by the response. Pavlov's (*488*) experiment on the conditioning of the salivary reflex in a hungry dog will illustrate the process. If the ringing of a bell or the application of an electric shock accompanies the presentation of food which causes a flow of saliva, then, on a later occasion, the ringing of the bell only or the application of the shock only will tend to cause the flow of saliva.

The process of insight is difficult to describe, but it would seem, according to Koehler (*350*, *349*), to consist of a period of observation leading to understanding and followed by an appropriate response. Thus Koehler's (*351*) ape in the well-known jointed stick experiment, after being unable to reach a banana through the bars of its cage with a short bamboo stick, retired to the back of its cage. In the process of handling two sticks it inserted one into the end of the other, observed the result and straightway went to the bars where with the now longer stick it drew in the banana and ate it. And Kellogg's (*337*) child, when seeing a screen placed between itself and some object it wanted, observed the obstruction, ran around the end of it, and obtained the object.

The trial-and-error theory would seem at first sight at least to be in sharp contrast to the insight theory. It applies a series of reactions more or less random in nature, but directed toward some end such as the obtaining of food, with the gradual restriction of the range of movement until the right response occurs as though by accident. Upon later occasions the correct response occurs more and more promptly until it follows at once upon the stimulus. Thus Thorndike's (*616*) hungry cat, when placed in a cage whose door could be opened by pulling a looped string, and in front of which a morsel of food could be seen, struggled to obtain the food. It scartched and clawed around the box, but mainly in the direction of the food, and in the course of its struggles it happened to catch the loop which opened the door. After many repetitions, the cat, when confined in the box, immediately pulled the loop and obtained the food. It had learned.

Common Gound of Learning Theories

Closer inspection of these theories shows rather striking resemblances. Guthrie (*235*, *190*) has pointed out that the illustration of learning by insight given by Wheeler is an excellent description of trial and error entirely acceptable to those who support the latter theory. Wheeler (*700*, *252*) says:

> When you train your fox terrier to sit up and beg, you reward him with a tidbit not thereby to vivify the muscular sensation of making the correct movements, but in order to provide the dog with a definite goal with respect to which it will execute the desired act. Dog-fashion, it will then understand what you want of it, for responding with respect to food goals falls well within the repertoire of dog insight! Dog insight is relatively feeble and slow of development, especially under artificial conditions, consequently considerable time will elapse before it will make its movements just as you want them. Meanwhile it is making numerous other movements all at about the same time, jumping, barking and running around (which of these is to function as the "tool" for the securing of food is the difficult problem you have imposed upon it. As the dog keeps trying, its insight into the situation grows, just as the human being on a higher plane solves a mathematical problem by continued performance with respect to a definite goal.

Durkin (*152, 83*), who studied human problem solving, saw no sharp distinction between insight and trial and error.

> Problem solving in human adults is never completely blind or random, although O may proceed to his goal by manipulating the material without seeing ahead the relation of his moves to the goal.... On the other hand, it is, except in the simplest cases, to some degree exploratory, and always requires some manipulation, if only for verifying a correct hypothesis. It is not that a new kind of process, that of seeing the relationship of the material to the goal, enters in at the level of so-called "insightful" thinking, but that that the process was there in nucleus, though but vaguely, from the beginning, in the "blindest" variety of trial and error. Whether this is an independent process or is based genetically on trial-and-error or conditioned response, is not established.

The final sentence of Durkin suggests a common ground not only between trial and error and insight, but between conditioning and the other two. Resemblances between trial and error and conditioning have been mentioned by other investigators also. The similarity is disguised by the fact that in conditioning the final response in the sense of the end to be attained, is predetermined and has only to be associated or connected with the new stimulus. But when attention is directed to the pattern of movements by which the response develops in the course of the conditioning, its variations from trial to trial become evident. The stimulus pattern likewise varies in its composition as the response is being established. Moreover, learning by conditioning resembles insightful learning in that the number of trials necessary to establish the response becomes fewer and fewer as the experimental conditions are more rigidly controlled. It would seem, therefore, that perfect control of stimulus conditions might be expected to establish the response in a single trial, just as happens in cases of "good" insight.

This brief survey of theories of learning and their similarities gives clues to the necessary conditions for learning which hold for all theories. In the words of Miller and Dollard (*431, 2*), "In order to learn one must want something, notice something, do something, and get something. Stated more exactly, these factors are drive, cue, response, and reward." The drive may be a need, a desire, or a habit. In the illustrations used above it was hunger. The cue may be the "tool" mentioned by Wheeler and derived from observation, understanding, knowledge (getting acquainted with or seeing into a situation), insight, or it can be just stumbled upon. The response, or the responses, may be immediate and adequate or variable and gradually approaching adequacy according to the conditions under which the learning takes place. What the organism gets may be a reward in the sense of direct satisfaction as in obtaining food, or relief from punishment as in the escape from an electric grid.

Motivation in Learning

"All behaviour is motivated." With this sentence Yong (*731, 1*) opens his extensive treatment of motivation. One has to accept the statement largely on faith for it is difficult, if not impossible, to control all motivating influences in experiments with animals, and it is impossible to do so in human research. For it can be said that an animal which learns a mazo, in the absence of hunger or other clearly identifiable motivation, is driven by the urge to explore, by curiosity, or perhaps just the urge to be active. If one averts the question whether it is possible ever to learn at all without motivation, he can comfortably accept the statement that one invariably learns more readily when motivated and the stronger the motivation up to some limiting point the readier the learning.

The so-called native drives, and many others whose origin is not so clear. The former are the easiest to work with and are the only possible ones to use in animal studies. A large body of evidence has accumulated concerning the motives and their relative strength in animals (*677*). The curves from the work of Ligon (*378, 42*) reproduced in Figure 2.1 are representative of the results obtained in animal studies. The data are in terms of the time in seconds required for groups of rats to run through a maze, when hungry (solid line) and when not hungry (broken line). There is a striking difference between the learning curves of hungry and satiated rats. It will be obvious that cases of motivation such as this one are in part anticipations of reward and as such are covered in what will be said concerning that

FIGURE 2.1
Effect of Hunger Drive upon Learning*

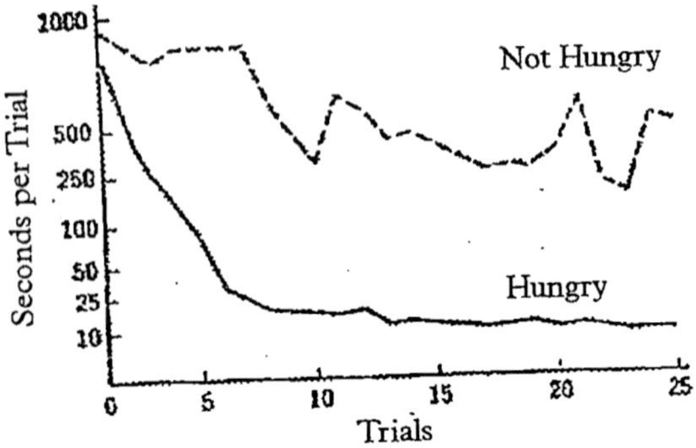

* Adapted from E.M. Ligon, "A Comparative Study of Certain Incentives in the Learning of the White Rat," *Comp. Psychol. Mon.*, 1929, 6, No. 28, 42.

aspect shortly. For although the animal may be driven by the pangs of hunger or because of some chemical deficiency to arrive at the food box on the first occasion, thereafter it seeks food. The overlap between drive and reward (or punishment) is particularly great in learning, and for that reason the former can be more appropriately discussed under Reward in this chapter. It will be enough to say at this point that motivation must be naturally present or must be provided if learning is to be achieved. A child's learning may be accelerated because he likes candy, wants to please his mother, to excel over his classmates, to avoid staying after school hours, to earn a new toy, to get information he wants for some purpose, or to pass his examinations. Which ones of the almost unlimited range of motives will be employed and which ones will be most effective in any specific instance are matters that need inquiry.

The Role of Understanding

Two kinds of processes are distinguished by Pear (*490*, 37) in the acquisition of skill, one being "blind learning" and the other "thoughtful". The former would seem to represent the extreme form of trial and error where understanding or cues are absent or impossible to obtain at the beginning of learning, and the latter would represent the case where the adequate cues are present at the outset of the process or are speedily found. *Training*, for Cox (*118*, 6), is a process in which cues or insight or understanding are provided for the learner by proper instruction from some competent person and to be distinguished from *practice* in which "the worker repeats the operation more or less mechanically at maximum speed." He makes a further interesting and important distinction within the same skill-forming process between a "thinking-out function" and a "putting-together function" (*118*, *18*). In an assembling task the latter can be distinguished from the former by "ensuring that at the outset the individual thoroughly understands how the parts are to be fitted together". Under ordinary circumstances, at least where some instruction is furnished, understanding would come first to be followed by the "putting together". Tasks differ in the relative importance of the understanding factor, from the case where the process is "blind" to the case where there is complete insight. Figure 2.2 from the study of Shuey (*564*, *332*), who tested problem-solving in kittens, gives a curve for "blind" learning, that is where cues were reduced to a minimum. Improvement is uniform throughout the extent of the curve, with no sharp decreases in time. Figure 2.3 from Cox (*118*, *111*) shows the curves for the task of assembling an electric lamp socket. The upper curve marked "without" shows the performance of a person who began without cues or understanding, but acquired it during the first few days, giving a

FIGURE 2.2
Problem-Solving in Kittens*

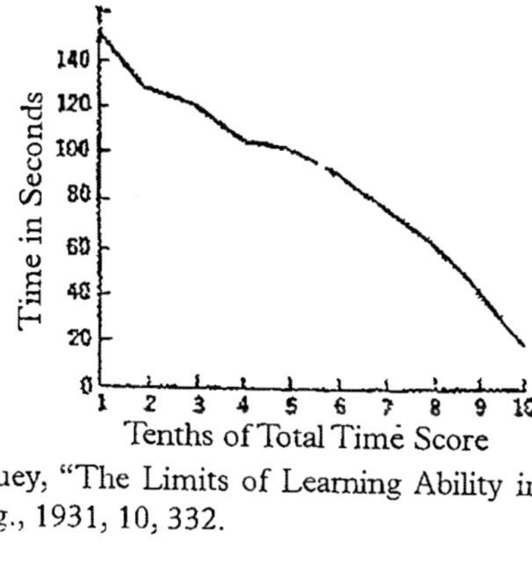

*From A.M. Shuey, "The Limits of Learning Ability in Kittens," Genet. Psychol. Monog., 1931, 10, 332.

FIGURE 2.3
Effect of Understanding upon Learning*

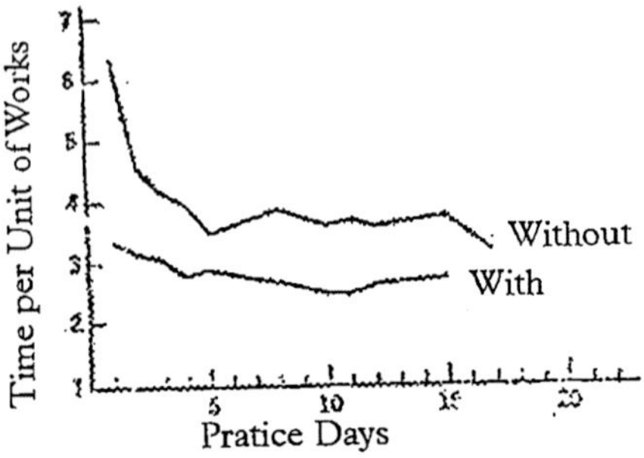

* Adapted from J. W. Cox, *Manual Skill* (London, Cambridge University Press, 1934), p. 111.

rapid fall in the curve. The curve marked "with" represents the performance of a person who had full understanding of the task at the outset, with the result that his curve begins about where the other subject had arrived after five days of training. Woodworth (*711, 146*) has prepared strikingly similar curves from the work of Twitmyer for learning of the blindfold maze by human subjects, some with understanding derived from previous visual inspection of the maze and some working "blind". The former saves the equivalent of the first third of the curve of the latter.

Tasks differ also in the necessary proportions of the "thinking-out" function and the "putting-together" function, to revert to the terminology of Cox. In Figure, 2.4 Cox (*118*, 124) shows an average curve for about forty subjects assembling electric lamp sockets without previous instruction. The early part of the curve covering the first three days of training shows by the rapid descent the development of understanding. The curve from this point on to the end marks the "putting-together" function. In contrast to this curve is the one given in Figure 2.5, also adapted from Cox (*118*, 124), showing progress in inserting screws into the lamp sockets. This is a purely motor function calling for coordination of fine movements but with the understanding factor at a minimum. The curve marks a slow but steady increase in speed from beginning to end.

FIGURE 2.4
Practice in a Function Requiring Understanding*

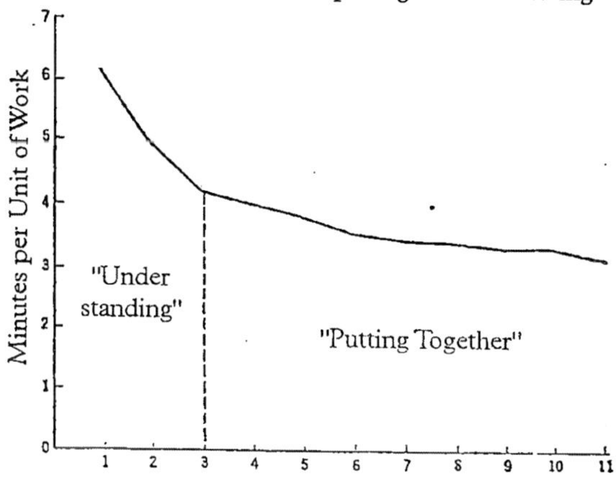

*Adapted from J. W. Cox, *Manual Skill* (London, Cambridge University Press, 1934), p. 124.

The practical conclusion to be drawn from an examination of these curves is that, for maximal efficiency, "training" should replace "practice". Instruction should be given and cues provided wherever possible. In the laboratory, a rat is put into a maze in order to study how it learns to avoid blind alleys and take the shortest route to the goal. If one were practically interested in having the rat make the run as efficiently as possible, all blind alleys might be closed until the correct path had been learned. The postman on a new route or the milkwagon horse would not be left to trial and error to find his way, but would be guided along it. The more complicated skill should be developed in the same way. The correct form in tennis and golf, in typewriting and in assembly operations, in adding figures and in reading, cannot be left to the *non-understanding* individual. What is correct must be worked out before hand and taught. This is one of the essential aspects of any industrial efficiency system, and of any good educational system. There are instances, of course, where correct cues cannot be provided beforehand as in meeting an entirely new and strange situation. In such cases under standing must be arrived at by the process of thinking or reasoning on the part of some one.

Repettion

Understanding is, however, not the whole of training. After the rapid fall in the curve of learning, progress continues as in Figure 2.4 and it continues likewise where only motor control is called for as in Figure 2.5. It is here that the response and the reward aspects of the learning process enter. The subject must actively react in order to improve, the rat must run in the maze, the child must try to write or to recite his lesson, the adult must swing at the golf ball. One of the oldest and best known of the so-called laws of learning is that of repetition or frequency of response. "Perfection does not come without practice." Recent research has shown, on the other hand, that repetition in and of itself will not inevitably bring about improvement. Its effectiveness seems to reside rather in the opportunity it affords for modification and variation of response and for the selection of the "correct" response where the initial cues are lacking or are inadequate. There are instances where learning occurs with one experience as in certain cases of conditioning and of insight. And there are also instances where no learning occurs in spite of many repetitions (*623*, 6 - 63), due perhaps to absence of an intention to learn, to lack of motivation, or to the presence of fatigue.

FIGURE 2.5

Practice in a Function Requiring Only Motor Skill* Practice Day

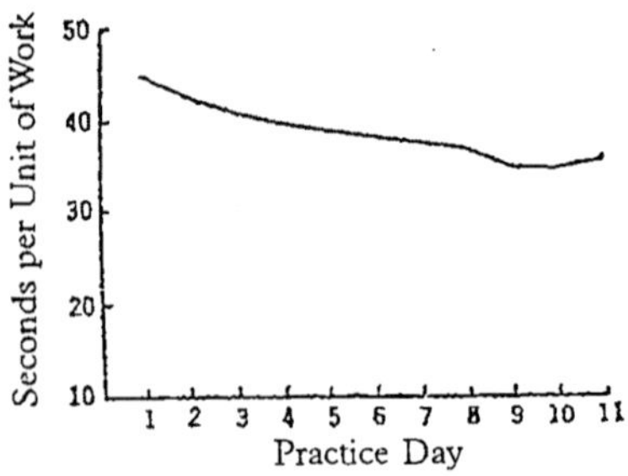

*Adapted from J. W. Cox, *Manual Skill* (London, Cambridge University Press, 1934), p. 124.

Intention to Learn

It is difficult to design an experiment in human learning where there will not be some intention to learn, although one can find many illustration from one's everyday experience of the dependence of learning upon intention to learn. For instance, the writer has in the course of certain experimental work named a series of 100 colours (five different colours, each repeated twenty times, arranged in random order) over 1,000 times in order to measure his speed of reading, and he never learned the list so far as to be able to recall even the first three colours. Here the intention was to gain speed in reading and not to remember. One's ignorance of situations which one meets daily during many years testifies to the importance of this intention to learn. The inability to describe correctly the face of one's watch is a striking example.

The few available experimental studies of "incidental" memory (*457*) (*556*, 4 - 15) have demonstrated the correctness of these more casual observations upon the necessity of the intention to learn. No small proportion of the success attained through the use of mnemonic systems comes from the intention thus created to pay attention to the material to be learned.

It is not easy to discover the shape of the learning curve in a situation where there is intention to learn, but without specific reward or without insight. Barton's (*29*) curve shown in Figure 2.6 approximates that condition. It represents progress of a group of students in typing where there certainly was a mild intention to learn but with a minimum of motivation, insight, and reward. The curve approximates a straight line with the usual fluctuations due to a variety of uncontrolled influences. But there is steady improvement.

This facilitating effect of intention to learn calls for an interpretation in more objective terms, if possible. Intention to learn means being interested in knowing something or doing something and attending to it. These in turn are reducible, in part at least, to increases in muscular tensions in the sensory mechanisms and very probably also in the machanisms (*184*, 367 - 394). There is some experimental evidence to suggest that such tensions do have a facilitating influence upon behaviour. There is negative evidence from the work of Jacobson (*310*) showing inefficiency of performance in a state of muscular relaxation, and positive evidence from the research of Bills (*40*)

FIGURE 2.6
Learning Curve for Typewriting

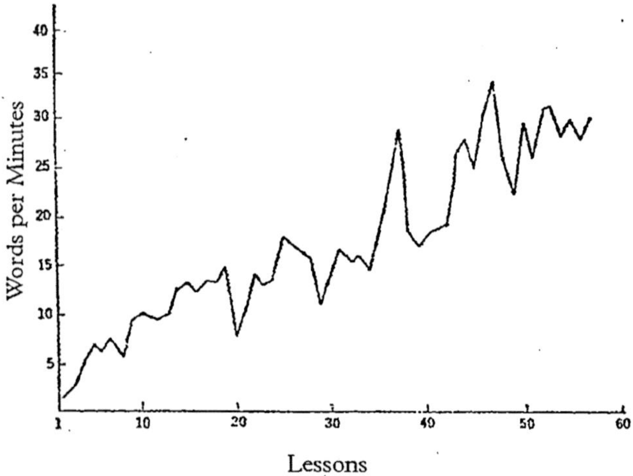

*From J.W. Barton, "Smaller vs. Larger Units in Learning to Typewrite," J. *Educ.* Psychol., 1921. 12, 473

and others on the reinforcing effect of muscular tensions, both those occurring naturally and those that are artificially created. The data obtained by Block (*49*) make it appear that there is such a condition as over-tension which when extreme may not only fail to facilitate but may even interfere with performance. Mere intention to learn is not likely, however, to create tensions of such magnitude.

Emotional Reinforcement

Emotional excitement may strengthen the effect of repetitions so much that in exceptional cases there is no need for more than one or a few repetitions of an experience. The psychoanalysts rest heavily upon such excitement to account for the devastating effect of emotional episodes. Guthrie (*235*, *103-113*) explains the reinforcement produced by excitement in terms of body tensions, or what Freeman (*184*, *433-459*) describes as "proprioceptive backlash". It would seem, though, in the light of the brief comments just made concerning the effect of strong tensions, that great excitement or too great excitement might impede learning. Certainly excitement vigorous enough to create confusion should do so. Instances of amnesia due to such a cause could, doubtless, be found. At any rate intention and mild emotional excitement are generally regarded as facilitators of the learning process.

Reward and Punishment

One of the best known of the so-called laws of learning and the one that has aroused the most controversy in recent years is the law of effect, which says that a satisfying after-effect tends to stamp in the response that produced, it, and that a dissatisfying after-effect tends to inhibit the response that produced it. There is a serious theoretical difficulty in accounting for such a retroactive effect of satisfaction or dissatisfaction upon the reaction that created it, as pointed out by Cason (*94*), but the fact remains that in practical life situations, in the training of animals, in the teaching of children at home and in school, and in the learning of skills by adults, rewards and punishments are effective in the long-run. The isolation of these influences from the complexity of factors affecting learning is difficult in the work with animals and particularly so in the case of human beings. For instance, reward or punishment once administered leads to the anticipation of the same in future trials, and provides one of the most common forms of motivation or incentive to improvement (*678*). The fact of the influence of motivation in learning having been established, one may question whether improvement is due to the reward or punishment directly or to the increased motivation. The same overlapping of influences undoubtedly occurs in animal training also, though probably not to the same degree.

The change in the rate of learning through reward, in a relatively pure form, is demonstrated in Figure 2.7 from the work of Tolman and Honzik (*648*). They ran rats through a maze, taking them from the food box at the end of the run without a food reward. After ten trials of this sort, the rats were rewarded with food at the end of each of the succeeding eight runs. The rewarded with food at the end of each of the succeeding eight runs. The records are in terms of errors made per trial and time

FIGURE 2.7
Effects of Reward upon Learning*

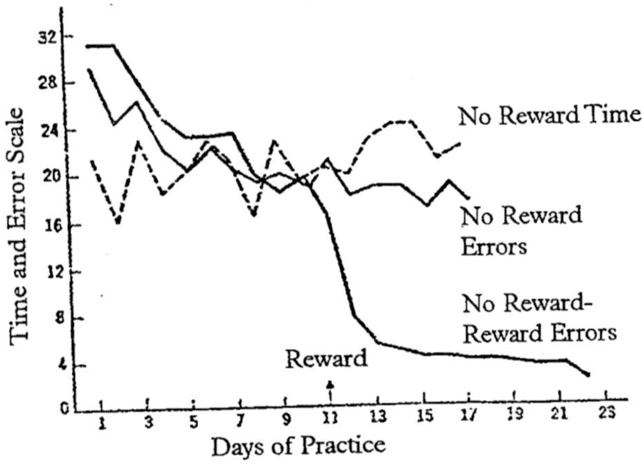

*Adapted from E.C. Tolman and C.H. Honzik, "Degrees of Hunger, Reward and Non-Reward and Maze Performance in Rats," Univ. Calif. Publ. Psychol., 1930,4. 267.

per trial. The rapid fall in the error curve upon the administration of the reward is obvious. It should be noted, however, that there is much improvement in error score during the first ten trials in the absence of the food reward. It is not possible to say whether some uncontrolled reward such as escape from the maze was at work in the early part of the curve or whether the improvement was the consequence of sheer repetition. Some vague motivation was certainly present for the animals did move around in the maze, but there can be motivation, of course, in the absence of reward or punishment. The influence causing reduction of errors in the absence of reward was not effective in reducing the time spent in running the maze, for the broken line in the chart, indicating time score, does not fall. Whatever may be the interpretation of the early part of the curve the fact remains that giving a food reward at the end of the run increased the rate of learning.

Guthrie (*235*, 153, 158) attempts to resolve the conflict between theory and practice in the use of rewards and punishments, at least so far as the process of conditioning is concerned, with the opinion that it is not the reward and the punishment in themselves that have the effect but what they make the animal do that counts. In support of this view he cites cases, exceptional to be sure, in which reward impedes the fixing of a correct response and punishment facilitates it. Thus, if one is training a dog to sit up and beg and the food reward, instead of being given to it while it is in the begging posture is thrown into a far corner of the room, the reward will fix the running for the food instead of sitting for it. Likewise, if a dog is being trained to jump through a hoop, a smack on its posterior, a punishment, administered at the proper moment, will send the dog through the hoop and tend to fix the correct reaction. An even more instructive instance is cited by Miller and Dollard (*431, 32*) in which a mother is teaching her child to play the piano. The child received no reward such as the sight of the mother's pleasure when correct notes were struck whereby these responses might have been reinforced. His only reward was permission to run away from the piano when his work was well done. Therefore the whole set-up emphasised escape from the piano rather than good work while at the piano.

These instances of failure of rewards and punishments to accomplish what is expected of them offer no argument against their use, but they do emphasise the necessity for their *intelligent use.*

Distribution of Practice

An efficient learning programme demands consideration of other factors than motivation, understanding, repetition and reward. A large body of research data is available on such questions as how one shall spend his available learning time and how he shall organise the material to be learned. If the exact influence of fatigue, practice, and a number of other factors involved in learning were known, one could arrange beforehand the time schedule that would be most economical for learning. But since we do not have such knowledge in sufficient detail, the problem has to be attacked empirically. Various tasks are set and a given amount of time allowed for learning. This time is differently distributed for different individuals, some spending theirs in one continuous work period, and others dividing it into portions separated by unoccupied intervals.

The conclusion that has been drawn from experiments of this type is that too great concentration or distribution of time is not economical. The learning periods should be short enough to avoid the onset of fatigue, and long enough to avoid the loss of too much time in getting warmed up to the task at the beginning of each learning period. No absolute rule can be laid down for all individuals, but it can be safely said that a moderate distribution of time always gives more economical results than spending the same amount in one continuous study period (*523*). The same facts are applicable to motor learning or muscular activity.

Interesting evidence concerning the proper distribution of time in a practical learning situation is derived from an investigation of chain assembly by Henshaw and Holman (*256*, 26). Four work schedules were tried in the training for this task. They were :

I. Sixteen ten-minute training periods of chain assembly per day with rest interval following each one, eight periods in the morning and eight in the afternoon with a lunch hour at noon.

II. Eight ten-minute periods at chain assembly in the morning, with eight periods in the afternoon spent in a rather similar task of cartridge filling.

III. Eight ten-minute periods of chain assembly each morning with no work in the afternoon.

IV. One ten-minute period only of chain assembly per day.

The results of these schedules are given in Figure 2.8 where the curves are in terms of the number of units per ten-minute period at the beginning of each day. The first point on the curve gives the standing of the groups at the beginning. The curves for programmer I, II, and III are practically indistinguishable. They show that whereas programme I had double the practice of programme III on each day, the rate of learning did not differ. Curve IV differs from the others in that the rate of improvement was very much slower, indicating that only ten minutes of practice per day was entirely too little for efficient learning. There are certainly extremes of dispersion and concentration beyon which it is not economical to go. Within these extremes other

FIGURE 2.8

Practice Curves in Chain Assembly*

I - Two 80-minute training periods — chain assembly
II - One 80-minute training periods — chain assembly
One 80-minute training periods — cartridge filling
III - One 80-minute training period — chain assembly
IV - One 10-minute training period — chain assembly

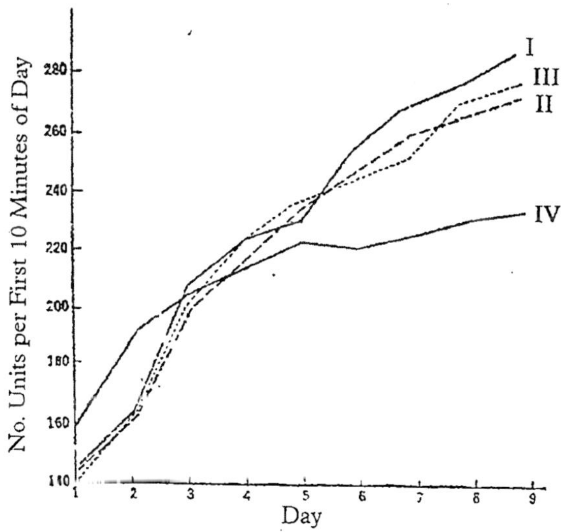

* Adapted from E.M. Henshaw and P. Holman, "Manual Dexterity," *Industr. Hlth. Res Bd. Rep.* 1933, No. 67, Part II, 26.

practical considerations will determine the programme, such as the date at which the trained person's services will be required. It is entirely possible, for instance, that no matter how much faster one might learn with the shortest daily practice, the learning time would have to be more concentrated to meet practical requirements.

Comparison of curves II with curves I and III suggests that the groups learned two related tasks without interference between them, for II is neither worse nor better than I and III. Caution should be exercised in the practical application of this fact, since the nature of the resemblances or differences between the two tasks would determine whether or not interference would develop between them.

Learning by Wholes and Parts

Investigation of the learning of nonsense and sense material, poetry or prose, seems to favour the learning of material as a whole rather than in parts. If one had a poem of sixteen four-line verses to learn, the correct way to learn it would not be to learn it one verse at a time, a procedure commonly followed by an untrained individual, but to read from beginning to end again and again until the whole could be repeated. There is only one drawback to this method, namely that a person is likely to become discouraged or lose interest when progress is apparently lacking, if he does not have sufficient confidence in the method. It sometimes happens that, in first using this schedule of learning, rather poor results are obtained, but if given a fair trial the time saved and the greater permanence of the result will show its real efficiency.

The reason for the greater economy of the "whole method" is said to be found in one of the most fundamental laws of learning, that one should always begin by doing a thing as nearly as possible in the way it is eventually to be done. Otherwise, it must not only be relearned in part, but old habits must be broken. In learning anything in sections, associations are formed between the end of a section and its beginning, but since repetition as a whole is the desired end, all such associations must be finally broken and correct ones formed. Learning the task as a whole in the first place forms only habits that will be needed in the perfected performance. Allowances must be made to cover differences among individual preferences and attitudes, the length of the material, the degree of uniformity in difficulty within the material, and the purposes to be served by the learned material. Nor is it certain that the laboratory findings are as applicable to the acquisitition of complicated skills as they are to the process of memorising. In any case the safest practical recommendation to make is to choose that method of learning that best suits the purpose rather than to apply a hard and fast rule. Children's learning should be supervised by those who can lay out the proper method for them.

Adjustment of Learning to Use

Emphasis upon practical considerations dictates freedom not merely in the choice of one or another method of learning, but in the degree to which learning shall be carried and in the form in which it shall be retained. Learning seems to most people to imply preparation for verbatim reproduction, which is a most exacting task, whereas the work of the world seldom demands that. There are occasions, to be sure, that require this type of learning, for example learning the multiplication tables and the spelling of words. But there are other kinds of material that should be accessible when required but that need not be carried in the mind at all times. In such cases one does not have to learn so completely that the facts may be recalled at any time, but only well enough so that they may be relearned easily when needed. Most of the knowledge acquired in school days has apparently gone completely from the mind, but only a small percentage of the original labour will bring it all back. Much of the education of the engineer, the professional man, and the teacher is of this kind.

There is a kind of material which need be learned only so well that it will be recalled along with some other definite thing with which it has been associated. The name of a person may be thus associated with the sight of his face, a telephone number with a particular name, a foreign word with the sight of the English equivalent: This type of memory calls for much less effort than absolute recall and in its place is just as efficient.

Some things need to be remembered only when they themselves are present. This form of memory is called recognition, and it is the most economical of all. It consists simply in knowing a thing or being familiar with it when we need it. For instance, it is far more important for one to know his fountain pen when he sees it, to be able to use it, than to know all about in at other times. In what way and how well a thing is to be learned must depend on the use that is to be made of it, for economy of effort demands that the means shall be employed that will be the most efficient and that will require the least expenditure of energy.

Simplification of Material to Be Learned

One of the greatest economies in learning comes from the adoption of simplified systems of material, such as spelling and measuring, in place of more complicated and unwieldy ones. It has been estimated (*209*), for example, that a system of simplified spelling would save approximately two years in the school life of a child. The value of a saving of this magnitude in terms of ability to read at an earlier age, of time available for other projects, and in terms of preparation for a life work shortened by two years, is difficult to compute. Gilbreth (*209*) promised even greater economies from the adoption of a simplified system of measurement such as the metric system. "Counting the English units bearing the same names as our own, we have in use four different sizes of pints, quarts, and gallons; three different sizes of gills; many sizes of barrels; and untold numbers of different sizes of bushels of things in different states, such as apples, potatoes, and the like; three kinds of ounces, drams, and pounds; two different sizes of hundredweight; four different tons; and two or three kinds of miles." It has been estimated that the United States spends unnecessarily each year 315 millions of dollars in teaching the old system of weights and measures and that a child of ten years who knows the decimal ratio can learn the essentials of the metric system in ten minutes. Similar economies could be attained in other directions if attention were addressed to gaining economy in learning, and with no decreased efficiency in other respects. Industry has achieved enormous economies by simplifying skilled operations and reducing them to standardised forms. What the efficiency engineer has done for mechanical work can be accomplished for the mental work of the child and the adult when the advantages of doing so are clearly understood. Any one who becomes thoroughly imbused with the idea of conserving human time and energy will go to the limit in advocating such radical innovations as a simplified universal language and a simplified universal calendar.

Forgetting

Although learning and remembering are entitled to major interest and attention, one should not lose sight of the importance of forgetting. Much is learned for temporary use only, much is incorrectly learned and should be changed, much is experienced against the will and should be forgotten. It appears that time alone will not erase our memories whether they be good or bad.

Forgetting, thanks to Freud, has come to be looked upon as an active and not a passive process, an interference with connections rather than a mere weakening of them with age. The long succession of researches into retroactive inhibition is interpreted in terms of the inhibitory effects of the newer upon the older. Besides this bare fact of interference is the discovery that its degree depends upon the qualitative relation of the new to the old – the greater the similarity, within certain limitations, the greater will be the interference (*339*) (*524*). Studies of the rate of forgetting during sleep furnish striking confirmation of forgetting as an active process, for it is found that a much smaller proportion what is learned will be forgotten if learning is followed by sleep than if the learner remains awake (*657*). The practical rule to follow if one wanted to remember something just learned would be to learn it just before going to sleep, to follow it with a period of rest or with a very different kind of activity.

What should one do, on the other hand, if he wished to forget? The answer would seem to be that he should follow his learning with similar learning. But if he wished to forget immediately after learning, then, except in a laboratory experiment, he should not have learned at all. Obviously, the instances in which one wishes to forget in everyday life are very different from this. There the proper rule would seem to be to get new experiences, visit new scenes, form new associations. The more associations one has with a given idea or object or reaction, the less likely will any one of them be to come to mind, other things being equal. The device proposed by Dunlap (150) for breaking undersirable habits such as nail biting, typing errors, and the like would seem to be a contradiction not only of the statements just made but of all the facts of learning. He advocates the elimination of such habits by practising them, and reports success in dealing with particularly stubborn cases. His technique demonstrates the potency of the intention to learn as a necessary condition of learning, for he instills into his subjects the *intention not to learn*. It is the clear consciousness of the purpose of the repetition along with accessory reeducation that makes his method effective.

Transfer of Learning

The practical outlook of this book makes it possible and advisable to pass over the earlier discussions concerning the transfer of training. Out of an active controversy covering many years there has evolved an attitude toward the problem which is healthful for both education and industry. Formal discipline in the early meaning of the terms is advocated by few persons today. The opposing view that no transfer occurs from one situation to another except where identical elements are present in the two is softened by the recognition of the nature of such identical elements. There may be habits of looking for relationships, of confidence in one's ability; there may be a knowledge of principles of good management; there may be a tendency to be alert; there may be a good emotional attitude or a successful technique. In every case of transfer there seems to be "something that you can put your finger on" (*715*, 362).

The most important point to remember is that the transfer of such elements is not a mystical process that occurs automatically. The relationships must be pointed out or detected; the applicability of the principles must be noted; the utility of the techniques must be discovered. It is the functions of education, and of technical instruction in particular, to teach principles and techniques so as to make them transferable. Even with all the devices at the command of the teacher, the actual amount of transfer in education and industry is not very great (*257*).

A new approach to the whole problem of similarity of skills and of the feasibility of transferring workers from one skilled operation to another has come about through current techniques of occupational analysis (*27*). Attempts are being made to break down jobs into unit functions and to build up jobs into families according to the similarity of their units. These procedures are being worked out in the hope of readjusting large groups of competent workers who have been deprived of employment through technological changes. Of more remote utility are the encouraging efforts to apply the techniques of factor analysis to the breakdown of jobs into functional units.

3

THINKING AND SUGGESTION

Habits, whether they are motor habits or habits of mind, have the character of routine implied in them. They have been developed in the course of a series of repeated reactions. Well-established habits closely resemble native responses, so much so that it is frequently difficult to distinguish between natural and acquired behaviour. When a certain situation is presented, a series of habitual responses may occur in a seemingly automatic fashion. It is well that this is so, for such action is by far the most economical form of behaviour. But all of our behaviour cannot be of this routine sort. The human environment is so complicated that new and strange situations are sure to arise for which no habitual responses have been established. Thinking becomes necessary.

The Nature of Thinking

When obstacles or difficulties interfere with the smooth flow of habits, some slight shift in the series of habits may be all that is necessary. But when no ready made response is adequate, the human being is said to think, to reason, to judge what to do. A new adjustment to this strange situation must be created. It is the capacity for adjustment to a changing environment that is said to distinguish man most clearly from the animal. Whether this statement be strictly true or not, the thinking form of human reaction may be illustrated most readily by contrasting it with the behaviour of an animal in a new and unusual situation.

When an animal is placed in one of the *puzzle* boxes used for studying learning, it attempts to escape by using many or all of its natural and learned reactions. These appear to be applied in a random, haphazard fashion, wrong movements being repeated again and again, until one movement or series of movements happens to meet the situation and makes escape possible. Or the animal may fail entirely to solve the problem. When a human being is made to face a similar problem, such as the need to escape from confinement, he may meet it just as the animal does, by trial and error". Or he may use a kind of mental "trial and error", in which the various reactions are tried out in consciousness, the unsatisfactory responses being discarded before they become overt acts. The only overt motor response may be the one that correctly meets the conditions of the problem. The most striking difference that an observer would note in the behaviour of the man and the animal would be the absence of motor manipulation in the case of the former. This case represents a kind of ideal fashion of solving a problem, for the customary difference would be that the human being makes relatively fewer and less random movements than the animal rather than none at all. In fact the study of human behaviour in the presence of puzzling situations reveals instances ranging all the way from the animal method of attack to the relatively rare case such as is cited above (*152*). The majority of cases would fall somewhere between these two extremes.

In dealing with strictly mental problems where overt action is entirely absent of long delayed, the thinking process differs from the "trial-and-error" process mainly in the systematic character of the trials. That is, the wrong response is not repeated again and again as in animal learning, but when tried and found wrong it is permanently discarded. Thus the range of possible reactions is rapidly narrowed down until only the correct response remains.

Thinking, therefore, is not a unique mental operation differing from all others and superimposed upon them, but, on the contrary, partakes of the nature of the simpler forms of behaviour. Hollingworth (*276*, 14), who approaches the problem of thought by way of sleeping and dreaming – with which it is usually sharply contrasted – says.

> In sleep thought ceases; in drowsiness, thought is seen making headway with the most meager equipment; in the dream the nature of thinking is

so clearly exhibited that only waking reflection can rob dream verdicts of their coerciveness.

Stages in the Thinking Process

An examination of the mental trial-and-error process will reveal the conditions upon which effective and economical thinking depends. The following illustration cited by John Dewey (*133*) affords excellent material for this study. A certain individual crossing a river on a ferry-boat noticed a long pole painted white, bearing a gilded ball upon its end, and projecting nearly horizontally from the upper deck. At once a question arose in his mind, namely, what is the function of that pole? Possible answers to the question began to crowd into his mind – memories of earlier experiences of somewhat similar objects. Each answer or suggestion was examined and tested in order to determine whether it was an adequate solution. These suggestions and the methods of trying them out were as follows:

1. It is a flagpole. The colour of the pole, its shape, and the presence of the gilded ball upon its end made the suggestion of flagpole acceptable. But the position of the pole seemed to be a very unusual one for a flagpole. Furthermore, there was no visible means of attaching a flag to the pole, such as a ring, pulley, or even a cord. And finally, there were two other vertical poles, each carrying a flag. If this were a flagpole, it, too would be bearing a flag. This suggestion of flagpole as a solution of the problem was considered inadequate and was rejected.

2. It is an ornament. The general appearance of the object made this suggestion acceptable as it conformed to earlier experiences of ornaments. But memory and observation supplied the further information that all sorts of river craft carried the same kind of poles. Among these were tug-boats and freight boats which showed no other attempt at ornamentation. These objections were sufficient to overthrow the suggestion as a correct solution to the problem.

3. It is a radio antenna. Such terminals, however, usually occupy the highest available point and have wire attachments of some sort. There were no wires visible. In addition, there would seem to be no good reason for equipping all tugboats, ferry-boats, and other river craft with radios. Finally, memory supplied the information that boats carried this sort of pole before the radio was invented. Therefore, this suggestion could not be accepted.

4. The pole might be a device to aid in steering the boat. In support of this suggestion it was noted that the pole was so located that the ball

seemed to be projected in front of the pilot house where the pilot could easily see it. The pilot being located on the front of the boat would need some form of guide as to the direction in which it was travelling. Here is a device that might be used to guide the boat somewhat as the gunner uses his gun sight in order to aim. Thus its position could be accounted for. As all boats would need some kind of aid in steering, the presence of such poles on all boats would be accounted for. The white color and the gilded ball on the end could be explained as a means of increasing the visibility of the steering device. The suggestion that the pole was a steering device seemed to fit all the conditions of the problem and was consequently accepted as the correct solution.

The Demands of Correct Thinking

This simple illustration of an ordinary adjustment to a strange situation contains all the elements of the thinking process.

1. First, a problem or difficulty must be clearly perceived. Where no problem is encountered there will be no thinking and the situation will be met with an habitual response. Where the problem is not clearly perceived the thinking will be erroneous. If it had not been observed that the pole lacked rope, ring, and pulley there might have been an immediate acceptance of the idea of flagpole.

Since thinking is difficult and since such a large proportion of our behaviour is or the habit sort, there is a tendency to see no problems but rather to accept the first suggestion that occurs, or to interpret each new and strange experience as though it were an old one. It is a characteristic of some minds that they have a mental habit reaction for every new problem. Minds of this type are said to be in a rut. The social consequences of such a substitution of mental habit for thinking on the part of all people are elaborately set forth by James Harvey Robinson in his *Mind in the Making (527)*.

It is not always mental laziness that is responsible for the failure to see problems. In many cases training is necessary. A scientific training is, in some measure at least, a training to see problems. The geologist is trained to see problems in rock formation, the botanist in flowers, the chemist in metals and soils that would escape any but such a trained observer.

2. Correct thinking implies a rich and varied experience out of which tentative answers may come. In the simple case cited,

there were memories of flagpoles and their customary position and equipment; of decorative devices and where they are commonly used; or radio apparatus, its usual character and position, and the approximate time that the radio was invented.

> The curious mind is constantly alert and exploring, seeking material for thought, as a vigorous and healthy body is on the *qui vive* for nutriment. Such curiosity is the only sure guarantee of the acquisition of the primary facts upon which thinking must be based. The most casual notice of the activities of a young child reveals a ceaseless display of exploring and testing activity. Objects are sucked, fingered, and thumped; drawn and pushed, handled and thrown; in short, experimented with till they cease to yield new qualities. Such activities are hardly intellectual and yet without them intellectual activity would be feeble and intermittent through lack of stuff for its operation (*133*, 31).

The important part played by range of information in intelligence tests is justified since they serve as indicators of the presence of the stuff on which thinking must depend.

3. It is a fundamental condition of thinking that there must be a reservoir of past experiences, but even then the suggestions may not come forth from it. Their utilisation will depend largely upon the systematic and orderly arrangement of one's memories. If, in the illustration given above, the previous experiences had not been recalled, thinking would have failed. Since all recall depends upon the functioning of associative mechanisms, the necessity of establishing numerous associations is apparent. Experiencing should be a process of assimilating, of relating new to old, of noting similarities and differences between new and old and not just a sponge-like soaking up of information. Each one of these operations means forming additional sets of associative connections which will increase the chances of recall in a variety of circumstances. Unless one's memories are orderly and systematic and variously interrelated, one cannot be sure that all fruiful sugestions will be submitted for the solution of a problem.

Graham Wallas (*673*) has described the surprising fact about thinking, that solutions to problems frequently come when least expected, when no effort is being made to solve them, and when the problems themselves have been apparently forgotten. The happy suggestion may come during a ramble through the woods, during strenuous mountain climbing, in that hazy state of mind that occurs when one is about to fall asleep, or even in dreams. Thinkers vary in the means which they find most effective for encouraging and eliciting these "flashes" of thought. About all that one can do is to provide the circumstances that are known to be conducive to such flashes, to be prepared to recognise them when they come, and to record them before they fade away. After all the material bearing upon a problem has been absorbed, it is well to drop the matter, to rest from mental labour or to take up the solution of some other and entirely different problem, and accept the illumination when and if it comes.

4. Not every idea that flashes into the mind proves to be a correct answer, so that each one must be carefully tested to determine whether or not it satisfies the conditions of the problem. To withhold decision until all the evidence has been submitted and tested of often an irksome task. If in the above illustration the first, second and third suggestions had not been carefully checked against observed facts, the conclusion would have been in error.

Individual Differences in Thinking

How shall one explain the great differences among people in their capacity to think and in the value of their thinking? The mind of the genius works much the same as the ordinary mind, and the steps in his reasoning are the same. There may, however, be differences within every stage of the process. One great difference appears in the number of suggestions that come to mind, owing to the varied relationships that are noted between the problem and previous experiences. The genius brings forth many recollections and "ideas" that would seem to the ordinary mind to have no connection whatever with the problem in hand.

Another difference has to do with the speed and facility with which the suggestions come. In some persons the suggestions come to mind with great rapidity and in others they come very slowly. On the whole, abundant and easily flowing suggestions are necessary to good thinking, but it sometimes happens that so many suggestions crowd into the mind that there is an inability to select from among them and to try them out. There is such a condition in thinking as never being able to reach a conclusion because of the impossibility of giving all suggestions an adequate test. The best thinking results from neither too few nor too many suggestions.

The quality of the suggestions is more important than their number of the speed with which they are presented. Some suggestions may be extremely shallow and represent only the most superficial relationships, whereas others are fundamental and appropriate. The quality of the suggestions depends to a great degree upon the manner in which the material is originally experienced. If only superficial characteristics of a situation are perceived and made a part of one's mental stock, the suggestions coming therefrom will also be superficial. But if one's natural curiosity and training lead him carefully to analyse and examine facts as they are presented, the suggestions arising to meet problems will be not only more numerous but of greater value. Intuition, or insight, as the terms are popularly used, is probably nothing more than having only relevant and pertinent suggestions offered as material for meeting new and strange situations. Contrasted with intuition as thus defined are the ravings of the insane. Their ideas are the results of the functioning of associative mechanisms, but the associations are of the most superficial sort, frequently nothing more than connections based on word sounds. Such material is worse than useless, so far as correct thinking is concerned. Most people's thinking lies somewhere between these two extremes, where much material that is superficial and useless is recalled but is promptly rejected and not allowed to slow down the process of examining the relevant suggestions.

Finally, there are great differences in the care with which the suggestions are tested. Genius has been defined as the "capacity for taking infinite pains", and it is here that tedious and painstaking labour must be expended. It is said that great inventors have been known to try out systematically thousands of suggestions before finding a correct solution to some puzzling problem. In contrast to this is the ready acceptance of the first solution that old habits and attitudes of mind will suggest, which is characteristic of usual careless thinking. Careful and systematic examination of relevant ideas is at the bottom of most great achievements of thought.

The Basis of Opinion

The need for a higher quality of thinking is everywhere evident. Our opinions, our beliefs, our judgments and convictions about matters of everyday life have been built up out of such a procedure as we have described, sometimes more complicated in the number of suggestions that are offered and examined, and sometimes very much simplified and contracted in one or other of the stages leading to a conclusion. What chance is there that our opinions, thus formed, are sound? How can the serious-minded citizen be confident of the stand that he takes on prohibition, the platforms of political parties, a protective tariff, the League of Nations, and the other grave international questions about which every one is supposed to have an opinion? The answer to this question is of the gravest concern in a democracy where vital decisions on matters of policy are up to the people. The least that an intelligent individual can do is to check his opinions and attitudes by putting to himself the following queries:

1. Do I rightly understand the question?
2. Is my experience with the question sufficiently broad, as the result of reading or other contacts, to enable me to have fruitful suggestions or "ideas"?
3. Do the suggestions that occur to me exhaust the fund of my relevant experiences?
4. Have I thoroughly tested each suggestion in relation to the problem?

Only when an affirmative answer can be given to each of these questions can reliance be placed upon a conclusion. Opinions on most of the questions of the day cannot stand this searching examination. The proper attitude should then be that of open-mindedness, a willingness to wait for further evidence, rather than a final acceptance of one or the other point of view. Along with this there should go a recognition of the possibility of the appearance of new evidence which will require the readjustment of many well-established conclusions. The world of knowledge is constantly expanding and our opinions should be fluid enough to permit the changes that such growth entails.

Rationalisation

Thinking is seldom a cold process of pure logic, but tends to be warmed by the trend of our desire. We *want* preconceived solution to be the correct one. This undercurrent of desire may determine the course of thought at almost every stage. It may give a favoured position to the suggestions leading toward the desired conclusion so far as recall is concerned, and may warp the testing of the suggestions so as to give undue weight to whatever will conform to desire. A case of such thinking known as *rationalisation* is reported by Leuba (*373*, 127).

> I know a laborer who is tormented by the desire to make money. Some time ago, he showed me a heavy mass of dark gray sand which he had extracted from the bottom of an old well. He thought the sand contained gold, and had spent much time and money in order to establish the truth of his belief. A desire for wealth was at the root of this man's conviction; but the desire alone would not have suggested the idea that the sand contained gold. It was of great weight and he had, moreover, observed in it brilliant yellow particles. Therefore, even though many reasons were urged against his conviction, he believed that he had found gold. He did not, of course, rest content at this point. He wanted a scientific demonstration of the truth of his belief, and accordingly he had the sand analysed. When reliable chemist reported the absence of gold, he placed samples in other hands. Despite several concordant negative analysis, this man has not yet altogether given up hope.

Lund (*389*) has gathered spectacular evidence of the degree to which people's current beliefs are related to their desires. He took a series of statements ranging from those that are accepted as axiomatic to those that have a peculiarly personal quality. These statements were rated in three ways, according to the degree to which they were believed, the degree to which they were supported by evidence, and the degree to which they were desired by the raters. When the correlation technique was applied to the three arrangements of the statements, it was found that the correlation between belief an evidence was +.42, that between desire and belief was +.88, and that between desire and evidence was –.03. Although one is not safe in inferring causal relations from correlation coefficients, the presumption is that one tends to believe what one wants to believe.

Suggestion

It was pointed out above that thinking is difficult and laborious and that it is used only when necessary to overcome obstacles that cannot be met by means of an habitual response. Rationalisation has been described as a short cut to a solution. There is one other way of avoiding the rigors of thinking that consists in accepting, without critical examination, the conclusions of some other person. This response commonly occurs when an opinion has been expressed by one who is considered an authority, as a teacher, preacher, or public speaker, or where it is printed in a book or newspaper. Although in many instances of no great importance it may be advisable to accept the opinions of others without testing them, it is a bad mental habit to do so generally. Authorities have been known to be wrong and much that is printed and spoken cannot be considered authoritative.

Suggestion is the term usually applied to the uncritical acceptance of an idea coming from another person. And people are said to be more or less suggestible according to the degree to which they are governed by the ideas of others.

Suggestion may be looked upon as a force to be guarded against or as a force to be employed. If one wishes to guarantee that his own behaviour shall be as effective as possible, he will choose the former attitude; whereas if he happens to be especially interested in controlling the behaviour of others, he will choose the latter attitude. Applied psychology should offer the material necessary for satisfying either demand.

Conditions Favouring Suggestibility

The so-called laws of suggestion which state the conditions under which suggestion may be most forcefully used, will, if thoroughly understood, serve both as an aid in the use of suggestion and as a protection against it. It is true, however, that most interest has been directed toward the former of these functions. For example, suggestion as a means of increasing the efficiency of the salesman has been widely exploited. No corresponding attention has been given to the protection of the potential purchaser against the influence of the salesman.

The most important facts about suggestion are the following:

1. The suggestion should be indirect, that is, it should seem to arise spontaneously within the mind of the individual and not to come from another. Few persons are willing to have their ideas and actions completely under the control of another person and will on that account alone often resist suggestions when they are made too bluntly. Suggestion is most effective when used to strengthen ideas already present, but which are prevented from leading to action on account of the presence of other conflicting ideas. In such cases the one idea may be strengthened sufficiently to lead to action without opposition. This is very much easier than implanting entirely new ideas. The following cases described by Sidis (566, 7) are good examples of indirect suggestion:

> A stump orator mounts a log or a car and begins to harangue the crowd. In the grossest way he praises the great intelligence, the brave spirit of the people, the virtue of the citizens, glibly telling his audience that with such genius as they possess they must see clearly that the prosperity of the country depends on the politics he favours, on the party whose valiant champion he now is. His argument is absurd, his motive is contemptible, and still as a rule he carries the body of the crowd.

> A huckster stations himself in the middle of the street, on some public square, or on the sidewalk and begins to pour forth volumes of gibberish intended both as a compliment to the people and as praise of his ware. The curiosity of the passers-by is awakened. They stop. Soon our hero forms the center of a crowd that stupidly gazes at the "wonderful" objects held out to its view for admiration. A few moments more and the crowd begins to buy the things the huckster suggests as grand, beautiful and cheap.

2. There must be a high degree of attention to the idea that is suggested. This is much the same as the earlier statement that there must be no conflicting ideas if a given idea is to lead to action. A high degree of attention to an idea may be obtained by the removal of distracting conditions of all sorts. It may be accomplished by restricting bodily movements with the consequent reduction in the stream of sensations therefrom or by reducing the number of stimuli of the special senses, especially of vision and hearing. The favourable conditions for inducing that

extreme state of suggestibility known as hypnotism (298) are the darkened room, the crystal ball, the regularly beating metronome, and the rhythmic stroking of the arm or head. One reason which has been offered for the great suggestibility of persons in a crowd is the restriction of bodily movement caused by the massing of the people. Recent research into mob behaviour (*423*) has shown, however, that it is an extremely complicated pattern of reaction and not to be explained by any simple formula.

3. The success of a suggestion depends upon its source. Prestige and authority are great factors in giving strength to a suggestion (*375*). The mere fact that some one in authority or one in whom we have great confidence does a thing is sufficient to give the suggestion of it great power. Thus, we are likely to follow the leaders in fashion, in politics, in all social manners and customs through the intensity of the indirect suggestions coming from these sources. A powerful factor in selling certain kinds of goods is the suggestion that the article is used by the President of the United States, by the King of England, that it is manufactured by the largest firm in the United States, or by the oldest firm, although none of these factors is in itself any real guarantee of the value of the commodity. In the suggestive power of prestige and reputation lies much of the power of great evangelists, great orators and entertainers. The prestige of the radio was beautifully demonstrated by the reactions of thousands of people to the Martian broadcasts, the "War of the Worlds" (*81*), when their fears could have been immediately allayed by reference to the radio programmes in their daily papers.

4. The force of a suggestion depends in part upon the frequency with which it is applied. Repetition tends not only to increase the strength of the suggestion by driving out competing ideas, but tends also to make the suggestion seem spontaneous. In the course of the repetition, consciousness of the external origin of the suggested idea is lost. Many a person has denied that he is influenced by advertising in the purchasing of foods and other necessities, and yet a canvass of these purchases shows that a large proportion of them are of the most widely advertised and trade-marked goods. It is very likely that advertising of the

publicity sort met on every hands has much to do with the inability of people to account correctly for the disposition to buy certain brands of goods rather than others. Repetition is said to be a favoured device of the political dictators in forcing acceptance of their ideas.

5. Positive suggestions are more effective than negative suggestions. It is more effective to say, "Do this," than it is to say, "Do not do that." Ideas tend more directly to the production than to the inhibition of action. There is a strong tendency to react to suggestion in the positive fashion no matter how it may be presented. This is well illustrated in the story many times repeated of the man who offered a large money prize to any person who could fry an egg and while doing so refrain from repeating to himself the word hippopotamus. No one ever succeeded in winning the prize, for the negative suggestion guarantees the positive reaction. The relative value of positive and negative suggestion has been much discussed in connection with advertising appeals (*387*), whereas the growing belief in the efficacy of positive suggestion is reflected in the striking decrease in the use of negative suggestions in advertising during the last two decades.

6. Cantril (*82*) points out still another condition favouring suggestibility which is found in the state of confusion existing in the minds of people regarding questions of social philosophy. Confused and bewildered persons whose foundations of belief are badly shaken and who need enlightenment and guidance will tend to accept them uncritically from any promising source. By playing upon condition of mind such as these, dictators have risen to power.

Individual Differences in Suggestibility

Numerous experiments have been devised for measuring suggestibility (*479*) (*701*), and attention has been directed thereby to the question of individual differences in this trait. One very definite conclusion has been reached, namely, that people cannot be classed into suggestible and non-suggestible groups. This trait is possessed in varying degrees just as intelligence is found to be distributed among the population. Furthermore, it has been found that a person who is very suggestible in one situation is not necessarily suggestible in another situation (*63*). It would seem that there are many suggestibilities rather than a single trait of suggestibility. As age increases it has been found that suggestibility tends to decrease. The exact relationship between intelligence and suggestibility is not known, but it is likely that there is at least a slight negative correlation between these two characteristics in the individual. As far as sex differences are concerned, no clear-cut differences between men and women have been discovered. Suggestion is a most powerful factor in those individuals who cannot or do not think for themselves. Waves of certain types of crime, waves of suicide by peculiar means, waves of kidnapping, waves of mania for dancing, and waves of style are in part at least to be explained by the power of suggestion upon certain types of mind.

Crowd Suggestibility

The suggestibility of people, when gathered into crowds, follows the same laws as that of the individual taken alone, but susceptibility to suggestion seems to increase in a crowd. There appears to be less resistance to suggested ideas and less repugnance toward being swayed by others. The conflicting ideas that help to determine the course of action in any one person taken alone are submerged in the group. Or, as one writer has aptly put it, "The intensity of personality is in inverse proportion to the number of aggregated men." Sidis (*566*, 300) thus describes the suggestibility of the crowd:

> There is a gradual limitation of voluntary movement, a condition of monotony and inhibition with a consequent contraction of the field of consciousness. When a preacher, politician, the stump orator, the ringleader, the hero, gains the ear of the crowd, an ominous silence frequently characterised as awful sets in. The crowd is in a state of overstrained expectation; with suspended breath it watches the hero or the interesting, all-absorbing object. Disturbing impressions are excluded, put down, driven away by main force. So great is the silence induced in the fascinated crowd, that very frequently the buzzing of a fly or even the drop of a pin can be distinctly heard. All interfering impressions and ideas are inhibited.

By referring to the conditions of suggestibility previously

mentioned it will be seen that here is an ideal setting for powerful suggestions to become effective. Often individuals are horrified at what they did as members of a mob. Religious revivals, political meetings, strike riots, and lynchings are all illustrations of what individuals, when collected into a large group and under the influence of strong suggestion, will do. Cantril (82) has furnished excellent descriptions of the patterns of mass action in a variety of settings, including lynchings, religious cults, social utopias, and great political movements.

Propaganda

The topic of propaganda deserves space in any chapter dealing with the control of ideas, not so much because it is a unique phenomenon but because it represents a deliberate, systematic, and organised large scale effort to control public opinion. When subjected to psychological analysis, skilful propaganda is seen to rest upon the full utilisation of the facts of suggestion and suggestibility such as have been discussed in this chapter. Its current potency is due not to the discovery of new principles but to the universality of the radio and motion picture, the public-opinion poll, and other means of rapid and widespread communication by way of which ideas may be disseminated and their influence gauged. The present state of social unrest is undoubtedly a contributing factor, heightening suggestibility, but whether this unrest is cause or effect of the power of propaganda is not so easy to determine.

What is it that distinguishes propaganda from education, publicity, news, or advertising? Lasswell (*365*) and his associates attempt to discriminate among these terms. Education is defined by them as a process of transmitting skill and *accepted* attitudes, whereas propaganda is a process of transmitting attitudes that are recognised as *controversial* within a given community. This is, indeed, a tenuous and variable distinction. Identical ideas spread at one time and place may be education, and at another time and place may be propaganda. The authors just mentioned say that the inculcation of respect for Martin Luther in a devout Prussian village is a process of education in terms of the village, but a process of propaganda in terms of the whole of Germany or of the world. To the casual onlooker upon the current social scene, the most obvious distinction education and propaganda resides in the greater zeal, enthusiasm, and vigor with which the propagandists prosecute their programme. Education in its process of spreading accepted views might learn much from those who endeavour to teach controversial ideas.

Social psychologists have been actively interested in the conditions which favour the inculcation of attitudes as contrasted with the educators who have till recent years concerned themselves with the teaching of mental and motor skills. The development of techniques for measuring attitudes in the form of tests and scales has been followed by a succession of studies of the relative effectiveness of the spoken and printed word, of the speaking person as compared with a recording of his speech, of the influence of age, degree of education, family background, economic and social status upon attitude change. Murphy, Murphy, and Newcomb (*449*) have made this material accessible to the reader in an extensive survey.

These brief comments upon propaganda may be closed with the observation that the mechanisms and processes that have been described in this and the preceding chapter can be enlisted equally well in the cause of education and in the cause of propaganda, in the cause of changing attitudes and in the cause of developing resistance to such changes.

4

WORK AND REST

Work and fatigue resulting from work come close to the daily life of every one. As a consequence they were among the earliest problems to be investigated by the physiologist and the psychologist. The concern of the psychologist has been indicated on several occasions in the preceding chapters. He has had to deal with fatigability as a possible source of differences in achievement between the sexes; he has had to look for fatigue effects in the quality and quantity of learning under various conditions; and more generally still he has been led to search for methods of work in which the fatigue would be the least. In doing these things he has accepted more or less directly the layman's notion of fatigue. The layman has no rigid definition, but he *knows* what fatigue is and believes that he regulates his behaviour so as to avoid it or recover from it when it cannot be avoided. He knows that fatigues is "being tired" and that when one is tired the proper thing to do is to rest. Such a meaning is satisfactory and safe under ordinary circumstances, particularly where there is no urge "to make the most of one-self". However, when pressure for increased output is exerted as in a war emergency, then doubts begin to arise because sometimes one feels tired when he has done no work at all, and sometimes he does not feel tired after a long period of work. He discovers, too, that the tired feeling occasionally disappears in the course of work instead of becoming more pronounced as it should.

The Concepts of Work and Fatigue

The foregoing statements suggest the need for a definition of the terms work and fatigue, if confusion is to be avoided. This is especially true of the former where a variety of meanings can be detected in everyday usage. For instance, work may mean a certain product such as a cord of wood sawed, a mountain climbed, or a chapter of a book written, and it may mean the process by which these results were achieved. Thus one may do a great deal of work without accomplishing much, when sawing wood with a dull saw, or when struggling to write a chapter when the "conditions are not right". Work defined as product also has a variety of meanings. There seems to be a distinction on the basis of utility such that if the product is useful it is called work, if it is not useful it is called "play" (*77*). Similarly, one can detect a distinction on the basis of necessity, work being that which is necessary and play that which is not necessary. There is a further common notion that work is necessarily unpleasant, whereas play is by its very nature pleasant.

Even when work is defined as process or function the meaning is not entirely unequivocal. In fact the meanings in terms of output have equivalent meanings in terms of function. *Doing* something necessary is work and *doing* something unnecessary is play. There is the tendency, too, to think of the work process as limited to that which leads to the desired or useful product. Thus in an experiment on a finger ergograph the rhythmic contractions of the finger that raise the weight are work, but there are contractions and tensions of other muscles which are just as real work so far as the organism is concerned.

The most serious source of confusion for both scientist and layman resides in the distinction between physical work and mental work. And this distinction appears in work conceived as product and as process. Physical work is thought of as something like pounds lifted, the result of the contraction of muscle and the movement of bones. Mental work is less tangible, like solutions to problems, and involves the functioning of the mind or perhaps the brain. The distinction is frequently drawn between solving a problem which is mental work and writing down the answer or speaking it, which is physical work. Benedict and Carpenter (*35*) measured the mental work done in taking an examination by deducting from the total energy expended in the process the amount that was later expended in just copying the examination paper as previously written. This residue was the cost of the pure mental-work process.

It may be convenient to use the terms mental and physical in reference to product. In terms of process, however, it would appear to be less confusing to classify work in terms of the amount of overt muscular activity involved such as heavy, medium, and light, or general and local. For research has demonstrated that even the purest thinking may be correlated with incipient speech movements, and that "mental images" may be recorded in terms of muscle tensions (*553a*). The acceptable scientific procedure would be to describe the task, the process, and the product and avoid such labels as work and play, mental and physical.

Most of the definitions of fatigue that have been proposed have been derived from common-sense notions, and emphasise one or another aspect of them. One rather widely accepted definition is that fatigue is the reduction in the output of work as the result of work, and which is recoverable by rest. In this particular definition the feelings of tiredness are not mentioned, but in others they have been recognised as potent factors in determining output of work. Thus Woodworth (*713*) said:

> Every one who has worked with the ergograph has certainly felt these sensations. Every one recognises that their tendency is to check contractions. Every one must have noticed the difficulty, amounting in untrained subjects to impossibility, of resisting this tendency. Yet few have recognised the sensations of fatigue as an actual factor in the determinations of the rate of fatigue.

Dodge (*140*), likewise, felt that feelings had a place in the concept of fatigue in that they acted as warning signals against overexercise of delicate mechanisms.

The lack of correlation between changes in output of work and changes in the feelings, along with other inconsistencies in definition, led Muscio (*454*) to reëxamine thoroughly the whole concept of fatigue. He gave expression to a point of view which has had a pronounced effect upon subsequent thinking and research. Starting with the widely accepted definition of fatigue as "a condition caused by work in which the capacity for work is diminished," he revised it at once by substituting the word "activity" for work, since, as he said, play as well as work may conceivably cause fatigue. His definition thus became : "Fatigue is a condition caused by activity in which the capacity for repeating the activity that caused it is diminished." He then noted that capacity for activity cannot be directly observed, but must be inferred from some expression of it. The most obvious expression would be output of work and a less obvious one perhaps would be feelings. But is output a valid expression of capacity? Dodge had shown that output at least within certain limits, is a function of the intensity of the stimulus, citing the changes in performance due to motivation in the form of incentives. He had shown also, and again within certain limits, that output is a function of the intensity of motivation toward competing kinds of activity, citing in this case the effects of distractions upon output. Hence, Muscio concluded that, at best, output only *tends* to be an expression of diminished capacity when there are no interfering factors. He arrived at a final definition as follows: "Fatigue is a condition caused by activity in which output produced by that activity tends to be relatively poor; and the degree of fatigue tends to vary directly with poorness of output." This definition he considered inadequate and scientifically unsatisfactory for two reasons. The first is that fatigue can never be directly measured but is a condition which must be *inferred* from diminished capacity, whereas diminished capacity itself must in turn be *inferred* from diminished output. The second reason is that the inference of diminished capacity from diminished ouppuc is insecure since the latter is known to depend upon a variety of influences such as distraction and motivation. Muscio concluded that the concept of fatigue had lost its utility by reason of its very remoteness from reality.

The Effects of Work

After making a critical examination of these and other difficulties inherent in the various interpretations of fatigue, Muscio recommended that the concept of fatigue be banished from precise scientific discussion, and that in its stead attempts should be made to measure the effects of work directly upon mental and physiological functions without the intermediary notion of fatigue. Although this recommendation implies primarily a shift of emphasis, it is a healthful one in that it forces attention upon the psychophysical mechanism of work and the changes which it undergoes while functioning. When the changes become known, and ready means of measuring their amount become available, the practical problem of efficient work will be easy of solution. The relative extent of the changes during different work conditions will show which ones of such conditions are the most favourable for work.

The functions in which changes may be sought as a consequence of work are numerous and varied. Although a complete account of the effects of work would call for the measurement of all of these functions, data on only one or several may be adequate for the solution of a particular practical problem. The functions whose changes have been measured or proposed for measurement at one time or another are output of work, strength, feelings, energy cost, pulse, blood pressure, weight, skin sensitivity, sensory acuity, and perceptual reactions. The point to note is that each or all of these should be measured for what the evidence would be worth rather than to provide the means of inferring a condition of fatigue. Thus at a time when high output is vital, that method of work could be cought in which the initial output was highest and the decrement from continuing it the least. It is conceivable that at another period, as in a time of labour unrest, the matter of most concern would be to find that method of work in which the feelings would be the least outraged. Or at still another period, as in a time of extreme food shortage, the important thing might be to get work done with the least expenditure of energy. Finally, it might well be that changes in the circulatory functions would be the most significant effects to search out if one were measuring the cost of work in conditions of extreme heat as in a boiler room. A knowledge of the correlations among these various measures would be of immense scientific and practical interest. If the correlations were very high one measure could serve as an indicator of the others, but even if the correlations were unknown or were known to be low, each measure could serve its own independent purpose. Some of these more common measures will be examined.

Effects of work upon sensitivity

Several tests of bodily sensitivity have been used from time to time as indicators of a change of condition during work. Underlying their use was the expectation that there should be a general decrement resulting from work, and that the sensitive receptor mechanisms should be progressively dulled. Notable among the sensitivity tests was the two-point threshold test or the esthesiometric index (*701*, I, 243-261), as it was called, to detect changes in discriminative power of the skin. It was widely employed at one time as a means of showing the fatigue of school children and for classifying them according to their endurance. The test was thought to be an indirect measure of sustained attention a function that ought to undergo a decrement in the course of work. After years of controversy over the question the test has been recognised to be so influenced by innumerable variables that it is no longer employed as an index of the effects of work. Since changes in the function itself have no practical utility no further attention need be given it here.

Visual acuity is another form of sensitivity that has been suggested from time to time as a useful index of change as a result of work. Requiring a high degree of fineness of muscular control, it might be expected to undergo deterioration during a period of work. Thus far no studies have definitely shown this to be the case. As the visual acuity test is usually administered, it suffers from the defect that it calls for only a momentary effort to which an individual can rise even under very adverse conditions. A more appropriate measure would be something like that employed by Ferree and Rand (*174*) in which the maintenance of maximal acuity was derermined over a period of three minutes. The visual acuity test deserves further consideration since it measures a function which has direct utility. This is especially true where, as in aviation, a high degree of visual capacity is of great importance, and where at the same time work under strain might be expected to create some decrement. In fact Ferree and Rand (*173*) have offered speed of accommodation for near and distant objects as a measure of fatigue of aviators.

Sensitivity of the skin to faradic stimulation is another measure that has been employed as an indicator of the state of the organism. An irritability curve covering a number of persons measured over a twelve-hour period by Grabfield and Martin (*226*) shows periods of high irritability (low threshold) between 10 and 11 a.m., and at 8.30 p.m., with a period of low irritability at about 4.30 p.m. This curve is reported to correspond very closely in its general features to curves for a series of crgograms and for a series of reaction times taken at various periods of the day. Large ergographic output and short reaction times corresponded to low threshold. The authors believed that the irritability index was not a measure merely of peripheral sensitivity but was an indicator of the general nervous condition of the subject. The test itself is subject to all the difficulties inherent in threshold measurement, particularly momentary fluctualtions in attention, and is therefore not very feasible for detecting the more gradual changes that might be expected to occur in the course of work.

The Effects of Work upon Muscular Strength

The Martin Strength Test (*400*) measures the amount of traction that certain muscle groups can resist. The test has been used primarily for determining standards of strength required for certain kinds of industrial work, but its author says:

> Variations of strength between the beginning and the end of a working period, particularly if they take the direction of a falling off at the end of the shift, are indicative of an impairment of physique which can be most readily explained on the basis of fatigue.

Table 4.1 gives a few sample figures showing percentage of change in strength as the result of a day's work of different sorts. There are two kinds of work, heavy and light, represented in the table, as well as two groups of workers, strong and weak, as measured by the strength tests. Plus signs mean increase in strength and minus signs mean decrease in strength. The table shows that heavy work causes a greater percentage of loss in strength than light work, and also that strong individuals suffer less than weak ones. It will be noticed that the strong group of workers increased their strength in one of the heavy tasks and in both of the light tasks, and that the weak group increased their strength in both the light tasks. There has been an inclination to doubt the value of a test for measuring physiological changes during work which shows an actual improvement after the "expenditure of much energy." Muscio (*455*) criticised the test because of the errors to which it is liable when administered under factory conditions and by different testers. A further criticism resides in the fact that the test calls for a momentary resistance to tension, and that the brief bursts of power needed in such a case may be possible even for a tired muscle group. However, the measurement would be warranted in so far as such strength as the test measures is a condition that might have utility on any given occasion.

Table 4.1
Changes in Strength during Work*

Operation	*Per cent Change*	
	Strong	*Weak*
Heavy – Swaging valves....	0.00	–4.60
Brazing heavy part.......	+1.00	–6.00
Light – Milling machine...	+ 3.20	+ 0.68
Drilling and burrring.......	+ 5.00	+ 1.60

*From E. G. Martin, "Strength Tests in Industry," United States Public Health Service Report No. 606, 1920.

Effects of work upon Attention control

It has been pointed out by numerous investigators that work involving a high degree of attention is likely to be more fatiguing than that which demands merely strength or speed. There are other reasons for believing, too, that attention is a highly sensitive barometer of general mental and physical efficiency. It was such a belief, in part at least, which led to the use of the various sensitivity tests mentioned above, since sensory thresholds were known to be affected by degree of attention. It is not surprising, therefore, that an effort should be made to find a direct measure of attention to replace the more indirect ones. Reversals of visual perspective, such as occur in looking at simple drawings of cubes and staircases, have been thought to be a function of attention, and these have been measured as indicators of shifting attention. According to Carr (*88*, 282) these reversals "occur automatically and spontaneoulsy even though one perspective may be the preferred one and in spite of any experimental or volitional control."

Ash (*17*) set up a reversible perspective test for measuring the fatigue caused by arithmetical computation. The speed of reversal for cubes and pyramids was measured before and after one hour of computation in the case of twenty-one subjects, one and a half hours for three subjects, and two hours for one subject. For this last subject the reversal time was longer after the work by 26 per cent, 51 per cent, and 104 per cent for the one-hour, the one and one-half-hour, and the two-hour work periods respectively. For the three subjects who worked for one and for one and one-half hours the average delay was 39 per cent and 53.6 per cent respectively, although one of these subjects showed greater delay for the shorter period. For the twenty-one subjects who worked only one hour, the average delay varied from 9 per cent to 146 per cent, with an average of 50 per cent. There was no instance in which the speed of reversal was greater after work than before.

Poffenberger* repeated the visual-perspective test, as used by Ash before and after physical work performed on devices of the ergograph type, involving either the hand, the arm, the leg, or the whole body as in rowing. In every type of work the combined records for all subjects showed fewer reversals after work than before work. However, the differences are too small and the variability too great to make the results anything more than suggestive. Thus, in the data for the leg work comprising eighty-six different measures and showing an average of 8.7 per cent fewer reversals after work, there were fifty individual cases of "slower after work" and thirty-six of "faster after work". Serious difficulties have been encountered in the practical administration of the test, as it requires well-trained subjects to get satisfactory results. One difficulty arises from the difference between voluntary and spontaneous reversals as pointed out by Hollingworth (*273*) since the effects of continued work seem to decrease speed of reversal in the former and to increase it in the latter.

Effects of work upon motor control

The fineness of motor control or coördination is such an essential factor in many forms of adjustment as to justify a search for its decrement in the course of work. This is particularly true in industrial operations where heavy labour has been so largely replaced by rapid movements of small muscles, and where slight deviations from proper control may result in serious error or accident. Ash (*17*) acted upon an observation made by McDougall (*406*) that in the use of a finger ergograph the fingers not immediately concerned in the lifting begin to respond as the contractions of the working finger grows weaker. As the work progresses the muscles of the wrist, arm, shoulder, and even of the face and neck become involved.

These accessory responses indicate a spread or overflow of excitation out of the immediately appropriate channels. Ash attempted to measure this spread of activity in the course of work. He modified the usual Mosso finger ergograph so that while the middle finger was attached to a weight of 13.2 pounds, the first and third fingers which are ordinarily held rigid were

FIGURE 4.1

The Effect of Work upon Motor Control*

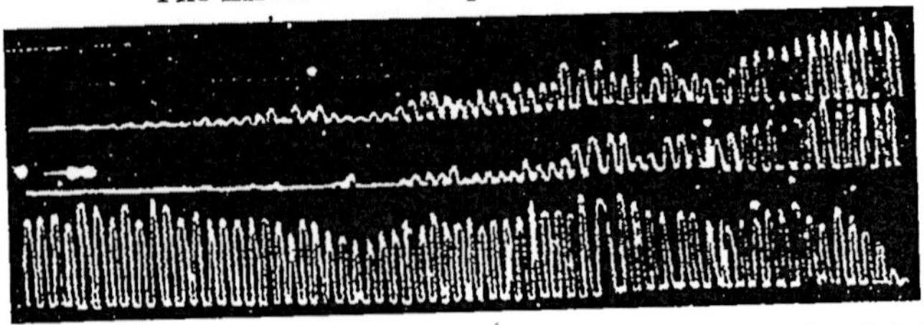

* From I. E. Ash, "Fatigue and Its Effect upon Control," *Arch. Psychol.* (New York, 1914, No. 31, 19.)

attached to springs of known tension. As the middle finger lifted the weight any movements of the first and third fingers would pull against the springs. Kymograph records were made of the movement of all three fingers and the amount of work done by each was calculated. Such a set of curves is shown in Figure 4.1, where *C* represents the middle finger lifting the weight, *B* the third finger, and A index finger. Table 4.2 shows the foot-pounds of work done in groups of five contractions. Column I is the index finger, Column II is the middle finger, and Column III is the third finger. Column IV gives sum of the work done by the first and third fingers. It may be noted from both the chart and the table that the spread of movement to the "non-working" fingers begins very early and is noticeable earlier than the reduction of output in the working finger.

TABLE 4.2
Spread of Motor Response in the Course of Work*
Foot-Pounds of Work in Successive Groups of Five Lifts

Groups of five Contractions	*I Index Finger*	*II Middle Finger*	*III Third finger*	*IV Sum of Index and Third Fingers*
1	.00	5.30	.00	.00
2	.00	5.50	.03	.03
3	.00	5.30	.11	.11
4	.01	4.81	.29	.30
5	.07	4.12	.17	.24
6	.07	3.78	.36	.43
7	.21	4.54	.52	.73
8	.29	4.88	.70	.99
9	.92	5.15	1.20	1.92
10	.53	4.40	1.01	1.54
11	1.19	3.85	1.01	1.20
12	1.79	4.33	2.23	4.12
13	2.11	1.36	1.82	3.93

* from I. E. Ash, "Fatigue and Its Effect upon Control," *Arch. Psychol.* (New York), 1914, 32.

Dodge (*140*) disclosed the increasing loss of motor control in a succession of rhythmic eye movements. The eyes, each with set of six external muscles, constitute an exceedingly sensitive and finely balanced coördinating mechanism. Any decrement in control should show itself in the character of the eye movements. Dodge instructed his subjects to shift their eyes rhythmically from one fixation point to another over an angle of 60 degrees, and photographed the series of movements upon a falling plate. Such a photographic record is reproduced in Figure 4.2 where the dash lines mark the sweep of the eyes back and forth, and

FIGURE 4.2
Effects of Work upon Eye-movement control*

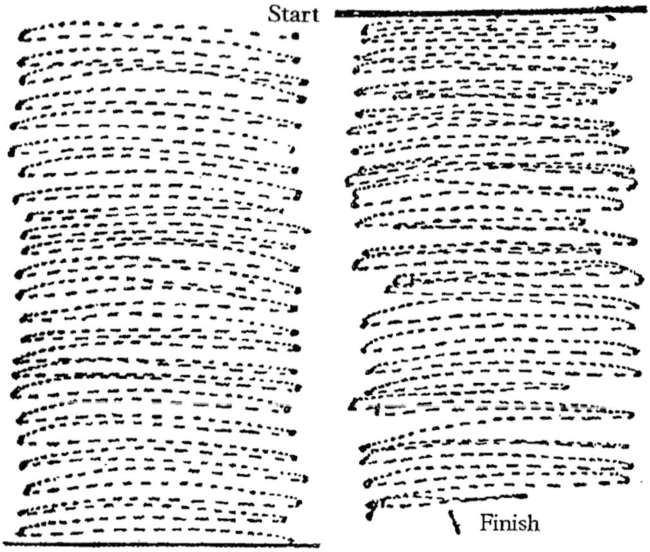

* From R. Dodge, "The Laws of Relative Fatigue," *Psychol. Rev.*, 1917, 24, 107.

where each dash and each space equals an interval of .008. In the early part of the record the curves are smooth and of uniform length and the dashes evenly distributed, indicating that the fixations are accurate and the speed of movement steady. The latter part of the record, on the other hand, shows increasingly faulty fixations, varying rates of speed, and unevenness of the paths traversed. All of these changes are indications of a deterioration in control which Dodge attributes to a central rather than a peripheral factor, since in binocular reactions the two eyes respond in the same way.

Weinland (*687*) attempted to follow the course of the variability of performance in the usual type of ergograph curve, obtained from the finger, arm, hand, leg, and the body as a whole (rowing). He had available the records of ten subjects, each furnishing a number of ergograms. Of the several types of variation in performance, he was particularly interested in the

FIGURE 4.3
Variability of Performance in the Work Curve*

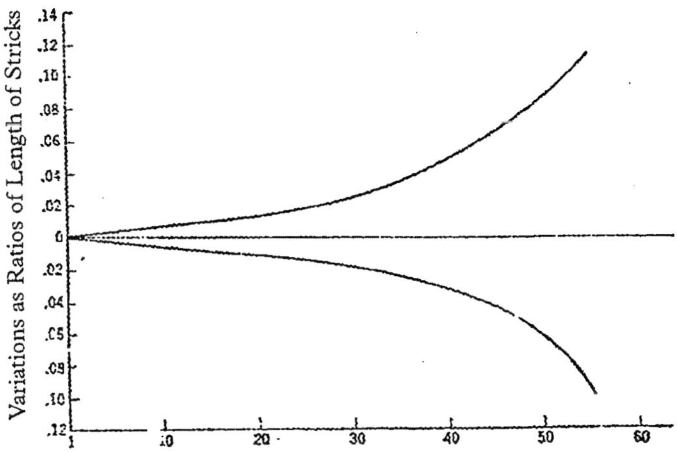

Units of Work Curve

* Modified from J.D. Weinland, "Variability of Performance in the Curve of Work," *Arch. Psychol.* (New York), 1927, No. 87. 23.

changes in output from moment to moment of the work period. He corrected for the increase in variability due to the gradual fall in the level of the curve by computing the variations of the individual contractions above and below a smoothed curve. Figure 4.3 presents a chart showing in terms of percentages the course of the deviations thus computed for an arm raising a twelve-pound weight at a two-second rhythm and continuing till the weight could no lognger be moved. The vertical scale shows the percentage of change from the smoothed curve taken as zero, and the horizontal scale marks the successive units of the ergogram. The varistion increases from zero at the beginning and may amount to as much as 20 per cent for some individuals at the end. The fluctuations are undoubtedly due to irregularity of motor control rather than to the condition of the muscle. The pattern of variation changes with the individual and with the particular kind of movement, although "the degree of variability within the work curve appears to remain comparatively constant for a given individual under particular working conditions." The steadiness of tempo of reaction was also found to vary in the course of work. It need scarcely be pointed out that fluctuations in motor control of the magnitude recorded in this experiment, accompanied by variations in movement rhythm, might have serious repercussions upon acievement. The size of the differences in variability among individuals, which would be expected and which were noted in this experiment, suggest the probable importance of selection for stability of motor control.

The concept of blocking in the course of continued work has been developed by Bill (*39*); and many of his experiments with such functions as colour naming, naming opposites, addition, and subtraction seem to support his view. Blockings are "brief periods when the subject is unable to react at all and must pause an instant before proceeding." He seeks the explanation for the blocks in the "cumulative refractory periods" of the functioning neural units, a theory of mental fatigue earlier proposed by Dodge (*140*) and elaborated by Robinson (*521*).

The point of particular interest is that the blockings are reported to occur more frequently and to become longer as work continues. Although these inert periods demonstrated by Bills are so brief and occur so frequently that they would not be readily detectable in the course of everyday activities, they represent a type of loss of control. If they were to become more and more persistent in the course of long continued repetitive work, they would have to be reckoned with as a factor in efficient performance. Search might well be made for evidence of such loss of control in operations resembling more closely the activities of everyday life.

Effect of Work Upon the Feelings

The discrepancy between the way one feels and the amount of work he is able to do is a matter of common knowledge. Its influence upon the formulation of concepts of work and fatigue has already been mentioned. The changes which the feelings undergo during work deserve careful examination both as possible signs of capacity to work and as indicators in their own right of the effect of work.

Thorndike (*619*) had five persons judge the quality of compositions continuously for four hours. Every twenty minutes during this period each person evaluated his feelings on a ten-point scale ranging from extreme distaste or discomfort to extreme interest, zeal, or satisfaction. He reports that whereas output remained substantially the same in quantity and quality, the satisfyingness decreased greatly. "These facts support the general doctrine that the effect of lack of rest is far greater upon whatever is the physiological basis of interest, willingness, or tolerability than upon the physiological basis of quanitity and quality of product produced."

Poffenberger (*499*) obtained substantially the same results when he computed the averages for ten to thirteen subjects working at four different kinds of tasks, equivalent forms of an intelligence examination, sentence completion, judging compositions, and addition. The work continued for approximately five and one-half hours, except for addition where the time was less. The total time was divided into units of approximately twenty minutes. At the beginning of the experiment and at the end of each unit, the feelings were evaluated on a scale of seven degrees, varying from (1) Extremely good to (7) Extremely tired. At the end of the fourteenth unit of work a rest period of ten minutes was introduced, at the termination of which the final unit of work was completed. The data for this whole experiment are presented graphically in Figure 4.4. Solid lines show output and broken lines show feelings. The output curves are plotted in terms of ratios of the initial score taken as 1.00 (left-hand vertical scale), and the feeling curves are plotted in terms of units of the scale above or below the initial feeling score which is taken as zero (right-hand vertical scale).

In every type of work these average curves show a considerable drop in the quality of feelings, regardless of the course of the output curves. It will be noted that the tasks differ markedly so far as output changes are concerned, ranging from a gain of 20 per cent in the intelligence tests (obviously practice effect), to addition with a loss of about 20 per cent; completion and the judgment of compositions remaining almost unchanged. The greatest change in the feelings occurs in the completion test in which output does not fall. One further fact should be noted, that the ten-minute rest improved the quality of the feelings by

Figure 4.4

Relation Between Output and Feelings in Four Forms of Mental Works*

Solid Line Represents Output and Dotted Line Represents Feeling Record

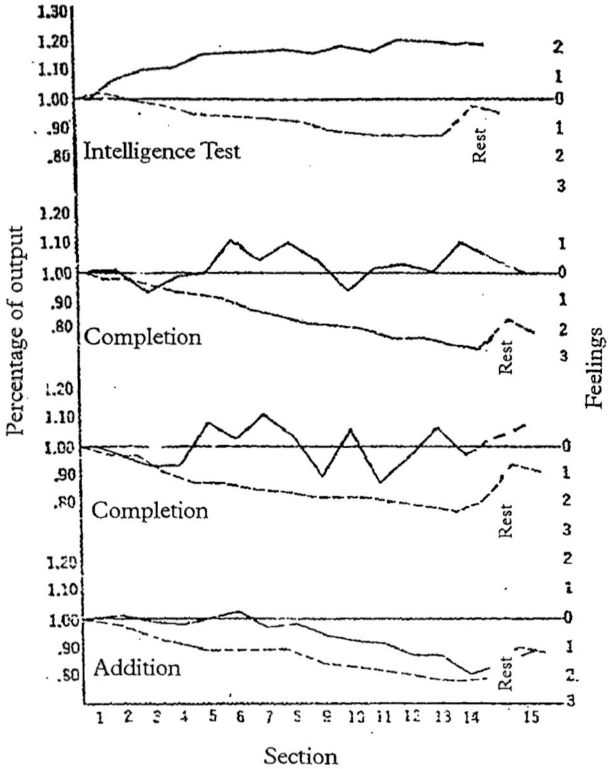

* From A. T. Poffenberger, "Effects of Continuous Work upon Output and Feelings," *J. App. Psychol.*, 1928, 12, 459-467

one scale unit or more, regardless of whether the output improved or not.

An inspection of the separate curves of output and of feelings for each individual provide one additional bit of suggestive information. In the intelligence test the subject who made the greatest gain in output had the least decrement in his feelings, whereas the one who made the least gain in output had the greatest decrement in feelings. The same is true in the case of the addition test. These facts are shown graphically in Figure 4.5

where the solid line represent output and the broken line represents feelings.

In order to discover whether the relationship between

FIGURE 4.5
Relationship Between Amount of Change in Output and Amount of Change in Feelings*

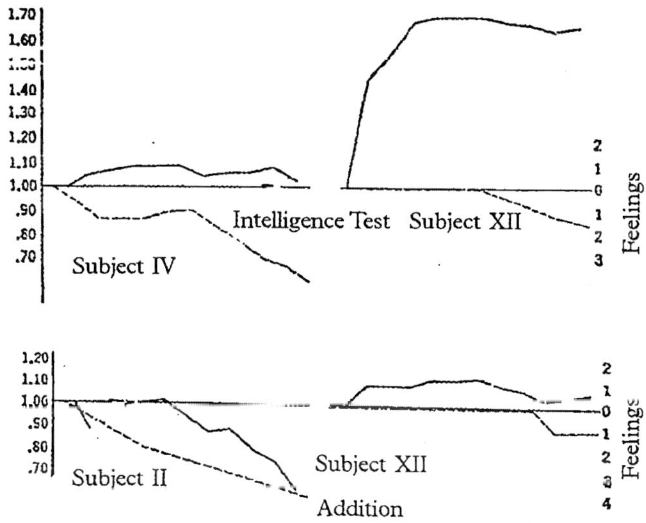

*From A.T. Poffenberger, "Effects of Continuous Work upon Output and Feelings," *J. Appl. Psychol.*, 1928, 12, 459-467.

amount of loss in output and in feelings shown in these two extreme cases would hold more generally, the four subjects showing the greatest loss of output were compared with the four showing the least output in regard to the amount of feeling change. The former dropped 2.0 scale units of feeling and the latter 1.25 units in the intelligence test; and the former dropped 3.25 units and the latter dropped 1.25 units in the addition test. With so few cases it is futile to compute the reliability of these differences, but the results do suggest that those persons who lose most in output may be the ones who will be expected to experience the greatest change in feelings and vice versa.

As suggested in the beginning of this chapter, changes in the feeling level may be a significant item of information, entirely aside from any relationship such a measure may have with quality or quantity or of output. Other things being equal, that type of work, length of work spell, distribution of rest periods, or condition of noise or of quiet which outrages the feelings the least would be the best one.

Effects of Work Upon Rate of Recovery

The effects of work may very well show themselves not so much in terms of amount produced as in terms of the time that is required to recover from a spell of work, or the degree to which recovery occurs in a standard time interval. Thus in a standardized type of work whose rhythm is specified by the speed of a machine or of a moving belt, the effects may appear in a failure to recover from a nights rest.

Mosso (*440*) in one of his early ergograph experiments found that, with a given load to be lifted, the finger became exhausted after lifting the weight thirty times. Complete recovery from this work required two hours of rest. When the work was stopped after the weight had been lifted only fifteen times, complete recovery was attained in only a half hour. Thus the recovery time is reduced to one-fourth by reducing the number of lifts one half. From these simple facts a hypothetical recovery curve can be constructed as shown in Figure 4.6. The horizontal scale indicates the number of lifts, whereas the vertical scale indicates the percentage of time required to recover from

FIGURE 4.6
Rate of Fatigue During Work

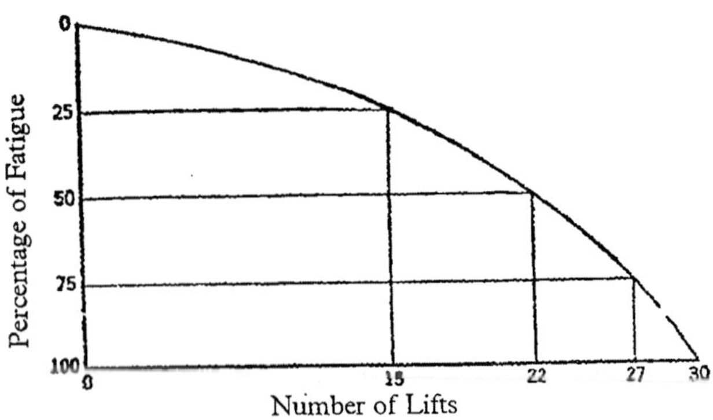

complete exhaustion (percentage of fatigue), zero being at the top of the scale and 100 per cent at the bottom of the scale. It appears that it took four times as long to recover from the second half of the work (the second fifteen lifts of the weight) as from the first half (the first fifteen lifts of the weight). It appears also that the last three lifts cost as much in time required for recovery as the first fifteen lifts. If recovery time be taken as the measure of efficiency, then carrying work to the limit of exhaustion would be uneconomical because the last few units of work would be too costly. On the other hand, the introduction of a half hour of rest would always keep the worker in that part of his curve where the cost per lift would be the least. The problem of efficient work reduces, therefore, to keeping the worker in the efficient part of his curve through the introduction of rest, adjustment of load, and so forth.

Crawley (*121*) measured the effects of work under varying conditions upon the degree of recovery during a standardised rest period and found that increasing output in a given work period would, under certain circumstances, be reflected in a decreased output after rest. A pair of ergograms taken before and after a rest of four minutes when the arm was lifting rhythmically a load of fifteen pounds. Since under the conditions of the experiment the output should be the same after rest as before it, the decrement in the second work period is attributed to failure to recover completely during the rest. The cumulative effect of a work and rest schedule which does not allow for complete recovery from any one work period is clearly shown in the curves obtained by Manzer (*394*). Work spells of rhythemical lifting by the arm of a 13.5 kilogram load until exhaustion, repeated fourteen times with a rest period of two minutes between work spells. Since all should have been the same as the first one except for the failure to recover from preceding work periods, the cumulative loss throughout the series is obvious.

The degree of recovery and, conversely, the degree of failure to recover from varios kinds of work with different rest intervals between work periods is shown in Table 4.2, which is also derived from Manzer. The work performed by a number of subjects was all of the egograph type involving either the finger, hand, arm,

TABLE 4.2
Recovery from Work*

	Original	After Rest		
		5 min.	10 min.	20 min.
Finger......	100	83	86	100
Hand.......	100	82	90	95
Arm........	100	90	98	99
Leg	100	85	100	103
Rowing....	100	72	75	77
Average....	100	82	90	95

* From C.W. Manzer, "An Experimental Study of Rest Pauses," *Arch. Psychol.* (New York), 1927, 90, 29.

leg, or the whole boxy (as in rowing). The rest intervals were five, ten, and twenty minutes in length. In each case the work done is expressed in percentages of the first work period which is taken as 100 per cent. It will be seen from this table that a five-minute rest did not bring about complete recovery in any type of work, but that ten minutes was adequate for recovery of the leg and twenty minutes for recovery of the finger. Rowing showed the least recovery after every rest period.

Sufficient evidence has been given to show that the effect of kind and quantity of work may be detected in terms of time required to recover or the amount recovered in a given time. The techniques employed in these studies are not appropriate for field studies, but they offer the sort of evidence from which a scientific study of work and rest programmer could well begin. Here the conditions were set so as to bring out effects in terms of recovery. In everyday life the loss per unit of work or per day might be so small as to be undetected, and yet the cumulative effect of months or years might assume disturbing proportions. Some of the series of ergograms obtained by Manzer showed no unrecoverd effect in the second and even in the third ergogram, but in the tenth the effect was unmistakable.

Effects of Work Upon Metabolism

If one looks upon the human organism as a machine and its functioning as a process which transforms energy, then the work that it performs can be measured directly in terms of such energy transformation, which is known as metabolism. The unit of measure generally employed for expressing the rate of the metabolic process is the *calory*, which is a heat unit. It denotes the amount of heat necessary to raise one gram of water one degree centigrade. As the amount of heat needed to do this is very small, a unit 1,000 times as large and known as the large calory is commonly used. It denotes the amount of heat needed to raise the temperature of a kilogram of water one degree centigrade. Thus the energy that the human body has to expend in performing any sort of task could be measured in terms of calories, and the differences in energy cost between various work programmes could be measured in the same way.

The direct determination of the amount of energy liberated by way of the heat generated is laborious and cumbersome, as it requires the subject to be confined in an elaborate calorimeter chamber. Fortunately, a substitute measure is available in terms of the oxigen which the body extracts from the air that it breathes. The energy releasing process is an oxidation process in which a kind of fuel, presumably glycogen, is burned and heat generated. Now this combustion process requires oxygen and the amount of it that is needed to release a unit of energy has been computed. Thus, as stated by Hill (*259*), one liter of oxygen is required to produce 5.14 calories (large) or, roughly, a fifth of a liter of oxygen is needed to produce one calory of energy. Fortunately, also, the human body has no facilities for the storage of oxygen which may be drawn upon as needed, so that the amount used has to be promptly replaced by extracting it from the inspired air. It is possible, therefore, to measure the amount of energy used in work even oven a short period of time, by determining the amount of oxygen used. There are numerous ways of doing this, each with its own advantages and disadvantages. The method which has the greatest flexibility and which allows the greatest freedom of movement while the measurements are being made, is illustrated in Figure 4.7, taken from Hill's study referred to above (*259*, 9). The subject inspires atmospheric air whose constitution is known and is remarkably stable. His expired air is captured in a suitable container. When the composition of this expired air is determined and compared with the inspired air, the changes which it has undergone can be computed. Atmospheric air has the following components:

	Per cent
Oxygen	20.93
Carbon dioxide	0.03
Nitrogen	79.04

If the expired air turned out to be;

	Per cent
Oxygen	16.93
Carbon	4.03
Nitrogen	79.04

Then 4 per cent of the oxygen would have been used; and if the total quantity of the air expired was known, the actual amount of oxygen could be found. It will be noted that amount of carbon dioxide has increased in this illustration by 4 per cent. The amount of carbon dioxide, too, could be used as an index of energy. However, it has one disadvantage which offsets certain advantages, namely, that the body can store large quantities of carbon dioxide; hence one cannot tell just how the amount released is related to the amount produced during a given time interval. The illustration shows a bag strapped upon the worker's back, and a mask covering his nose and mouth. Flexible rubber tubing leads from the mask to the bag, and contains a valve permitting passage of air into the bag but not in the reverse direction. The mask also contains an opening to the outside air, and is fitted with a valve so that air may enter but not leave the mask thereby. Thus the expired air accumulates in the bag. There remains only the process of analysing this expired air, measuring its amount and computing the change. This is a laborious process, but it can be accomplished under ordinary working conditions with an estimated error of 1 per cent. How extensively this measure of the effects of work has been used in recent years is indicated in the survey of the literature on the subject up to 1932 by Page (*480*) whose annotated bibliography contains 625 references.

FIGURE 4.7
The Measurement of Energy Expenditure During Work*

*From A. V. Hill, *Muscular Movement in Man* (New York, Mc Graw-Hill Book Co., 1927), p. 9.

The energy expended in various forms of human locomotion is shown in Table 4.3 which is compiled from data of Hill, Long and Lupton (260), and Douglas and Priestley (*144a*). The first column of figures gives the speed of travel in miles per hour; the second gives the cubic centimeters of oxygen consumed per minute; and the third gives the amount consumed per mile of travel. All the figures are rough estimates and not all the data are taken from the same subjects, so that too much importance should not be attached to small differences. However the table shows that the energy measure is sensitive enough to pick up differences in cost resulting from variations in performance of work.

Schubert (*541*) attempted to measure the metabolic cost of a unit of work at various stages of the work curve, somewhat as Mosso did in terms of recovery time. Among the many obstacles that he encountered was his inability to stabilise sufficiently the output curve over a succession of work periods to make possible the comparisons of the cost of different quarters of it. To meet the difficulty he chose such a lead to be lifted and a rhythm for lifting that the output remained uniform throughout the work period. That is, the work curve approximated a straight

TABLE 4.3
Energy Expended in Human Locomotion

Activity	*c.c. of O_2 per Minute*	*c.c. of O_2 per Mile*
Lying down in post-absorptive states	237	......
Standing still	328	......
Walking 1.66 m.p.h.	606	21816
2.00 m.p.h.	668	20040
3.00 m.p.h.	907	18140
4.00 m.p.h.	1182	17730
5.00 m.p.h.	2125	25500
Running 6.50 m.p.h.	2868	26472
7.50 m.p.h.	3395	27160
9.00 m.p.h	3834	25534
10.00 m.p.h.	3910	23460

horizontal line. He then looked for evidence of changed efficiency only in the cost per unit of work. But the work conditions that gave a uniform output were also the conditions that enabled the worker to maintain a "steady state" so far as expenditure of energy was concerned. The only evidence of changing cost that he could detect was in the slightly longer period required to return to the resting metabolic rate from work done in the latter stages of the curve. This problem that Schubert attacked is sufficiently important to warrant a modified attack upon it. The field study by Waller reported suggests that the unit cost of the work should increase in the later stages of the work period.

Effects of Work Upon Output

The most commonly used measure of the effects of work and the one which has the most immediate utility is the amount of work done. The objective of work is to produce something, whether it be a formula from the thinking of the mathematician or an automobile part from the worker in industry. However, the earlier parts of this chapter show that other effects cannot be entirely neglected.

The effect of work is not always and necessarily a decrement in out-put. Laboratory studies of the work process usually do

FIGURE 4.8
Warming- Up Phenomenon*

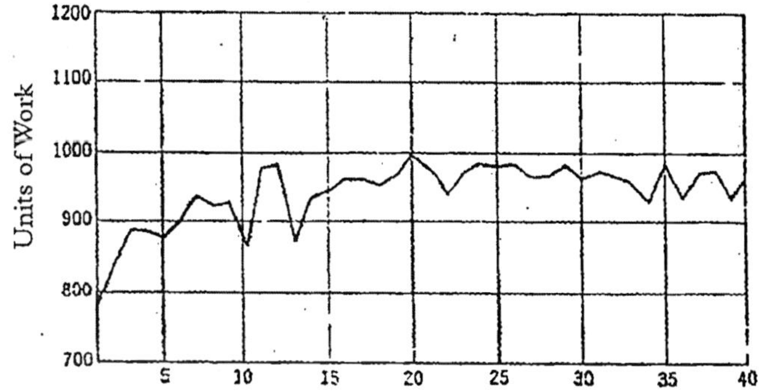

Half Minutes

*Adapted from E.S. Robinson and W.T. Heron, "The Warming-Up Effect," *J. Exp. Psychol.*, 1924, 7, 81.

show such a decrement but that is because conditions are deliberately arranged to produce it. Thus ergograms generally show a progressive loss because the load to be lifted and the frequency of lifts are set so as to show a decrement within a convenient time interval, since the investigator is interested in decrement. Even under such circumstances there is frequently an early stage of the work curve which shows an increase in output. This is known as the warming-up period. It is clearly indicated in Figure 4.8, which is the work curve for a very simple task from a study by Robinson and Heron (*526*). Here the influence of practice, which might well cause such an increase, has been eliminated. The vertical scale shows the units of work done, and the horizontal scale shows the consecutive half-minute units of the work period. The maximal rate of work was not reached until the end of sixteen such units. The work begins to decrease in quantity at about the twenty-sixth Half-minute. Work curves obtained from industry and covering periods as long as a half-day or a day show similar initial increase in output. This is particularly clear in Figure 4.9, which is a composite curve for medium-heavy machine work and in which output is expressed in terms of the percentage of the maximum of which the plant is capable. It will be observed that the high point of output for the

FIGURE 4.9
Output Curve for Medium-Heavy Work During an Eight-Hour Day*

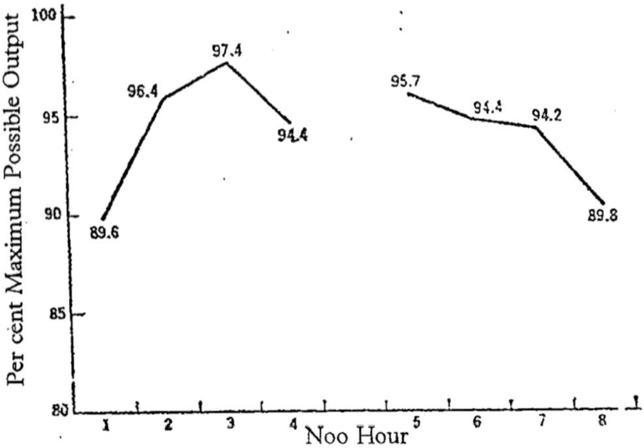

*Adapted from *Public Health Service Bulleti in, U.S. Pub. Health Service,* 1920, No. 106 74

day is not reached until the third hour of the morning. Although other factors than mere warming up are undoubtedly at work in such instances, that, too, contributes something to the total effect.

The work curves just mentioned, which portray the course of output for moderately heavy work, do show a decrement over the course of the whole work period such that the final hour may be as much as 10 to 15 per cent below the maximum. But not all work curves show such loss. In fact work curves for light, high-speed operations may portray a pattern just the reverse of these. For instance the curves shown in Figure 4.10, taken from Wyatt (*724*), tend to have their high points at the beginning and end of the period with a low level of output somewhere between these extremes.

Individual Differences in Capacity for Continuous Work

It is natural that people should differ markedly in their capacity for continued work, since the work process is found to involve so many of the bodily functions, each of which varies in efficiency from individual to individual. The range of individual differences is as great in respect to work as in any other where measurements

FIGURE 4.10
Output Curve for Seven-and –One –Half Day-Light Work*

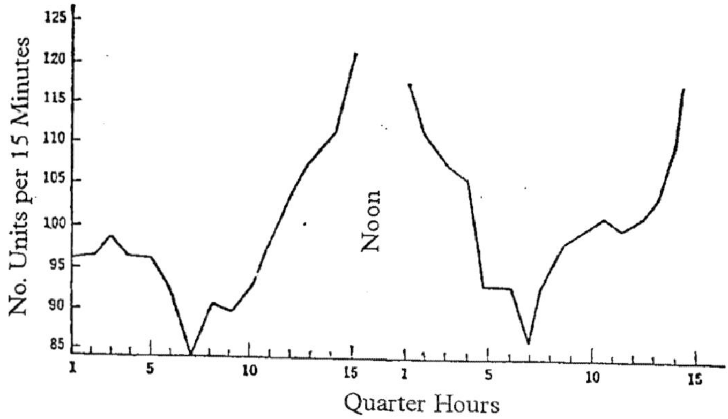

*Adapted from S. Wyatt, "Incentives in Repetitive Work;" *Industr. Hlth. Res. Bd. Rep.*, 1934, No. 69, 18.

are available. Some persons seem able to maintain a work schedule that would be impossible for others. There are individuals who become exhausted after taking a few steps and who figure prominently in spychopathology. Figure 4.11 presents the work curves of four men who lifted a 24-pound weight every two seconds by bending the arm at the elbow, each one continuing the work as long as he could. The vertical scale shows kilogrammeters of work done at each lift, and the horizontal scale indicates the number of separate lifts. Although the four began at about the same level of performance the best one did more than twice as much work as the others. All the men were in good health and had some previous training in the work. Strength, undoubtedly, is an important factor in such a performance as this, yet many other factors, some of them mental, play an important part.

In comparing the efficiency of individuals it is well to remember that there is useless as well as useful work, and that some persons do much more useless work per unit of useful work than others. As far as energy is concerned, the useless work is just as costly as the useful. The person who worries or is otherwise emotionally upset, who works under high tension, who fidgets or

FIGURE 4.11
Individual Differences in Output of Work

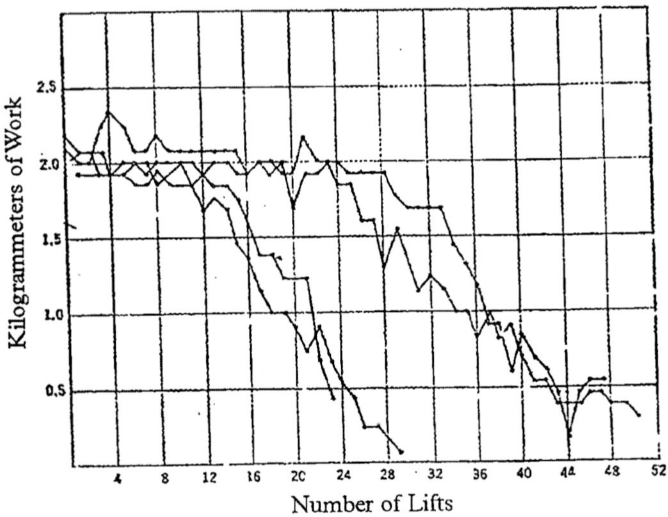

keeps his whole musculature under strain while at work expends his energy needlessly. In selecting persons for a given type of work, therefore, it is not enough to determine the soundness and strength of the working parts, but it is necessary also to know something about their habits of work.

Proneness to Accident

An individual peculiarity that has come to attract unusually wide attention is the proneness to accident. It has, indeed, become customary to speak of "accident prone" automobile drivers (*44*) (*167*), meaning roughly those who have two to three times as many accidents as the average driver. The use of the term need not, however, be restricted to automobile accidents for it covers equally well the accident repeaters in industry. It will be futile to seek for any single cause for the behaviour of such individuals, although the hypothesis of Drake (*146*) is worth thorough testing in that it has the support of common sense. It is that individuals whose level of muscular reaction is above their level of perception are prone to more frequent and more severe accidents than are those individuals whose muscular reactions are below their perceptual level. In other words, the person who reacts quicker than he can perceive is more likely to have accidents than is the person who can perceive more quickly than he can act. Bingham (*44*) presumes a native factor to be found in mental dullness, emotional instability, and defects in the special sensory and motor mechanisms. He mentions also temporary conditions such as illness, lack of sleep, fatigue, worry, and anxiety leading to absent-mindedness. The data that have been reported on the effects of continuous work upon motor control would lead one to expect increasing accident rate with increasing duration of work. And the additional fact of individual differences would lead one to expect great variability in the effect of work upon the control needed for avoidance of accidents. Properly controlled research should be able to tease out the effect of this so-called fatigue factor, and to determine its relative importance among other contributary circumstances.

Rest

Continuous activity has been found to affect certain functions in the direction of a lowered level of achievement, interpreting the term achievement very broadly. Under properly controlled conditions output is reduced, satisfaction is diminished, and motor control is less adequate. The data presented in this chapter show, too, that where these effects of continuous work obtain, rest will tend to restore the achievement to its pre-work level. This statement holds for output, feelings, and accuracy of control.

One further assertion is commonly made, although it is less firmly established in evidence from research, namely that the more complete the rest the more thorough is the recovery. Recovery from the effects of work would, then, be most rapid and complete during a period of absolute inactivity. Such a state, however, can only be approximated but never attained since there is activity of some degree during every waking moment (*342*). Many of the muscles of the body are active, if in no other way than in supporting the body's weight. Consequently, all rest might be conceived as a change of activity in the direction of a reduced amount. Even during sleep there is not perfect rest, as the body movements and dream activity clearly show.

Kleitman, Cooperman, and Mullin (*343*) have obtained records of normal sleepers by means of an elaborate recording system attached to a bed. They found normal subject to make from thirty to sixty shifts of positions per night, with a period of about thirty seconds of activity per hour in units of five to ten seconds. These results confirm the earlier figures of Johnson (*326*). It will be granted, nevertheless, that sleep approaches more nearly to complete rest than does the normal waking state. It should be noted incidentally that Jacobson (*311*) finds it entirely feasible to establish in the waking individuals a state of relaxation approximating that of sleep. Individuals differ in the ease with which they can induce the state of relaxation in themselves, but apparently it can be learned by any one who will practise according to the programme of Jacobson.

The effects of rest may be taken at their face value or an attempt can be made to explain them. If this is done the explanation may be made on one or another level, psychological, physiological, or chemical. It is usual to explain them on the physiological level and to consider sleep as the phenomenon to be studied as it represents the maximal resting state.

Practically all the physiological theories of sleep attribute its onset either to a diminution of available energy-producing materials or to an accumulation of the waste products of metabolism. The actual state of unconsciousness is variously accounted for (*342*). Studies that have been made of circulatory processes during sleep support the view that it is a period of repair. For instance, Shepard (*560*) found that the amount of blood in the cerebral blood vessels increased during sleep, suggesting the probability that the increased circulation makes for the effective repair of brain tissue.

According to the waste and repair theory the amount of rest (sleep) that is needed would be a function of the amount of waste. This should differ not only with the kind and amount of the work done, but with the individual. Some persons seem to preserve the balance between waste and repair more perfectly than others, hence they need less rest and sleep. Thus rest periods in the midst of work to be most effective must be adjusted to the work and to the individual.

5

THE EFFECTS OF DISTRACTION UPON ACHIEVEMENT: NOISE

The behaviour of living organisms cannot be considered apart from the environment in which their reactions occur. Native endowment and training up to the moment of action lay the conditions and predispose for certain kinds of behaviour, but the particular quality and amount or reaction that actually occurs depend upon the interaction of these forces. Environment is here used in a very broad sense and includes the envelope of air surrounding the body, as well as its clothing, the quality and quantity of the illumination, natural or artificial. It includes the individual's human and animal neighbours and all the stimuli that are playing upon his special senses. The list is, consequently, extremely long, although the influence of many items in the list is too slight to be practical importance. It is essential, however, to go beyond the general notion that some environmental factors are good or bad, and to find out to just what degree one's daily work and play are affected by them, and just which ones are vital enough to warrant efforts toward their control in particular circumstances. The search for means of increasing efficiency in business, in industry, and in the public schools, and for means of raising the level of general health and comfort has led to the investigation of some of these environmental forces, with interesting results. Noises, smoke, gasoline fumes, quality, quantity, and sources of light, temperature and humidity, the rhythmical alternation of day and night, and many others are objects of attack in research laboratories and in the field. Some of the more important of these conditions will be examined in this chapter.

Attention and Distraction

Distraction should be thought of as a form of attention. In every waking moment something is being attended to. And at every moment there is a great variety of objects competing for attention. These are facts resting upon the nature of the inherited sensory and motor mechanisms. It is equally natural that only one of these objects or a limited group of them should be attended to at one time and that attention should tend to shift from one of them to another. The objects which can be attended to are of the most varied sort. They may be experienced by way of the distance receptors, the eye, the ear, and the nose, the sights, sounds, and odors of everyday life; or they may be objects in contact with the body, thus affecting the receptors in the mouth, skin, the muscles, and internal organs, bringing tastes, experiences of warmth and cold, contact of clothing, pains, sense of movement, and fatigue; or they may be memories or products of the imagination.

Attention, by its derivation, means "to be drawn to" or "to be attracted to". Out of all the complex of objects exerting their attracting power, one or a few of them will be most effective and will be attended to. All the others then become potential distractors of the attention, in that they tend to draw the attention toward themselves. Thus, what is at one moment the object of attention may at another be a distractor. There is, therefore, no real difference between "attractors" and "distractors". The distinction usually made is a kind of utilitarian one, namely that those objects that attract attention when one wants to or ought to be attending to something else are distractors. For example, when I ought to be studying, my neighbour's good music is a distraction. When I want to read, the bright light on the wall is a distraction. But both the music and the light may cease to distract me and begin to attract me when I intend to pay attention to them. When at work at a rapidly moving and dangerous cutting machine, I may be distracted by memories of a foolish mistake of the evening before or by the imagination of myself speeding over country roads in an automobile that I can never afford to purchase. A kind of moral distinction is also sometimes made between what I want to attend to and what I ought to attend to. The former are distractors and the latter attractors. It is not always safe, therefore, to think of distractors as unpleasant or undesirable from the point of view of the individual affected. Although it is necessary to understand these essential characteristics of distractions, it will suffice for the present to list as distractors only those objects, feelings, memories, and ideas which tend to interfere with work.

This struggle for attention implies more than a mere subjective conflict. Attention is inseparably bound up with adjusting movements and tensions that involve not only the muscles regulating the sense organs, but also the voluntary musculature, as indicated by respiratory, circulatory, and other organic reactions. Such muscular responses consume energy and lead to strain and weariness just like any other kind of muscular work. In fact the conflict between antagonistic muscle groups is especially likely to lead to such effects because the parts are under a constant tension, even when no overt movement occurs. For example, if a flickering light source lies within the field of vision while one is reading, one set of muscles tends to turn the eyes toward the light and another tends to draw them in the opposite direction. In such a case the eyes may remain adjusted to the book, but the muscles will be under constant tension. Accurate measurement might, in this case, show an unsteadiness of the eyes owing to the fluctuations in the success of the conflict. Tensions in other voluntary muscles are usually present and seem to give aid in directing the attention. Although evidence of such conflict is particularly clear in the case of vision it is, nevertheless, present in attention to any class of stimuli.

If the average person were to be asked whether or not distractions of any sort are advantageous, his reply would most likely be that they are not, for the term distraction implies an interference or disturbance. Evidence could be adduced of the disturbing effects upon efficient work of an aching corn, an itching nose, an ill-fitting collar, a broken finger nail, the hum of conversation, or the rattle of a type-writer. Still, there is the opposite view popularly expressed in the saying that "a dog without fleas would die", and the testimony of persons who seem either entirely unaffected of even benefited by a limited amount of distraction. At the present time when a search is being made for causes of inefficiency, and when business offices are filled with clicking typewriters, when industrial plants are resounding with the noise of huge machines, and the streets are filled with the sounds of traffic, the question of the real effect of distractions is worthy of careful study. Whether the distractions be great or small, the problem remains the same, namely, are distractions harmful and if so, why ?

Adjustment of Effort To Task

Experimental studies have tended to minimise the influence of most kinds of distraction. This conclusion has been reached by measurements of work products obtained under conditions that are distracting in comparison with conditions that are free from distraction. A peculiar difficulty is encountered in the interpretation of these studies. It is a matter of common knowledge that when conditions are made more difficult an individual will usually rise to the occasion and overcome the difficulty. Experimental evidence supports this belief. One practically never exerts himself to the limit, either mentally or physically, so that there is a reserve of effort which may be drawn upon to overcome obstacles (*313*). When motivation is built up, output of work will increase in nearly every instance and regardless of the kind of work. The use of such effort reserves is responsible for the effect of incentives to action, whether it be memorising a poem or acquiring an act of skill. Disturbances in one's environment *may* act as a stimulus or incentive to greater effort in order to overcome them, with the result that output of work does not decrease.

The tendency to adjust behaviour to the size of the task is one of the most interesting of psychological phenomena. A very simple case of it occurs in the size-weight illusion, in which the relative weight of two objects is estimated. One of these objects is large and the other small, but they are of exactly the same weight and similar in appearance. When lifted one at a time in the hand, the large one seems light and the small one seems heavy. It is not uncommon to have persons report that the small one is four times as heavy as the large one. There is an involuntary adjustment of the effort to the *expected* weight, with the result that the small one is lifted with relative difficulty and the large one with relative ease. In learning, similar adjustments are found to occur where it sometimes happens that a large task is learned better than a small one, because the small one is taken too lightly or the large one is taken too seriously. These may be thought of as cases of over-and under-adjustment.

Adjustment to Physical Load

An adjustment of a somewhat different sort occurs in certain physical-work experiments. For instance, if the person is instructed to squeeze a hand dynamometer once with all his force, he will do a certain amount of physical work. If, however, he is required to make fifteen consecutive contractions with all his force, the first contraction will produce less work than when only one contraction is called for. The data [A.T. Poffenberger (unpublished)] from seven subjects in an experiment of this sort show that when one contraction is required there is an average of 68 kilograms of pressure exerted, but when fifteen are called for there is an average of only 52 kilograms. Since the persons presumably "used all their force" in both cases, the difference is the result of an involuntary adjustment to the size of the task. The most striking evidence of such adjustments is to be found in the experiments of Morgan (*437*). The task consisted in exerting the "maximal effort" possible in lifting a weight which varied from 2,000 to about 6,000 grams (approximately 4 to 13 pounds). The time required for lifting should increase at a known rate as the weight increases if the effort exerted remains the same. The dotted line in Figure 5.1 shows this increase in time that *should have occurred* with the different weights, whereas the solid lines show the changes in time that *actually occurred* with one group of 5 subjects and with another group of 11 subjects. The horizontal scale indicates the weights and the vertical scale shows the lifting time in thousandths of a second. It appears, then, that the lifting time tended to remain constant; therefore the effort exerted must have been adjusted to the size of the load, so as to keep the time fairly constant. An increase of 300 per cent in the load produced an increase in time of only about 16 per cent.

FIGURE 5.1

Changes in Rate of Lifting with Increase of Load*

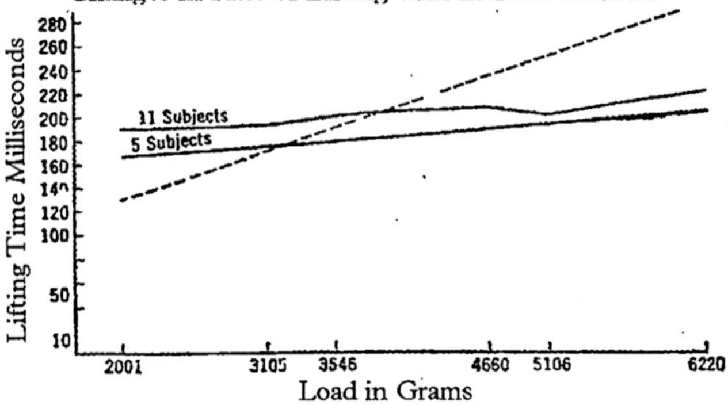

*From J.J. B. Morgan, "The Overcoming of Distraction and Other Resistances," *Arch, Psychol,* (New York), 1916, No. 35, 70.

The tendency to adopt a certain rate of work regardless of the magnitude of the task is called by Morgan the "congenial pace". It varies for different people, but all show the adjustment to some degree. Some tend to set a pace that is too rapid for their strength, whereas others adjust themselves far below their powers. The adjustment process was especially clear where the weight was gradually decreased. In several cases the decrease in force exerted was so considerable that when the weight was changed unexpectedly from 2,000 to 6,000 grams the force being used was not sufficient to move the weight at all. An interesting type of adjustment is described as follows :

> Subject Si, in his very first pull, made a score with the weight 6,220 grams of 100 sigma. (Sigma is the symbol for 1/1000th second, now more commonly designated a milli-second.) He threw himself into it with all his might. When it came up so quickly, he expressed his surprise that the weight was no heavier, and his next trial was 871 sigma. He was then told to do his best and pull all the time as hard as he did in the first trial, but either he could not or would not, for his times ranged from 206 to 261 sigma. This again goes to show that a subject expends energy in proportion to the idea he has of the difficulty of the task.

Subsequent research reported by Bills and Brown (*41*) has demonstrated that the "congenial pace" is not a simple and inevitable adjustment toward maintenance of a fixed time pattern as in Morgan's study, or toward a given effort as in the author's data. The set is rather a flexible adjustment which may owe its presence to a variety of conditions, such as the instructions of an experimenter, the presence of competition, a previous pace or schedule of work, or the mere knowledge that one is taking part in an experiment. The set may be in the direction of giving a maximal initial performance, of enduring over a long period, of maintaining uniformity of quality or quantity of output. One cannot predict just what the set will be in a given instance unless he is acquainted with the circumstances under which the work is being done. Thus Bill's and Brown had subjects doing simple addition problems with a set for one or another of four lengths of work period, one, two five, and ten minutes. Although the data do not have a high degree of reliability, they found the initial performance (first quarter/minute) to increase with length of task, and the decrement during the first minute to increase with length of task.

Measuring the Effects of Distractions

Such evidence as just been presented makes it obvious that the effects of distractions cannot be safely measured in terms of output of work alone if one is really interested in the efficiency of the performance. Doing one's best, instead of being a fixed quantity, seems to be surprisingly variable. If a given level of output is maintained upon the introduction of some distracting influence there may or may not be a change in efficiency.

Where there is a falling off in output upon the introduction of "disturbances", the findings should be taken as evidence of a decreasing efficiency. Adjustments cannot entirely overcome the resistance in every case, so that a residue of effect will sometimes manifest itself. In the curves of Figure 5.1, there is not a 100 per cent adjustment of effort to increase in weight, although if one estimated the load in terms of the time required to lift he would make a very serious error, indeed. Furthermore, the adjustment is not always immediate, and under some circumstances may develop rather slowly. This is clearly demonstrated in the adaptation to changes in industrial working conditions, where an adequate adjustment may require as much as five or six months.

What should be the ultimate measure of the effect of distractions? The fundamental problem is one of cost in relation to output. A distracting noise that one apparently disregards by an added effort so as to keep up a normal flow of work may still be detrimental, if it is using additional energy. A useful measure of distraction would, then, be one directly in terms of energy consumed. It is possible, however, to approach the problem in a somewhat less laborious fashion. If overcoming distractions means using additional energy, how is this energy used? The extra work must consist either in the activity of mechanisms tending to inhibit the response to distraction, or in the increased activity of other mechanisms. The latter manner of consuming energy may be detected by looking for accessory muscular movements in the presence of the distraction.

Measuring Adjustment in Terms of Accessory Movement

Morgan (*437*) found just such evidences of extra effort. He studied the effects of noises upon work requiring a high degree of attention and little susceptible to improvement from practice, and carried his tests over a fairly long period of time. Moreover, he attempted to measure the economy of the work as well as mere output. His findings are applicable, therefore, to experience with disturbances in everyday life. The work performed by his subjects consisted of a kind of translation of letters into numbers or numbers into letters by way of a code that varied in complexity in different sections of the experiment. Output was measured in terms of the time required for translating a given number of units of work, and the accuracy of the translations. Effort was measured in terms of the character of the breathing, the rate of breathing, and the amount of pressure exerted upon the keys which were struck in recording the translations. Additional measures were attempted but were found too difficult to control under the circumstances. The noises came from a great variety of electric bells and buzzers, the largest being an eight-inch fire gong. A series of six phonograph records was also used at times.

Figure 5.2 gives a graphic picture of the effects of the noises, and from it a number of important facts may be noted. The vertical scale indicates seconds of time required for a unit of work whereas the horizontal sections indicate the alternately quiet and noisy periods. In the quiet periods is shown the speed of the last forty reactions, in sets of ten, immediately before the noise is introduced, and in the noise periods is shown the speed of the first forty reactions immediately after the noise is introduced. The records of only four subjects are given as samples. In the case of every person, the introduction of the noise slows the translating time. Recovery from this is rapid, however, so that the speed soon equals that of the quiet period. In three of the four cases shown, the speed at the end of the noise period is greater than at the end of the preceding quiet period. When the second quiet period begins, that is, after the noise has ceased, the speed of two of the subjects is decreased, showing that the shift from noise to quiet is disturbing for a few moments for some persons. When noise is introduced the second time, the disturbance is again evident and the recovery rapid. Three of the four cases again show a faster speed at the end of the noise period than at the end of the preceding quiet period. The records of errors show no inferior grade of work during the noise and are too few to have any significance.

Concerning the results from eight persons subjected to this experiment, four of whom are charted in Figure 5.2, the author says:

FIGURE 5.2
The Effect of Noise Upon Output*

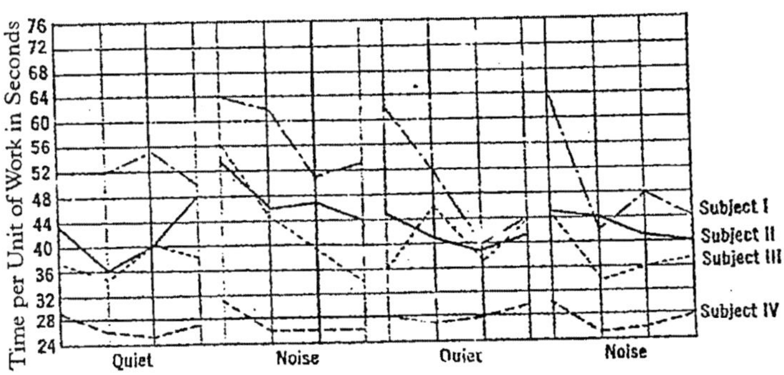

* Compiled from J.J.B. Morgan, "The Overcoming of Distractions and Other Resistances," *Arch, Psychol,* (New York), 1916, No. 35.

At first thought it may seem to follow that a noisy condition is more favorable than a quiet one. If six out of the eight make a better time during noise than before the noises were introduced, and if six out of eight make slower time after the noises stop, might it not follow that noises have a dynamogenic effect, spurring the subject to increased activity? This might be a legitimate conclusion were it not for the initial retardation at the beginning of the noise periods. If the influence were one of simple dynamogenesis, it does not seem plausible that the first effect should be one of interference. If a motor is going at a certain speed and more current is turned on, it does not first stop or slow down and then take on speed and exceed its former motion, unless the direction of the increased currents reversed.

It is not, therefore a legitimate interpretation of the data to ignore the slowing effect or pass over it lightly and say that in general the effect of noise is a stimulation; just as it would not be a proper treatment of the data to average the whole period together and conclude that the noise had no effect.

After giving each feature of the results due weight we do not conclude that a noisy condition is just as conducive to good work as a quiet one. Our work thus far has simply served to show that noises have *some* effect upon work, and that the effect is a complex one.

The production curves should now be checked against the curves suggesting excess energy expenditure in order to see whether the adjustment to the noisy condition involves additional cost. For this purpose the production records of all subjects are averaged and these, with all the energy measures,

FIGURE 5.3
Effects of Noise Measured in Terms of Effort*

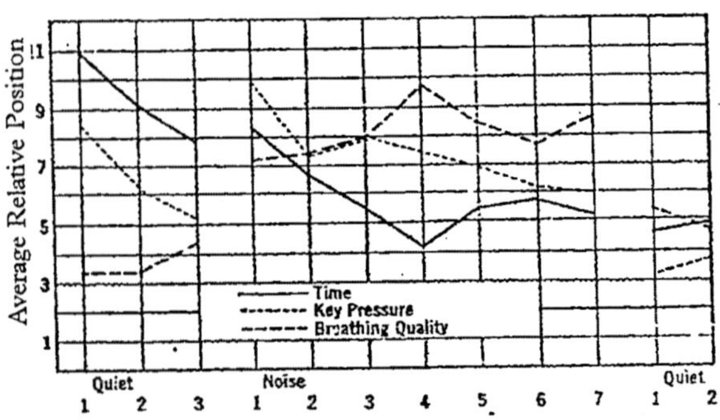

* Complied from J.J.B. Morgan, "The Overcoming of Distraction and Other Resistances," *Arch. Psychol.* (New York), 1916, No. 35.

breathing quality and rate, and key pressure are reduced to a common standard. The data thus combined for all but the breathing rate are shown in Figure 5.3. The vertical scale represents the common standard for all measures,* and ranges from zero to twelve. Along the base line are shown in succession three quiet periods, seven noise periods, and two quiet periods. The noise periods represent the combination of bells and buzzers and the six phonograph records in the order in which they were presented.

The output record (in terms of time per unit of work) shown a disturbance at the beginning of the noise period with a gradual adaptation and improvement in speed during the series of disturbances. The key pressure records, on the other hand, show that greater effort was exerted throughout the noise period than in either the second or third quiet period, with the greatest effort at the beginning of the noise period. The tension measured in this way is greater with the harsh noises than with the phonograph records. The breathing curve gives evidence only of the degree to which the breathing is disturbed through articulation, and shows, therefore, the extent to which this aid to attention had to be used to resist the noise distractions. The rising curve shows that most of the persons did not discover the value of this aid at once, but hit upon it gradually. The curve reaches its maximum in the middle of the noise period. When the quiet period follows the noise period, the key pressure is reduced and the breathing shows absence of articulation.

Measuring Adjustment in terms of Energy Expenditure

The indirect evidence which Morgan found for excess energy expenditure under noise distraction suggests the need for more direct evidence in terms of metabolic cost. Several studies of the sort have been reported. Laird (*354*) measured the energy cost

---

* The average relative position of any one noisy or quiet condition among the twelve conditions of the experiment. The noisy conditions were: (1) mixed noises; (2) phonograph record of concertina solo; (3) phonograph record of ocarina solo; (4) phonograph record of humorous dialogue; (5) phonograph record of humorous monologue; (6) phonograph record of tenor solo; (7) phonograph record of bass solo.

of typing under noise conditions simulating those of the usual busy office by the technique illustrated in Figure 4.7. Part of the time the hard plaster walls of the laboratory were covered with a sound deadening material presumably absorbing about 50 per cent of the reverberation, and part of the time they were left bare. In the former case the metabolic rate was 52 per cent above the resting level, and in the latter it was 71 per cent above the resting level. The difference of 19 per cent was attributed to the reduction in noise level through the sound absorbing walls. So far as output of work was concerned there was an increase in speed per letter written of 4.3 per cent when the noise level was reduced. Without inquiring into the significance of a saving in energy of 19 per cent, the results, in conjunction with the change in output, do show a tendency to meet the adverse working conditions with an increase in energy expended.

Vernon and Warner (*665*) in seeking to develop a test for distraction measured both output of work and oxygen consumption in the course of reading and arithmetical computation under noise and quiet conditions. Their results on output confirmed those of Morgan that every type of noise or music, from a phonograph, metronome, bells, or a combination of sources, reduced somewhat the time required for a given amount of work. Metabolism measured in terms of cubic centimeters or oxygen absorbed per minute showed an increased absorption over resting of about 1 per cent for reading with noise and about 5 per cent for arithmetical work with noise. The combined records of two subjects taking part in this experiment are shown in Figure 5.4. It appears from these curves whereas metabolic cost of the noise is greater than the final quiet period, it is actually less than the first quiet period. Vernon and Warner accepted the former as the better base from which to calculate the cost of noise. However, they concluded that the excess cost is so slight in any case that its estimation is useless as a routine test. Since the investigators were convinced that noises ought to be distracting, they finally resorted to subjective estimates on a five-point scale. Even with this measure, loud continuous noises did not seem to disturb, the only change of consequence coming from intermittent noises introduced into a process calling for concentrated attention.

FIGURE 5.4
Metabolic Cost of Work with Noise*

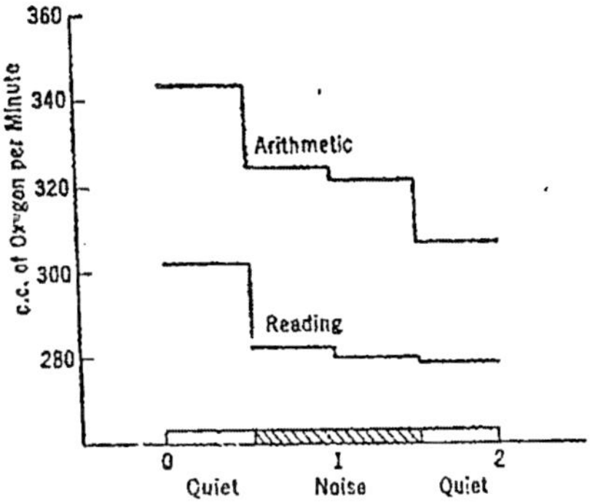

* Adapted from H.M. Vernon and C.G. Warner. "Objective and Subjective Tests for Noise," *Person. I.*, 1932-3, 11, 144.

Harmon (*241*) also studied the metabolic cost of doing mental work such as adding columns of figures in a quiet room, in a room where the noise from a large number of typewriters was reproduced by way of phonograph records, and where the noises of a busy city were similarly reproduced. When the noises were first introduced there was a temporary reduction in output of work and in accuracy accompanied by an increased metabolic rate per unit of work done. This is what one would expect from the work of Morgan and of Laird. It has been further confirmed by Poffenberger and Rounds* using the same setting as Harmon but with the introduction of certain additional controls.

Upon the expectation that the increased metabolism during work under distracting circumstances would result from increased muscle tensions, Davis (*128*) undertook to look directly for evidence of such tensions in the presence of noise. His findings are illustrated in Figure 5.5. His eighteen subjects did no specific mental task, but sat either in quiet or noisy surroundings. First there was a five-minute quiet period followed by two minutes of noise, then two minutes of quiet, two minutes of noise, two minutes of quiet, and two minutes of noise. Muscle action potentials of the forearm served as the indicators of tension. The curves of the figure represent such action potentials

* A.T. Poffenberger and G.H. Rounds (unpublished).

taken at the end of the third, fourth, and fifth minute of quiet, at the onset of each noise, and at the end of the first and second minute of each noise. Thus reading along the base line, one sees the three samples during quiet, then a sample at the beginning of the noise, and the two other samples at the end of the first and second minute. This is followed by one sample during quiet. This cycle is repeated twice. The experiment was run on five successive days and these are shown on the chart. Only the curve for the first day should be noted at this moment. It shows a sharp increase in action potential level at the onset of the noise in each instance. Here then is direct evidence of an effect of noise in a response of the peripheral muscles, along with which one might well expect an increase in the metabolic rate. These expectations are confirmed by Freeman (*182*) who measured output, metabolic rate, and muscle tension, and who found a decrease in accurate solution of problems, increased metabolic rate, and increase in muscle tension under noise stimulation.

Is Increase in Effort Essential in Adjustment to Distractions?

The experiments of Harmon and of Poffenberger and Rounds were continued over many days and the most striking finding of both investigators came from a comparison of results from day

FIGURE 5.5
The Effects of Distraction Upon Muscle Tension*

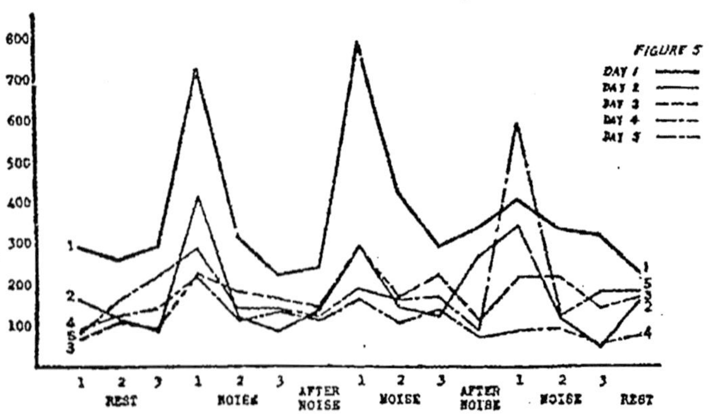

*6 From R. C. Davis, "The Muscular Tension Reflex and Two of Its Modifying Conditions," *Ind. Univ. Pub., Science Ser.*, 1935, No. 3, 13.

and from week to week. It was found that both the reduction in output and the increase in energy cost were only temporary and that in a surprisingly short time the worker returned to a normal output and normal cost per unit of work. The curves of Davis for successive days given in Figure 5.5 show a similar adaptation. Although it is difficult to follow with the eye all the points on the separate curves, each day has high points during noise which are lower than those for the preceding day. There is a striking difference in level between the first and the fifth day. Still more striking perhaps is the change within a given day. The greatest effect of the noise is immediate. On the first day the peaks of the third cycle are much lower than those of the first or the second cycle.

One is thus faced with the question as to how distractions are "mat" or adjusted to and whether the adjustment is always costly to the organism. To put the matter in still another way, do distractions really create inefficiency?

Introspective reports taken during the distraction studies may throw light upon the problem. Distractions have generally been defined in objective terms. A noise is produced while one is working at arithmetic problems, lights are flashed while one is listening to words to be memorised, high atmospheric temperatures are introduced while one is judging the quality of compositions. Are they distractions? Strictly speaking they are distractions or distractors only if they distract. Many of the introspective reports show that when the objective conditions for distraction are present, the subject is not distracted. He may say that he "paid no attention," he "was no bothered," or he did not "notice the supposed disturbers." In such cases no increased effort seemed to be necessary and the output, as would be expected, was normal.

To account for the fact that distractors sometimes do not decrease output of work, and may even increase it, by saying that distractions do not distract is merely raising another question that demands an answer. Why do environmental conditions that are called distracting not distract? How can the organism "not be bothered" or just not pay attention? One suggestive bit of evidence to meet these questions comes from the research of

Davis, just described, in which action potentials decreased during a five-day distraction experiment. Whether such changes in muscle tension as he recorded are causes or consequences of the adaptation cannot be stated definitely at this time. But if the former can be shown to be the case, then it would be a good guess that the peripheral sensory mechanisms together with the voluntary musculature taking part in the sensory adjustment process performed a protective function against distractors. By a reduction in tension (relaxation) they would transmit the otherwise disturbing stimuli at a reduced level of intensity, a level too low for effective competition with more favoured events.

If the tentative explanation just given seems to be weak or faulty, another is available that is almost exactly opposite in its implications. It may be introduced by the observation that not all conditions of distraction are resolved by ignoring them, or by not being bothered. The effort clearly demonstrated by Morgan is the response more commonly noted, particularly at the onset of the disturbance. Thereby the subject seems somehow to keep his performance to a prescribed level, or, in attempting to do so, exceeds it.

Utility of Effort

What is the utility of the added effort in maintaining a level of achievement or in raising that level? Is such effort merely the subjective experience of wasted energy? The answer is not immediately obvious from a casual examination of the accessory mechanisms that are thus brought into action. It is the old physiological and psychological problem of dynamogenesis, but some light is being thrown upon it by current researches. The work of Freeman (*185*), who measured the specific tension patterns in groups of muscles by means of mechanical levers, and that of Jacobson (*310*) and Davis (*129*), who measured muscle tensions in terms of action currents, establish without question the existence of the tensions during effort. The work of Bills (*40*) and of Block (*49*), who deliberately induced muscle tensions in the course of mental work and measured their effects upon performance, gives quantitative evidence of the reinforcement that may thus be produced. And the work of Hartmann (*245*)

(*246*) and others (*206*) (*537*) in their demonstration of the increase of subjective intensity of certain sensory experiences as a result of the simultaneous stimulation of other sense organs gives a hint of the possible mechanism of reinforcement in the presence of sensory distractors. If the stimulation of *other* sensory mechanisms raises the subjective intensity level of those experiences mediated by the sense having dominance at the moment, the latter should thereby become the more effective. In certain favoured circumstances, therefore, the expected consequence of so-called distractors should be an increase in the efficiency of behaviour. Are these favoured circumstances to be found in the states of muscular tension such as those whose effectiveness has been demonstrated by Bills?

Two types of explanation for the meeting of distractions have now been offered: one was derived from introspective reports of certain subjects who were not distracted and from the study of the process of adaptation to distractions showing a reduction of muscle tensions with time; and the other derived particularly from the study of that period immediately following the onset of a distraction and showing a reinforcement by way of the activation of accessory mechanisms. These two views, seemingly antagonistic, may be tentatively reconciled in either one of two ways.

The whole complex process of reacting to competing stimuli may be conceived as a process of sensory conditioning. Cason (*95*); after determining the subjective intensity of certain visual and auditory stimuli when presented separately, gave his subjects what he called a conditioned response training. This consisted in "evoking simultaneous visual and auditory responses a large number of times." Before the training, a stimulus affecting either one of two senses had the effect of increasing the subjective intensity of the other, thus supporting the findings of Hartmann mentioned above. "But after the conditioned response training, a stimulus affecting one of the two senses had the effect of decreasing the intensity of the other simultaneous sensory response." Thus, our two supposedly conflicting interpretations would seem merely to cover the two stages of an adjustment process, the first a reinforcing and the second a weakening one. There would remain to be explained just why in the first case the "appropriate" stimulus would be reinforced and why in the second case the distracting stimulus would be weakened. However, one need only appeal to the concept of "dominance" as elaborated by Razran (*512*) to account for such selective action in the phenomena of conditioning.

Or one may accept the increased tensions noted by Morgan as authentic and interpret the reduced tensions demonstrated by Davis as a *shift of tensions* to now muscle patterns with a reduction of tension only in those muscles on which measurements were at the time being made. The decreasing metabolic cost as adaptation to the distraction progresses would indicate merely that the later tension patterns were less extensive or less complicated patterns or functioned more economically than the earlier ones. The tension pattern would shift but would never disappear. There is evidence for such shifts of pattern in the experiments of Freeman (*185*) and of Jacobson (*310*). And the data of Jacobson give some support for the view that a tension pattern is always present during metal activity, since such activity is reduced to a minimum during a state of muscular relaxation.

The research of Bagchi (*22*) upon the adaptations of brain patterns to continuous and repeated sensory stimulation may have some bearing upon a possible interpretation of our findings if only to prevent the drawing of too hasty conclusions. He found, in the first place, that only 46 per cent of the first presentations of sound produced any change in the brain wave pattern, and in the second place there is an adaptation process as a consequence of which the pattern quickly returns to normal in the presence of the continuing or intermittent stimulus. After disposing of the view that the adjustment of brain waves is to be attributed to the adaptation process within the neural elements involved, Bagchi concludes:

> All these considerations would lead one to conclude that the arrival of nerve impulses from the peripheral mechanism at the brain is not the only important factor in reducing the brain waves. The cause of the variation lies in how and when the peripheral impulses strike the brain. It appears that the particular location or state of the whole cortex, or rather a complex pattern of the organism with its physiological and psychological components, determines whether or how much of hc influence of the incoming stimuli is going to be admitted, modified, or thwarted.

The Effects of Noise upon Efficiency

This long and perhaps tedious discussion has been necessary in order to prepare an adequate answer to such a very simple question as "What is the effect of noise upon efficiency of work?" For a casual search of the literature brings one first to the research of Morgan which shows that noise effects cannot safely be measured in terms of change in output. The phenomena of adjustment come at once to the foreground and lead to the search for a real measure of distraction. The inevitable conclusion seems to be that no stimulus in itself can be called a distractor. Whether or not it will distract depends upon the characteristics of the organism that receives it (*295*). And even if it is at one moment a distractor, the extent to which it shall continue as such depends upon the stimulus-organism relationship. Not only are there the usual differences that are to be expected from individual to individual, but within the individual there are variations from stimulus to stimulus and from moment to moment in reaction to the same external situation. These statements are borne out by data from the survey or Weston and Adams (*697*) who charted the output of a group of ten weavers, over a period of twenty-six weeks. On thirteen alternate weeks the weavers wore ear plugs that reduced the noise level from 96 decibels to 87 decibels, and on the remaining weeks hearing was unimpeded. The authors report an average improvement in personal efficiency of 12 per cent from the reduction in noise level. Individuals, however, gave widely varying records. Moreover, the effect upon output could not be inferred invariably from the introspective reports of the sensitivity or immunity to the noise. Figure 5.6 gives the contrasting average daily records of two workers whose introspective reports did accord with their output. The solid line in each case gives the subdued noise output and the broken line the noise output. Worker B said noise disturbed her, whereas worker L said it did not. For the former the quieter period gave consistently better performance, while for the latter there was no consistent difference between the two noise levels.

In spite of the uncertainties of prediction just indicated, a few facts are worth noting:

1. It should be remembered that the experiments that have been quoted do not cover long periods of continuous noise such as one finds in numerous industrial plants and business offices. What the wear and tear under such circumstances would be must be left largely to speculation.

2. In general those stimuli are most disturbing that effect the sense organs that are directly involved in the work, rather tan relatively inactive organs (*164*). Thus if one's work involves constant conversation or constant use of the telephone, a high level of noise would be equivalent to a certain degree of deafness. It would lower the efficiency of hearing.

FIGURE 5.6

The Effects of Noise upon Industrial Output*

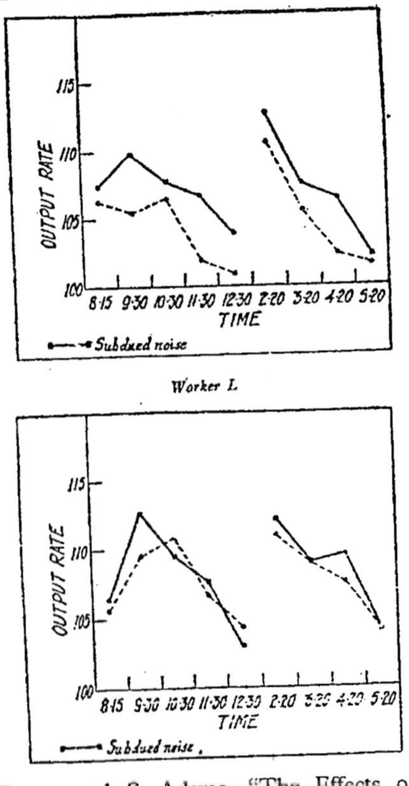

*From H.C. Weston and S. Adams, "The Effects of Noise on the Performance of Weavers," *Indust. Hlth. Res. Bd.*, 1932, No. 65, pp. 49 and 50.

3. The disturbing effect of noise tends to be directly related to its suddenness of unexpectedness (*37*). One must say that this only tends to be the case, however, because there are occasions when the expected sounds, as those occurring at a regular rhythm, are the more disturbing.

4. In general it would seem that stimuli that are meaningful carry the greatest distracting power because one is drawn to attend not merely through the intensity but through the quality of the experience (*353*) (*437*). However, there seem to be exceptions to this statement, notably in those cases where students can do intense mental work in the vicinity of a blaring radio. Instances have even been reported in which they complained of inability to study when their radios were out of order.

The Effects of Music upon Performance

Such meaningful stimuli as have been used in the study of distraction are more properly called sounds than noises for they may comprise music and the spoken word as in conversation. The literature upon the effect of music usually emphasises its facilitating influence, for music has been used to incite to action since the time of the early Greeks. Instances will readily come to mind such as the use of the marching music of military bands and the rhythmic songs of labourers (*137*). The whole question of the reinforcing power of music has recently come to the fore with the increasing ease of the reproduction and amplification of sound. One frequently reads reports of the use of music delivered over a public address system for increasing the output and satisfaction of dock workers, industrial labourers, and of office employees. The expectation of beneficial results rests mainly upon the belief that boredom is owing to the consciousness of uniformity and repetition, so that whatever will "take the mind off" will reduce the boredom. It should be noted, among other things, that the activities most commonly reported to be reinforced by music are the motor processes of industrial operations in which auditory components are lacking or are at a minimum. Wyatt and Langdon (*726*) tested the effect of music upon such an operation. It was the making of paper "snappers," the completion of each one requiring about thirty seconds. The output of twelve young workers was recorded at fifteen-minute intervals during the day. Five morning conditions were tested over a period of ninety-five day as follow: Thirty days without music; then fifteen days with seventy-five minutes of music in one single session; then fifteen days with thirty minutes of music followed after a half hour by forty-five minutes of music; then ten days with four thirty-minute periods at half-hour intervals; and finally twenty-five days without music. The data for the whole experiment are set forth in Figure 5.7. The solid line gives the average hourly output of all subjects for each day, whereas the broken line gives the weekly average. The music, produced by a phonograph, increased the average output, but the amount varied. The largest increase, 6 per cent, resulted from morning music; the smallest, 2.6 per cent, from one period each in morning and afternoon; and an intermediate change of 4.4 per cent from four periods in the course of the day. Although the averages show consistent improvement from the music, individuals differed in their reaction to it. The majority of the workers benefited, but there were several who were either not effected at all or were affected adversely. These results are consistent with the findings of others concerning distractions.

FIGURE 5.7
The Effects of Music upon Performance*

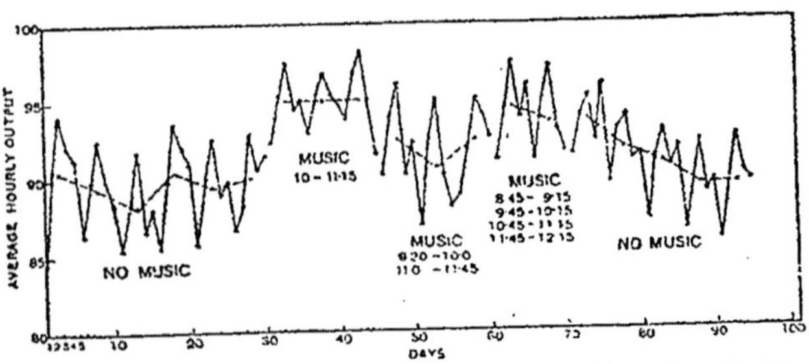

*From S.Wyatt and J.N. Langdon, "Fatigue and Boredom in Repetitive Work," *Industr. Hlth. Res. Bd.*, 1937, No. 77, 33.

Humes (*301a*) studied the effects of phonograph music upon the output of eighty-eight female assemblers of radio tubes over a period of many weeks. His interest was focused upon the scrappage rate and its correlation with the presentation of slow music, fast music mixed programmer of slow and fast music, and not music at all. It should be noted that the experiment was conducted in the plant where it had been customary for years to furnish music regularly during the day. Both slow and fast music showed less scrappage than the absence of music or than mixed programmer. Other results were less clear-cut, the mixed programmer, for instance, making for improvement only when certain tube models were being assembled. Employee morale was reported to be higher with music than without it. The author exercises commendable caution in interpreting his results, pointing out reversals of effect, the specificity of the effect, and also the possibility that non-musical factors might have influenced his results.

Other Distracting Influence

In addition to noises, two other sources of distraction have been rather extensively dealt with in business and industry, namely, visual distractions arising from defects in the system of illumination and from the presence of polished surfaces of desks and machines, which reflect light; and ventilation distractions arising from the discomfort of hot, cold, and humid atmospheric conditions. In so far as the effects of poor lighting are not limited to eyestrain and its consequences from conditions unsuitable for the needed acuity of vision, they are probably the effects of the distracting power of poorly distributed lights. And in so far as ventilation conditions do not produce a direct organic effect showing itself in loss of appetite and weakened physical condition, they also are reducible to the distracting influence of bodily discomfort.

There is one other source of distraction which is not found in the external environment. It lies rather in the realm of memory, imagination, and day dreams of the individual. For whenever the mind at work tends to be down off into "wool gathering" excursions it is suffering distractions just as real as if it is attracted to a loud sound.

It seems scarcely worthwhile to attempt to catalogue other distractions, in the light of our analysis of distraction at the beginning of this chapter. They are so much a product of the interaction of the individual and his working conditions, rather than a characteristic of the objective situation, that a distraction in one set of circumstances turns out not to be a distraction in another set of circumstances.

The practical rule would seem to be that, owing to the uncertainties of predicting results, where work of high quality or in large quantity is to be done the environment should be as free as possible from distractions of all sorts. In certain industries where efficiency methods have been introduced, not only such simple distractions as lights and sounds, uncomfortable and ill-suited clothing have been eliminated, but more complex mental distractions such as fear of accident have been removed by safety appliances, fear of sickness by introduction of methods of sanitation, fear of leaving dependents unprovided for by the introduction of insurance schemes. If the reports are to be accepted, efficiency is increased by these means. The rule will apply not only to highly organised industries, but the individual may find means of eliminating from his own environment many apparently slight distractions which in the course of weeks or months might conceivably make a considerable drain upon his energy.

6

THE PSYCHOLOGY OF MUSIC AND MORALE

Music is one of the least tangible products which can affect the human sense organs, yet it is also one of the most effective. Although it is fleeting, while we experience it we may be led to high resolves or passionate action. Shakespeare has said,

> The man that hath no music in himself,
> Nor is not moved with concord of sweet sounds,
> Is fit for treason, stratagems, and spoils.

Evidences of musical instruments are found among the remain of almost every early people and primitive tribe. But ancient music of the best sort was far different from that of modern times. The ancients had not learned the wonderful effect which can be obtained by simultaneously sounding several notes that "chord". They had no harmony, but produced only the melodies or simple tunes. Moreover, they knew nothing about key, failing to appreciate the facts which even the young beginner learns today. It was not until the year 1600 A. D. that the first real opera and the first oratorio came into existence, while the beginning of the eighteenth century really marks the birth of most music as we know it now.

Too many children as well as adults, however, are today developing the idea that music is the bizarre product of a gilded derby hat hung over the end of a trumpet, the mouthpiece of which is being blown by an individual who appears to quality admirably as a contortionist. Our public schools cannot alone devote sufficient time to the musical development of the child, so his fundamental tutelage in melodic patterns should come from the homé.

It is gratifying to parents and teachers to realise that musical ability, and especially musical appreciation, need not be considered as inherited talents. Aside from the necessity of having normal hearing and an extraordinary larynx if he hopes to become an outstanding vocalist, the average person can be taught good music or jazz. His tastes will be largely a result of his environment.

Conradi found that even young English sparrows, when reared by canaries, developed trills and a fair imitation of canary song. In the passage below we find his observation of one of his subjects.

> On September 26, when the sparrow was a little over three months old, he was for the first time observed to give a trill. It was short and musical and was given a number of times in succession. These short trills were at first only rare but they increased in frequency during the year. When he gave them he would sit still on his perch and give them one after another very modestly. Now (Dec., 1904) he gives short trills interspersed with other notes, punctuating the whole by turning complete circles and semi-circles on his perch.
>
> None of these sparrows ever had the characteristic call note of the wild species, but by and by adopted those of the canary. They imitated the canary perfectly except that their voice did not have the musical finish.

It is interesting to speculate upon what would result if all the adult sparrows were suddenly to be annihilated, and their eggs placed in canary nests. Would the sparrow's chatter depart forever from the earth? It would seem quite possible to invest the new generation of sparrows with the language of the canary, much as the immigrants take on the speech of their new country, and drop the old. But the practical value of Conradi's work lies in the fact that if the raucous chirping of English sparrows can be moulded into melodic sweetness by the canary environment during the infancy of the former, then it seems rather logical for us to expect our far more intelligent boys and girls, men and women, to react favourably to an environment rich in good music.

The Place of Music in Building Morale

If we stimulate a child's imagination to noble deeds and high resolves at the same time that we expose his ears to a specific piece of music, and if we continue doing this on several subsequent occasions, the music will eventually cause him to think and act in an idealistic fashion even though we arc no longer present to incite his imagination with words. This is simply the phenomenon of the conditioned reflex. We react hilariously or religiously not so much because of the tempo of the music and its particular melody, but because of the conditioned habits that have become attached to it. Indeed, in medieval times a writer of a mass would simply pick out a popular melody to which he fitted his religious utterances. Some of these melodies, such as *The Red Noses and Farewell, My Lover*, later gained sacred connotations. The reversal of this process is observed in the parodies of religious music which we often hear.

Parents and teachers who early capture the child's fancy in a web of melody are able to weave into the fabric of that young personality a cultural morale which will buoy up his spirit throughout all the years ahead. Indeed, the effect of music in building morale has been of marked historic significance. The Jewish nation during the captivities sustained its hope by the psalms which were sung to a musical accompaniment. The *Merseillaise* has lifted the spirits of muddy, bedraggled French legions from defeat into victory. In fact, it has inflamed the soldiers so violently that there have been times when its use has been forbidden.

In Revolutionary days *Yankee Doodle* kept the weary colonial troops in step and served as a rallying song for flagging hearts. And during the days before the Civil War the American Negro escaped the misery of his unhappy lot, in a partial degree at least, through his folk songs. Even so thorough-going a realist as Marshal Foch declared during the Word War I, "Morale is more important than material." An ancient tale of Greece corroborates this viewpoint. When Sparta, hard pressed by its enemies, sent to Atnens for aid, the Athenians did not want to succor their sister state, for they were jealous of her power and hoped that she would be defeated. Fearing to refuse outright, however, they sent as their representative the poet Tyrtaeus, a man of music and not of action. Tyrtaeus, however, composed ringing martial songs under whose inspiration the Spartans gained a great victory, much to the surprise and chagrin of the Athenians.

It seems quite probable that wars could not continue without music, which serves as an auditory stimulant to the emotions and submerges psychical fatigue. Even in industrial life it serves to eliminate the ennui that results from monotonous work. Music is offered employees through the medium of amplified phonograph records and radios, with beneficial consequences. Since much industrial work becomes so routine that it does not occupy the workers' full attention, music serves as a melodic escape by which their thoughts may dwell on pleasanter things. An occupied mind is usually a contented mind; hence, music by serving as an outlet for surplus cerebral activity, lessens industrial unrest and dissatisfaction.

From the psychological standpoint, therefore, the chief functions of music in building morale consist first of all in serving as an objective stimulus for re-arousing former emotional states. As a consequence of these re-aroused emotional states, the individual usually feels more excited and energetic. The simultaneous release of adrenaline with its accompanying increase in blood sugar places the human organism on a war basis physiologically. A second value of music in morale is its capacity to occupy the unused attention of workers in industry, and thereby reduce their boredom. The third factor has national significance, for the leaders of a crowd realise that the individuals will react emotionally as they did during the learning of the music. Thus, *The Star Spangled Banner* will instantly unify in emotions and thought the listeners who have come up through the American public schools.

Jazz vs. Classical Music

In talking about good music we refer not alone to those products of the old masters, such as Beethoven, Gounod, and Rossini, but also to many of the pieces which we hear from our better popular orchestras. After all, the criterion of musical excellence is not sheer complexity of architectural pattern, for *Old Folks at Home*, though fairly simple in this regard, holds all the essential elements of a perfect art form. But classical music is usually of complex kind, and is therefore considered a more "intellectual" type of music. There are certain fairly obvious reasons for the greater "wearing" qualities of classical music.

First of all, its mechanics is not so apparent; hence, the listener's curiousity is stimulated for a longer period of time. The central theme or motif of classical music is interwoven with sub-melodies, so that it might be compared to a rail fence covered with beautiful vines, in contradistinction to a single strand of barbed wire that we shall liken to jazz. Classical music, moreover, is akin to poetry in that it attempts to protray a number of emotions with an artistically developed climax. Jazz is simple and adapted for the feet. Because it usually is accompanied with verses, we are able to daydream along trains of thought set up by the romantic suggestions of the words, and consequently are less aware of the early monotony that otherwise results from the melody itself.

In the realm of poetry we are appreciative of this same difference in regard to metrical feet. Note the greater singsong monotony of the first of the two following quotations in contradistinction to the second.

1. Mary had a little lamb.
   Its fleece was white as snow.
2. Strongly it bears us along on swelling and limitless billows.

Nothing before and nothing behind but the sky and the ocean.

After a few repetitions of the first pair of lines we are tired of them. We can repeat the second set of lines two or three times as often without noting a similar degree of fatigue and ennui. Usually the dactylic hexameter is well suited for majestic compositions, which explains its use in Latin and Greek epic poetry. In this connection Gilliland and Moore performed a very interesting experiment to determine if equal boredom and dislike would result from hearing both classical and jazz music repeated twenty-five times. Four phonograph records were employed in the experiment and always played five times daily in the following order:

A. Bethoven's Fifth Symphony, First Movement.

B. Tschaikowsky's Sixth Symphony, the "Pathétique", First Movement.

C. Fox-trot – "That's It —A Fox-Trot."

D. One-step – "Umbrellas to Mend."

The complete experiment consisted of the five successive playings at five different periods, making a total of twenty-five hearings of each. The subjects were practically unacquainted with all four pieces. Only three of the college men ever remembered hearing either of the classical numbers, and only four felt that there was anything familiar about either of the two jazz pieces. At the first trial the experimenters had their subjects rate the four musical numbers on a ten-point scale of enjoyment value. At the conclusion of the whole experiment the students again rated the four pieces using the same scale. The first and last ratings are given below:

	First	Last
A......	5.88	6.00
B	5.60	6.04
C.....	5.00	4.01
D.....	4.37	4.50

The experimenters' conclusions follow: "The first is that since the strongly marked rhythm of street music has such an immediate stimulating value, it is important to select as our first music for the child or the musically immature, pieces that have a strongly marked rhythm, as well as melodic, harmonic, or structural merit. It is the rhythm that will first get the child's spontaneous attention, and the other musical values will gradually unfold themselves to him as he hears the selection repeatedly. The second conclusion is that since good music apparently tends to develop interest when it is heard repeatedly with an unprejudiced mind, it is important not to inject any moral controversy into the matter of appreciating music."

The chief psychological difference between jazz and classical music, therefore, lies in the fact that the latter is less monotonous because of its greater complexity, and because it usually develops a structural climax of a more imposing sort than is found in jazz.

Because of the fact that verses frequently accompany the jazz melodies, the monotonous effect of the latter is not so apparent as otherwise would be true, for the listener may be revelling in daydreams set up by the sentimental words and thus pay less attention to the tune. To either type of music, however, may be conditioned habits of merriment or sorrow and gloom, dependent of course upon the emotional state of the person when he first became familiar with the given melody. Much of the Italian's pleasure in opera which he hears in America is comparable to an American's pleasure in hearing *My Country' Tis of Thee* in Moscow, namely, its resurrected sentiments of home and parents and other loved ones. The structural merit of the music is probably of less concern to either in contrast to these conditioned emotions.

Music and Emotional Conditioning

Every reader knows that when certain musical pieces are played, he remembers old sweethearts, when others are heard, he recalls school days' experiences, while another group of songs carries him back to recollections of his mother, or a church, or may be a funeral. To the melody of one song have become attached the emotions which he felt when he first learned it, or which he underwent repeatedly as he listened to it. The reader may hum or whistle a stanza of *The Star Spangled Banner*, and find a peculiar emotional state returning which, upon analysis, may involve recall of a schoolroom, a particular teacher, flag day exercises, soldiers marching, and many other former experiences. Frequently he has forgotten the specific childhood scenes but retained only the emotions to which they gave rise. Now hum *Nearer My God to Thee*, and note the marked change in emotions. At the completion of a stanza, change to *Love's Old Sweet Song*, and follow this with Dixie.

One of the differences between language and music is the fact that words tend to be specific in their symbolism, whereas music is non-specific. Despite our individual differences in the conditions under which we learned "lamb chops", we are much more nearly alike in our reaction thereto than we are in reacting to *Marqueta.* Moreover, the word "beefsteak" may re-arouse our memories of "lamb chops", but *Dixie* can never re-arouse our emotional memories that have been conditioned by *Marqueta.* Emotions are not subject to recall, therefore, even though they are subject to re-arousal by their specific stimuli.

The fact that words accompany the melody aids greatly in setting the thoughts of the listener into the desired patterns. Since music is a non-specific form of symbolism, an entirely new melody leaves us rather unaffected during its initial rendition. If we can drift away into a dreamy sentimental mood because of its saccharine verses, we may begin to enjoy the piece the first time. Otherwise, our enjoyment must await the process of conditioning in which pleasant emotional states that were produced by our companions and the situation, become attached to the particular melodic pattern. This conditioning is similar to that by which a child learns to like or shun spinach, except that music tends to have more emotional experiences connected with it since we usually encounter it in exciting social situations.

Because strange music neither arouses old memories nor causes a concerted participation in its rendition, the minister who selects hymns which are unknown to a large percentage of his audience is making more uncertain his chances of influencing them by his sermon. The real function of music, from the speaker's standpoint, is to weld his audience into a unified whole and assure that similar emotions are re-aroused. The sooner he can get the cooperation of action and of thought of his assembled parishioners, the easier it will be for him to give an effective address. The school teacher, chorister, and voice instructor may profitably train their subjects to sing new pieces, but the minister, public speaker, politician, and propagandist should seldom attempt this task.

In concluding our discussion of music and emotional conditioning, we might say that except for its rhythm there is probably little intrinsic pleasure in music for the child who first hears it, but it soon becomes clothed with definite emotional significance, particularly if the music is heard in the same general situation each time during the learning period. The verses which accompany much popular music help speed this emotional conditioning. Music with verses written or sung in a foreign tongue, however, as opera, is slower in winning favor with the masses.

The Educational Potentialities of Music

For too many people music is looked upon simply as something to which they can dance. Music has conditioned their feet to the actions of shuffling, but has left their minds relatively unaffected. It is largely for this type of person that jazz has been evolved.

These persons have never been taught that the notes themselves have a language of their own. They need to join the classes of alert youngsters who have been pleasantly initiated into the game of picking out the bird calls in Beethoven's *Pastoral Symphony*. We should let them hear the rumble of thunder and the sharp lightning flashes of the storm in Rosini's *Overture to William Tell*, or let them test their interpretive capacities on the tonal dialogue in *The Sorcerer's Apprentice*, Paul Dukas' adaptation of Goethe's ballad.

Moreover music can become an emotional outlet of great value to the child, even before he outgrows his adolescence Here is Larry Benson, for example, a neighbour high school lad who comes home from a basket ball defeat feeling irritable. He sits down at the piano, and the first chords which he strikes are fierce loud, and vindictive. Martial music surges from the strings, and the listener feels that war is imminent. But after a time the music undergoes a transformation. It becomes more calm and subdued, and may finally pass over into some rollicking songs of youth.

In this instance Larry has vented his feelings *via* the music, and his emotional catharsis has cleaned out his ugly mood, leaving him in a much more friendly state of mind. His younger brother and two sisters have also been saved from probable irritable verbal attacks, for youngsters, like adults, are prone to project their ill will upon their weaker associates.

But the principal educational significance of music lies in the fact that the conditions under which we learned a piece tend to be resurrected in our memory when we later hear it. Governments rely on this fact when they get out the bands in time of war and strike up some of the stirring martial airs which they know all citizens have experienced in their grammar school days. They know that loyalty to the fatherland, a desire to protect home and mother, and a hallowed regard for the integrity of the country will be stirred into activity more quickly than if they sent skilled orators into our midst. A combination of fiery speech on top of musically inflamed emotions is almost certain to produce the desired action.

Emotions, however, can be utilised in the interest of peace and creative enterprises. We can condition children to unselfishness when we present certain songs to them until eventually the music itself will suggest those same attitudes. Note the emotional reaction to "Silent Night". And because music cannot be debated verbally, it is an especially powerful weapon to employ. It is always operative as suggestion; therefore, the most intelligent people have difficulty evading its emotion-arousing action. There is only one way to combat music and that is to use music in rebuttal. We cannot argue against the mood which is resurrected when one of Sousa's marches is being played by the band. But we can set rival bands to playing, and cause an emotional impasse to result. Those interested in peaceful adjudication of international disputes may more profitably spend their money and vocal energy on "peace bands" and blowing the cornet than on haranguing crowds while military, music is still audible on the horizon.

In yet another way, we may employ music to the profit of the individual and the race. It is not necessary that men and women be motivated to dancing behaviour when music is played. They may, instead, be conditioned to thinking. Rather than indulging in sentimental "jags", they may engage in creative thought. A certain prominent inventor states that he gets his cleverest ideas while reclining on a couch listening to music. Since the erotic moods may be sublimated into great poetry or art, as we have many examples to bear witness, those same moods when re-aroused by certain melodic patterns, can also, if so trained, be led into creative thinking.

The chief function of music, however, will probably always remain an emotional one. It serves as an escape from the unpleasantries of mundane existence, permitting us to flee to a make-believe world. The task of parents and teachers, therefore, consists of conditioning the child so that in this make-believe realm he does not indulge solely in emotional revelling and erotic debauchery, but diverts his emotional impulse into constructive channels.

In respect to the educational potentialities of music, therefore, we may conclude by stating that they pertain chiefly to the energy which is released under the revived emotions which are conditioned by the music. This energy can be sublimated into constructive thinking as well as into dancing over a ballroom floor, depending upon the previous training of the individuals. Since much of the poetry and art of the world has been evolved because of the emotional fervor of the poet and artist, it is possible to re-inflame a temporarily sluggish mind, much as the weary soldier's gait is speeded up, by appropriate melodies and thereby produce energy and incentive for creative thought. In addition to this educative potentiality of music, there is also the mental exercise occasioned in observing the portrayal of emotions by means of melody.

The Role of Music in Propaganda

Propaganda means essentially the spread of a particular doctrine without the hearers' immediate recognition of the source or motives behind the doctrine. It is apparent, therefore, that propaganda employs suggestions, for in so doing it avoids the possibilities of debate, conflict, and resistance. Whenever it can appeal to sentiments, it does so. The difference between sentiments and ideas consists chiefly in the fact that sentiments have an emotional colouring. Thus, the word "house" represents and idea whereas "home" is an example of a sentiment, for it has a host of emotional memories fastened to it, as Fdgar Guest's poem so well illustrates.

We have just pointed out that music cannot be combated by words. It leads to no angry debates. The subject is practically helpless when exposed to music, for he does not realise what is going to happen to him and cannot check the revival of old emotional states when their stimulus is offered. We were not conscious of the emotional ties when they were originally being fastened to the given musical piece, so it is almost impossible for us to focus upon them now. And the average citizen does not even make the attempt.

Since the aim of propaganda is to develop or re-arouse sentiments and then suggest action, music becomes one of its best tools. It is a short cut to action, eliminating a more lengthy reasoning process. Even in a religious meeting, for example, it becomes a quicker method of increasing the offering than does speech. A man or woman who is "cold" emotionally can more quickly be aroused by an appropriate melody than otherwise.

In 1940, after Roosevelt had won his third term by "peace propaganda", we saw both music and art used on the nation for war purposes, as in World War I, when it elected Wilson in november, 1916, on the plea, "He kept us out of war," and then was eager for battle on April 6, 1917. We have previously pointed out the helplessness of people before a musical attack, and the necessity for developing a counterattack with other music to which the opposite moods and tendencies to action have been attached. Since different moods may also be conditioned to the same melody, however, the propagandist must keep this fact in mind. To *The Star Spangled Banner* and military marches young men and women are usually incited to action that involves marching, cheering, and enlisting. But older women who have watched their husbands, sweethearts, and brothers leave for war to the accompaniment of these same tunes, may react with sadness, avoidance, and pain.

It is theoretically possible, therefore, for the school teachers of a nation to condition their students adversely to the military music of their country so that the adult generation would be helpless in inciting the youth to warfare by means of those military airs. Both the nationalists and the pacifists must accordingly vie for the cooperation of teachers and parents if they wish to condition the present children of the country so they will be warlike or peaceful a generation hence.

Music, therefore, become one of the most effective weapons of the propagandist, for it usually encounters no "sales resistance" on the part of the auditors, so it quickly arouses their emotions and renders them more ready for impulsive action. If group singing occurs, they are welded into a unified whole, ready for their leader to propose action. In the following sections we shall discuss some of the other instruments of the propagandist, particularly in the visual realm.

Propaganda vs. Advertising

The advertiser buys space for his message, and the reader knows that he is reacting to a commercial appeal. He can be on his guard, therefore, and employ reason, although suggestive advertising attempts to prevent his doing the latter. Propaganda, however, endeavours to hide its real nature at all times. It comes out as if it is educational matter with no ulterior purpose than the enlightenment of its readers or hearers. But it differs from true education in that the latter aims to present all aspects of knowledge with no hidden political or financial motives behind the process.

Probably because of its uses during the war, propaganda now has an unpleasant connotation. But propaganda may be good or evil depending upon the motive behind it. The political campaigns of a nation, the advancement of religious sects, the militarists and pacifists, these are only a few of the organisations and enterprises which employ propaganda. Indeed, the historical meaning of the word identified it with the foreign missionary work of the Catholic Church, for three centuries ago Pope Gregory XV founded the great Propaganda College to care for the interests of the Church in Non-Catholic countries.

In discussing the two great social dangers in propaganda, Dodge says:

> The first is its concentrated power of destruction of the established order. Great destructive power in irresponsible hands is always a social menace. We have some legal safeguards against careless use of high-powered physical explosives. Against the greater danger of destructive propaganda there seems to be little protection without imperiling the sacred principles of free speech.
>
> The second social danger is the tendency to overload and level down every great human incentive in the pursuit of relatively trivial ends. To become *blasé* is the inevitable penalty of emotional exploitation. I believe there may well be grave penalties in store for the reckless commercialised exploitation of human emotions in the cheap sentimentalism of our moving pictures. But there are even graver

> penalties in store for the generation that permits itself to grow morally *blasé*". One of our social desiderata, it seems to me, is the protection of the great springs of human action from destructive exploitation for selfish, commercial, or other trivial ends.
>
> The slow constructive process of building moral credits by systematic education lacks the picturesqueness of propaganda. It also lacks its quick results. But just as the short cut of hypnotism proved a dangerous substitute for moral training, so I believe we shall find that not only is moral education a necessary pre-condition for effective propaganda, but that in the end it is a safer and incomparably more reliable social instrument.

Propaganda and advertising employ several similar devices for effecting their ends. Cartoons, for example, are frequently a means of advancing some form of propaganda in much the manner that cuts are useful to the advertiser. Propaganda, like advertising, also appears in the newspapers and magazines, but is frequently designated as publicity. The difference between publicity and advertising is the fact that publicity attempts its purpose without having to pay space rates. The publicity stunts of actresses and actors, for instance, are aimed at gaining a few columns of newspaper space without the necessity of paying thererfor. Indeed, in many cases the individuals in question do not dare pay for space, for it is deemed unethical. Publicity, of course, tends to be more effective than paid space matter for the reader is in a more credulous state of mind concerning it. He expects business firms to praise their own products as a matter of policy, but he does not expect outsiders, such as newspaper reporters, to do so unless they are really good. In many instances, the advertiser himself also gains some free publicity in the medium carrying his advertisements. This result is especially likely to follow if there are human interest aspects of the manufacture or sale of his product, and also if the newspaper is desirous of retaining his account.

In summarising, therefore, we may state that propaganda is more secretive than advertising in regard to its source and its purpose. Accordingly, it engenders less resistance, for the public is seldom aware of the propaganda as such. In consequence, propaganda is a great power for good or evil depending upon the organisation and motives behind it. As Dodge points out, however, it may partly defeat its own end by an excessive emotional stimulation of the public until the latter becomes blasé.

How to Develop Propaganda

Those organisations which depend upon propaganda as a means of guaranteeing their economic stability and continuance have usually created a special department whose function is propaganda, usually called by its less unpleasant title of publicity. We have publicity agents for the members of the stage, for politicians, for universities, for public utility companies and similar businesses. Sometimes the men who function as such bear the titles, "Public Relations Counsellor", "Manager", or "Personal Secretary". The majority of individuals cannot afford to employ special men or women for this task, but must rely upon their own ingenuity in this regard.

Whether the motives behind propaganda are laudable or reprehesible depends upon the particular case and is not for us to decide herein. There are certain laws of propaganda, however, that are fundamental. The writer does not subscribe to Dunlap's views that the following rules "read like a catalogue of social shame," for this presupposes that psychological laws are evil, a tenet which we do not hold. We shall cite the six basic laws that Dunlap gives in regard to propaganda.

1. If you have an idea to put over keep preseting it incessantly. Keep talking (or printing) systematically and persistently.

2. Avoid argument, as a general thing. Do not admit there is any "other side"; and in all statements scrupulously avoid arousing reflection or associated ideas, except those which are favourable. Re-serve argument for the small class of people who depend on logical processes, or as a means of attracting the attention of these with whom you are not arguing.

3. In every possible way, connect the idea you wish to put over with the known desires of your audience. Remember that wishes are the basis of the acceptance of ideas in more cases than logic is.

4. Make your statements clear, and in such language that your audience can repeat them, in thought, without the need of transforming them.

5. Use direct statements only when you are sure that a basis for acceptance has already been laid. Otherwise, use indirect statement,

innuendo, and implication. Use direct statement in such a way that the attention of the audience shall be drawn to it sufficiently to take it in, but not sufficiently to reflect upon it.

6. For the most permanent eventual result, aim your propaganda at the children; mix it in your pedagogy. Follow the example, in this respect, of Ivory Soap and Prohibition.

To illustrate how propaganda is developed and utilised by industrial and commercial firms, we shall cite an authentic case. The cherry growers and canners in one of our midwestern states had a large crop and much canned goods of which they were unable to dispose. They were faced with a considerable financial loss. A newspaper man from St. Louis evolved the scheme of conducting a state cherry blossom festival, following the method of the state apple blossom festival already in existence. To this festival, which would be heralded throughout every county in the state and neighbouring Commonwealths, the governor and members of the state legislature would be invited, and a beauty contest would be staged at which time the most attractive girl present would be crowned Queen of the cherry blossom festival.

The growers and canners agreed to the newspaper man's proposal provided he could line up enough publicity men around the country for the later phase of the problem. He proved his ability by showing a long itinerary with cooperating organisations all along the route. The cherry blossom carnival was staged and it was a great success locally. The Queen was chosen. To Chicago she went, accompanied by the proper cortege. Her publicity director had already made contact with the publicity department of one of America" greatest railroads. The latter gladly cooperated in the venture since it meant opportunity for its railroad to gain some free advertising. The Queen, gracefully draped on the observation platform of a famous passenger train, would make a lovely picture, especially if the name of the train or the rail-road could also show in the photograph.

Since the Cherry Queen of a neighboring state was visiting Chicago, the newspapers could be enlisted in the project. The railroad office arranged for the pictures. To make the people "cherry conscious" and also whet their appetites in that regard, some views were later shown of the girl presenting a huge cherry pie to the mayor. The railroad offered her free transportation anywhere it had a train, so she headed for New York. Another pie was presented to its mayor, after which she called upon governors, and finally even obtained an audience with the President, presenting him with one of her enormous pies. If any newspapers were hesitant about participating in the scheme, they soon became willing when they learned that some paid advertising was to follow.

Whether we are trying to motivate our fellowmen by printed or spoken words, however, we must never permit our vocabulary and histrionics to race too far ahead of the audience's present emotional state. In short, we must not "emote" or wax unduly excited before a "cold" audience. Instead, we should consciously exercise self-restraint while endeavouring to incite the crowd by specific emotion-arousing stimuli and concrete episodes. Avoid too many superlative epithets! Narration, involving nouns and verbs with but a few striking adjectives, seems to arouse an audience more successfully than a piling up of descriptive adjectives like "unjust, inequitable and un-American" as in the following quoted editorial.

Mr. Hearst has written some of the most beautiful and effective prose I have ever seen in the English language, but in the editorial below he shows his personal indignation so quickly that the "cold" reader audience hasn't had the time to develop a similar incensed mood. Consequently, it reacts with surprise at the author's apparent excitement, instead of focusing its attention on the object of the latter's diatribe. Since an emotion is the psychological end result of a series of provocative episodes or stimuli, it cannot be foisted upon a cold audience like a military fiat or law. The crowd must be slowly worked up to the same emotional state by seeing or hearing the same type of specific incidents that originally inflamed the leader. To arouse an audience, therefore, employ the inductive method instead of the deductive!

Income Tax System Has Become Greatest Racket In The U.S.

To the Editor of The Chicago Herald and Examiner:

Please carry on sustained crusade morning, evening and Sunday against the present Bolshevist system of income taxation.

> The income tax system has become the greatest racket in the United States and the government the biggest racketeer.
>
> The system is in itself unjust, inequitable and un-American. It paralyses enterprise and penalises honesty.
>
> The rich evade the tax, the poor escape it and practically the whole burden of oppressive taxation is borne by the worthy middle classes.
>
> ★ ★ ★ ★
>
> Does anybody benefit?
>
> Yes, indeed—a standing army of snoopers, gougers, collectors, extorters, tax lawyers and dodgers, ex-government officials with a pull and incumbent officials with open minds.
>
> To support these gentry in ease and affluence is what the tax is for.
>
> Your fellow citizens are exploited, your business prostrated, your country plundered to encourage excessive governmental extravagance to support an unnecessary and dangerous bureaucracy, and to make a burdensome despotism out of our free democracy.
>
> ★ ★ ★ ★ ★
>
> There are two great historic failures and political evils which this country can indelibly engrave on the blackest pages of its record.
>
> One is the wholly ineffective and un-American policy of prohibition and the other is the inequitable, tyrannical, Bolshevistic policy of confiscatory income taxation.

The essential steps in the development of propaganda, therefore, consist of presenting the ideas in the form of suggestions, and then repeating them whenever possible. Dunlap's six rules are an excellent formula in this regard. A seventh rule should state that whenever music can be utilised, the process becomes easier. Songs may be written whose verses are propaganda itself, in which case the public will often do the repeating for months or years thereafter, and thereby help spread the propaganda at little further cost to those behind it.

How to Combat Propaganda

It is quite probable that the man who could best see through the sleight of hand tricks of a great magician like Thurston would have been Houdini. In short, the best way to see behind the illusions and pleasing display to the mechanics underlying them would be to gain a mastery of the technique involved in producing those same illusions and propaganda. Dunlap had this in mind when he dedicated his rules of propaganda not to the propagandist but to the public on whom propaganda is employed. The unfortunate situation in respect to propaganda is the fact that emotions are stimulated whenever possible, so that even the intelligent person is frequently caught off his guard, and stampeded with the less discerning. Moreover, the development of new "tricks" are likely to fool those who are skilled in detecting all the old ones.

There are about 13,000 daily, semi-weekly, and weekly newspapers in the United States disseminating information which is often coloured by the dictates of the personal, political, or financial predilections of the publisher, and the exigencies of the advertising and political situations in the respective communities. According to Kent about 75 per cent of all the county press is straight Republican, with the other 25 per cent being Democratic. These two print media serve as partial checks upon each other's propaganda. Unfortunately, most readers don't subscribe to both papers in their town. But these few are probably a large percentage of the shifting voters who determine

TABLE 6.1
Showing the change in percentage of the vote polled by the Republican party. (Adapted from Rice.)

Presidential Elections	*Change in Percentage of vote polled by republican party*	*presidential Elections*	*Change in percentage of vote polled by republican party*
1856-1860..........	6.8	1904-1908............	4.8
1860-1864..........	15.2	1908-1912............	1.0
1864-1868..........	2.4	1912-1916............	1.0
1868-1872.........	2.7	1916-1920............	14.4
1872-1876.........	8.1	1920-1924............	6.5
1876-1880.........	1.0	1924-1928.............	4.0
1880-1884.........	0.1	1928-1932.............	18.6
1884-1888.........	0.4	1932-1936.............	3.2
1888-1892.........	5.2	1936-1940.............	8.4
1892-1996.........	8.3	1940-1944.............	1.2
1896-1900.........	0.8	1944-1948.............	0.6
1900-1904.........	4.7		

the ultimate victor in an election, since the majority of people do not change from the political affiliation of their parents. In Exhibit 50, Rice shows the fluctuations in the percentage of votes polled by the Republican party. In only three instances was the change more than 10 per cent. In 1948, we saw slightly more than 45,000,000 votes divided between Truman and Dewey in a ratio of 52.4 per cent to 47.6 per cent.

The popularity of radio, television and the 17,000 moving picture theaters in the United States shows what forces for moulding public opinion are resident therein. Prior to television 100,000,000 patrons per week went to the movies. In the schools, churches and other institutions, there are also an estimated 70,000 motion picture machines of the 16 mm. Type. Even before television, Professor Ernest W. Burgess summarised the observations of 3,237 teachers of more than 100,000 school children, and concluded that 50 per cent of the children were affected by the movies, which then ranked third in influence upon their lives, as the following order will show: (1) the home; (2) the school; (3) the movies: (4) the church.

Even the news reels may be "coloured", either by means of captions, speaking, or by the selective process by which one phase of a situation is shown, and others ignored. In the war pictures that were permitted to reach the American theaters in 1917 and 1918, the doughboys were consistently pictured in happy roles, eating, playing baseball, grinning, fondling pets and French orphans, or dancing with petite French girls. The bleeding eyeless sockets of those blinded by shrapnel, the violent contortions and gasping for breath of the dying gas victim, and the rotting arms and legs and heads of boys who had been blown apart were, of course, censored.

Before the introduction of the "talkies", it was possible for the meaning of any film to be altered simply by a clever rearrangement, cutting, and rewriting of the captions and titles. Today those who write the lines spoken by the moving picture performers can also inject propaganda into the films. From general psychology we have learned the ease with which illusions can be created. If the announcer in the movie tells us to note the surly behaviour of a foreign crowd when an American arrives, we have a mental "set" thereafter for anything that fits the idea of surliness, and may misconstrue innocent actions and behaviour which are characteristic simply of a curious crowd. If we are told that an approaching lion is stalking its prey, we see ferociousness and cruelty in every move of the beast even though he is a toothless pet in a California zoo, gamboling playfully after his trainer. International hatred or goodwill likewise can be materially influenced by the announcers who describe travelogue pictures. In order to show how the same print matter may be used in behalf of diametrically opposed courses of action, we shall quote a Democratic and a Republican editorial cited by Strong, which appeared during the presidential campaign of 1920. The Democratic editorial ran as follows:

> "Mother of America! Mother of Pennsylvania! Mother of Pittsburgh! Do you want your boy to go to war? Is the roll of battle drums sweeter in your ears than the song of his voice in the home? Would you rather have his hands in fierce grip on gun in battle's rack than have his arms in love about your neck? That is the question you must answer to your God and your fellow-man when you go into the voting booth on November 2. Do not let demagogues confuse you. The issue is plain: A vote for the league is a vote for peace: a vote against the league is a vote for war. Mother of an American boy! The munition makers of the world are arrayed against American participation in the League of Nations. They are snatching at your vote, because with it they may claim the body of your first-born. Mother of a Pittsburgh boy! The question comes home to you! Your boy was not born to be food for guns."

> The Republican Advertisement Stated in Part:

> "Women! For your own good vote the Republican ticket... The American woman asks of her country: That it be a secure place for her home and for her children and that it be security with honour. That it give her children opportunity to lead their lives even better than she and her husband led theirs. That it be just in its relations with other nations, and merit the pride which the best of its citizens have in it, in its history and its ideals. A policy which has these purpose will have the support of American policy and has been Republican policy from the days of Abraham Lincoln. The Republican policy is to protect the security of the United States by preserving its right to make decision regarding its action in the future as events in the future demand. The Republican party is unwilling to pledge now that it will protect European boundary lines and to deprive Congress of the power to say in each case what the action of the United States will be."

In combating propaganda we can rely in part upon its own limitations. Professor Dodge has so clearly delineated these that we shall quote him in this regard.

> There are three limitations to the processes of propaganda that we have been considering. The first is emotional recoil, the second is the exhaustion of available motive force, the third is the development of internal resistance or negativism.
>
> The most familiar of the three is emotional recoil. We know only too well what will happen if we tell a boy all the things that he likes to do are "*bad*" while all the things that he dislikes are "*good.*" Up to a certain point the emotional value of bad and good respectively will be transferred to the acts as we intend. But each transfer has an emotional recoil on the concepts good and bad. At the end a most surprising thing may happen. The moral values may get reversed in the boy's mind. Bad may come to represent the sum-total of the satisfactory and desirable, while good may represent the sum total of the unsatisfactory and undesirable. To the pained adult such a consequence is utterly inexplicable, only because he fails to realize that all mental products are developments. There is always a kind of reciprocity in emotional transfer. The value of the modified factor recoils to the modifying factor.
>
> The whole mechanism of the transfer and of the recoil may best be expressed in terms of the conditioned reflex of Pavlov. The flow of saliva in a dog is a natural consequence to the sight and smell of food. If concurrently with the smelling of food the dog is pinched, the pinch ceases to be a matter for resentment. By a process of emotional transfer on being pinched the dog may show the lively delight that belongs to the sight and smell of food. Even the salivary secretions may be started by the transfigured pinch. It was the great operating physiologist, Sherrington, who exclaimed after a visit to Pavlov that at last he understeed the psychology of the martyrs. But it is possible to so load the smell of food with pain and damage that its positive value breaks down. Eating values may succumb to the pain values instead of the pain to the eating values. This is the prototype of the concept bad when it gets overloaded with the emotional value of the intrinsically desireable. The law of recoil seems to be a mental analogue of the physical law that action and reaction are equal and in opposite directions.
>
> The second limitation to propaganda occurs when the reciprocal effects of transfer exhaust the available motive forces of a mind. Propaganda certainly weakens the forces that are appealed to too often. We are living just now in a world of weakened appeals. Many of the great human motives were exploited to the limit during the war. It is harder to raise

> money now than it was, harder to find motives for giving that are still effective. One of my former colleagues once surprised and shocked me by replying to some perfectly good propaganda in which I tried to tell him that certain action was in the line of duty, to the effect that he was tired of being told that something was his duty, and that he was resolved not to do another thing because it was his duty. There seems to be evidence that in some quarters at least, patriotism, philanthropy, and civic duty have been exploited as far as the present systems will carry. It is possible to exhaust our floating capital of social motive forces. When that occurs we face a kind of moral bankruptcy.
>
> A final stage of resistance is reached when propaganda develops a negativistic defensive reaction. To develop such negativisms is always the aim of counter-propaganda. It calls the opposed propaganda, prejudiced, half truth, or as the Germans did, "Lies, All Lies," There is evidence that the moral collapse of Germany under the first of our paper bullets came with the conviction that they had been systematically deceived by their own propagandists.

As for legal control of propaganda, we encounter so much of the latter which is intangible and not specifically stated that it is impossible to restrain it as the *Printer's. Ink* Statute curbs dishonesty in advertising. Moreover, by word of mouth it spreads rapidly, so we often are unable to ascertain the origin of the rumors and whispering campaigns which are frequently heard. When large corporations with unlimited wealth enter upon a propaganda campaign they employ experts to conduct it, and stay within the technical statement of the law. Those alert citizens who may be aware of the mechanics and motives behind the apparently innocent publicity and legislation are frequently bought off. The process of silencing an opponent is not done so blatantly as to be offensive. It may be as subtle as the propaganda campaign itself.

Suppose that Professor Brown, a specialist in the field of public utilities, is to make a report to Congress at its next session on the subject of governmental ownership. If a large holding company fears his possible censure, one of its executive is likely to take Professor Brown to dinner, and say:

> "Professor Brown, we have been intensely interested in your economic research during the past few years in the field of public utilities, and feel that it would be desirable for us to have a man of your scholarly insight and scientific ability on our staff. We do not want to take you away from

> pedagogy, if you feel an aversion to leaving the teaching field, but should be happy to have your valuable criticisms and advice in the role of economic consultant."

No mention would be made of the future report to Congress, for the public utilities executive realises that men will feel hesitant in reporting adversely concerning the companies from which they are receiving large retainer's fees. This method of silencing the opposition is simply a bit more subtle than the obvious gift of automobiles, stock, or cash. Some of the experts in the employment of large industrial concerns are hired to prevent rival companies from getting them, or to check their unfavourable testimony before juries and legislatures. If this method were confined only to the commercial field, it would not be so pernicious, but our universities are frequently subverted from their inherent obligation to offer both sides of a question with scientific impartiality. A public utility company or a labour union will make a "gift" of $50,000 to a university for research in its field. There are no strings attached to the bequest, so the professor conducting the investigation is theoretically free to report the facts as he finds them. Actually, however, he may go through a psychological change, and fail to observe certain things that would be detrimental to the company or union paying for this survey.

The chief safeguards, therefore, by which we may hope to obtain protection from pernicious propaganda are: (1) a thorough training of youth in honesty and morality; (2) a through training in the technique and laws of propaganda; (3) counter propaganda; (4) freedom of speech and of the press; (5) an endowed, impartial press and radio; (6) bureaus of information, like the U. S. Bureau of Standards.

Utilising Advertising in the Interest of Morale

During the economic debacle following the crash in the stock market in 1929, the continued advertising campaigns of such firms as General Motors, the cigarette trade, and the soap and food manufacturers not only exercised a wholesome influence by retarding the rapidity of onset of the depression, but blazed the way for more rapid recovery therefrom. Independent business organisations spent money on full page newspaper and magazine advertisements pointing out the folly of becoming panic-stricken, and re-affirming the virtues and basic economic stability of this country.

The newspapers themselves aided this movement by donating pages for advertisements whose sole function was the encouragement of the public concerning the fundamental integrity of American business. Economists and financial experts cautioned and advised the public with reference to stocks and bonds. Banks spent millions of dollars advertising themselves in an effort to bolster the public's waning faith in such institutions.

In times of social need it is also a laudable custom for American business firms to donate space in which the copy explains the nature or virtues of another organisation coming before the people with a drive for funds. The Red Cross and Boy Scouts have been frequently afforded such courtesies and assistance. But retail dealers have also performed an admirable social service in the small country towns. It has been customary there for the merchants to unite and rent a moving picture projection machine and films so they may hold a show on one or two nights each week during the summer months. A screeb is frequently stretched across the main street. No charge is made to the farmers and their families who fill the street during the movie.

As a variation of the above procedure, in those towns that have a little movie house, the merchants may rent it, and hold their programme inside. To cite a specific case, in Covington, Indiana, a country seat of 2,500 population, the merchants pay $55 for the use of the local movie house, machine, operator, and films for an entire day – Wednesday. Any farmer or townsman is entitled to a free ticket for his whole family to see the show if he makes a purchase during the day at any of the stores cooperating in the venture, and practically every merchant is participating. The theater remains open until all have seen the movie.

This type of advertising is of social benefit as well as financially profitable. The average contribution from each merchant is approximately $ 1.00 yet there have been as many as 1,800 people who have seen the show in one day. Farmers drive in with their entire families, and the poor folks in the town who could not afford a movie from one year to another are given tickets to enjoy this weekly treat. Farmer's children who have never seen a moving picture show before are given an opportunity to watch the antics of Mickey Mouse and other comic characters, and their parents enjoy first class plays. The writer saw a picture in this little theater which he had seen in one of Chicago's finest theaters only a few weeks before. The plays presented are high grade "talkies" of the same sort as those for which Chicagoans pay 50 and 75 cents. In some small towns the merchants rent the theater for two successive days, and entertain the public accordingly, since the cost to the retailers for the second day is relatively small.

In discussing this type of advertising with one of the Covington merchants the writer was pleased to hear him say:

> "Although it pays for itself financially, it would be worth a dollar a week to most of us just as a combination toward improving the morale of the community. These farmers work hard, and haven't enough ready cash to take their families to a show. Prices of crops are low, and much of the land is mortgaged. The farmers and their wives now come in here in the afternoon or evening, and know that they have a good time awaiting them.
>
> They see a picture that would cost them $2 or $2.50, counting all their children, and have a chance to forget their troubles. We try to have a good comedy each week and a first class main picture to go along with it. They are entertained in the regular theater of our town, and accorded the same courtesy as if they were paying for their tickets.
>
> We issue them tickets with their purchases. They present these at the door. If the theater is full, they line up on the sidewalk and wait for the next showing. To some of the poor people from down along the river we give tickets whether they buy or not. They need some sort of amusement, you know"

Whenever advertisers can render such services to the public, as well as sell them worthy merchandise, they are doing a two-fold good. Since it is essential that people receive a certain amount of amusement and relaxation, advertising can often give them this without detracting from its primary purpose. Indeed, the improved morale may even increase buying.

The Relationship of Morale to Success

We have previously mentioned Marshal Foch's statement that morale is more important than materials. In maintaining a victorious army made up of various races, many of which did not even speak the same tongue, Hannibal also demonstrated his realisation of the significance of morale. He instituted boxing, wrestling, and gladiatorial combats to keep up the martial spirit of his troops when they were passing through the Alps route to Rome. In the recent World War we saw a similar appreciation of the importance of morale, and concerted effort to produce it. Moreover, the sales conventions to which manufacturers are willing to bring distant salesman and pay their expenses are held for the sake of increasing the enthusiasm and confidence of the sales force. Enthusiasm, confidence, and hope are vital factors not only in war, and business, but in medicine as well. The patient who believes in his physician, or is confident that he will get well, is much more likely to do so. The man who gives up, who admits defeat, is beaten before he commences.

In London some years ago an experiment was performed with five soldiers to determine the influence of their mental state upon their physical strength. They gripped a dynamometer as hard as they could to register their maximum handgrip strength. For the five men the average was 101 pounds. Then they were hypnotised, after which they were told that they were very weak and feeble. They were again given the dynamometer and told to grasp it as strongly as possible. Their average now was only 69 pounds. Then they were given the opposite statements, namely, that they were powerful, Herculean, after which their average strength of handgrip was 140 pounds.

Several important conclusions may be drawn from this experiment. In the first place, a negative thought, such as a feeling of failure or defeatism, leads to marked lessening of physical strength. On the other hand, a positive thought leads to more than average strength. The belief that they were strong actually increased their physical strength almost 40 per cent above their normal capacity, while the belief that they were weak reduced their strength 30 per cent below their best normal record. Although we can probably never attain such a concentration of attention in the focal circle during our normal state as in the hypnotic trance, we tend to go in the direction of the 140 pounds or the 69 pounds when we are respectively confident or fearful of defeat.

The football team, the business man, and the salesman are more likely, therefore, to attain success when confident than when afraid, provided they do not ignore other necessary requirements for victory, such as adherence to training and attention to details. The overconfident football team does not go down to defeat because of this mental attitude, but because it is careless and has avoided the severe training periods as much as possible, and also because it is running against another team which is likewise confident.

Every factor which equips a boy or girl with beneficial habits is thereby eliminating just so many occasions for lack of confidence later in life. We have previously explained that confidence is in large measure a matter of habit. The story of Half-Way Hurley illustrates this point. But physical health also aids in the development of a victory morale. The weary, sick, or enfeebled persons are not sure of themselves and aggressive. They stand back to let the virile individual go ahead, and give way before the counter attacks of customers, debaters, and opponents of all sorts.

Education is also of marked value in building a winning morale. The college man and woman have the advantage over the non-trained person not only in the possession of more book knowledge but especially in the self-assurance and poise which come with knowing that they have at least been "exposed" to all the advantages and information that their associates have received. The non-college man and woman may occasionally be better educated than their collegiate neighbours but lacking the college training, they do not know that they are, so they step aside in deference to the fearless behaviour of the college folks. Part of the benefit of a college training is the realisation of what our opponents do not know, for we feel that as a general rule they do not possess any educational equipment which we do not also have. This attitude enables the college students to attack a new problem with the feeling that they have at least a 50-50 chance against anybody. The non-college people tend to feel that they have perhaps but a 25-75 chance.

The buoyant influence of music in building a winning morale has been treated heretofore in this chapter when we mentioned that the singing of the *Marseillaise* had at times been forbidden because of its inflammatory effect upon the soldiers. And in industry as well as in the home we find that music can produce happiness and pleasure, both of which reactions are conducive to a feeling of confidence.

Although the person with a defeatism complex may occasionally succeed because of some clever idea or a "driver" at home who forces him into the battle constantly, the man who possesses a winning morale, a confidence in himself, coupled with an intelligent appreciation of the difficulties which beset him, is far more likely to win the coveted rewards of life and ultimately leave this stage with a confident smile for whatever may lie ahead. The development of this type of spirit is one of the functions of education and a duty of parents and teachers in general.

References

Adler, M.J., "Music Appreciation: An Experimental Approach to its Measurement" (*Arch. Psychol.*, No. 110, 1929).

Allprot, G. W. & Postman, L., *Psychology of Rumor* (Holt, 1947).

Bartley, S. H., *Beginning Experimental Psychology* (McGraw-Hill, 1950).

Brandt, H.F., "A Scientific Approach to the Study of Magazine Readership" (*Amer. Psychologist*, 3, 1948).

Brooke, E. E., *You and Your Personality* (Harper, 1949).

Buck, P.C., *Psychology for Musicians* (Oxford, 1944).

Cattell, R.B., *Personality* (McGraw-Hill, 1950).

Conradi, E., "Song and Call Notes of English Sparrows when Reared by Canaries" (*Amer. J. Psychol.*, 16, 1905).

Cuvelier, A., *La Musique et L'Homme* (U. de France Press, 1949).

Dietsch, R. W. & Gurnee, H., "Cumulative Effect of a Series of Campaign Leaflets (*J. Appl. Psychol.*, 32, 1948).

Dockery, F. C., & Lane, G. G., *Psychology* (Prentice-Hall, 1950).

Dodge, R., "Psychology of Propaganda" (*Relig. Educ.*, 15, 1920).

Doob, L. W., *Public Opinion and Propaganda* (Holt, 1948).

Dunlap, K., *Social Psychology* (Williams, 1925).

Farnsworth, P.R., "Sacred Cows in the Psychology of Music" (*J. Aesthet.*, 7, 1948).

Gaston, E.T., "Psychological Foundations for Functional Music" (*Amer. J. Occup. Ther.*, 2, 1948).

Gesell, A., *et al. Child Development* (Harper, 1949).

Gilliland, A. R., & Moore, H.T., "The Immediate and Longtime Effects of Classical and Popular Phonograph Selections" (*J. Appl. Psychol.*, 8, 1924).

Guilford, J.P., & Holley, J. W., "A Factoral Approach to the Analysis of Variances in Esthetic Judgments" (*J. Exp. Psychol.*, 39, 1949).

Gundlach. R.H., "Factors Determining the Characterisation of Musical Phrases" (*Amer. J. Psychol.*, 47, 1935).

Jersild, A. T. & Bienstock, S.F., "Development of Rhythm in Young Children" (*Child Developm, Monogr.*, No. 22, 1935)

Harsh, C.M., & Schrickel, H.G., *Personality* (Ronald, 1950).

Hearest, W.R., "Income Tax System has Become Greatest Racket in U.S." (*Chicago herald-Examiner*, Mar. 13, 1932).

Kent, F.R., *The Great Game of Politics* (Doubleday, 1923).

Kraines, S.H., *Managing Your Mind* (Macmillan, 1943).

Krout, M.H., *Introduction to Social Psychology* (Harper, 1942).

Larrabbe, H. A., "The Formation of Public Opinion Through Motion Pictures" (*Relig. Educ.*, 15, 1920).

Lawton, G., "Mental Hygiene at Senescence" *(Ment. Hyg.*, 23, 1939).

Lebarre, W., "The Psychopathology of Drinking Songs" *(Psychiatiy*, 2, 1939).

Lehman, H.C., "Some Examples of Creative Achievement During Later Maturity and Old Agr" (*J. Soc. Psychol.*, 30, 1949).

Link, H.C., "The Ninety-Fourth Issue of the Psychological Barometer and a Note on its Fifteenth Anniversary" (*J. Appl. Psychol.*, 32, 1948).

Macdougall, C.D., "The American Press's Influence on Public Opinion" *(Int. J. Opin. Attitude Res.*, 3, 1949).

Mitchell, S.D., "Music in Mental Hospitals" *(Hosp. London*, 44, 1948).

Mitchell, S.D., & Zanker, A., "The Use of Music in Group Therapy" (*J. Ment. Sci.*, 94, 1948).

Moss, L., "Social Science and the Gallup Poll" *(Int. J. Opin, Attitude Res.*, 3, 1949).

Rice. S.A., *Quantitative Methods in Politics* (Knopf, 1928).

Seashore, C.E., Psychology of Musical Talent (Silver, 1919).

Shils, E.A., & Janowitz, M., "Cohesion and Disintegration in the Wehrmacht in World War II" *(Publ. Opin. Quart.*, 12, 1948).

Soden, W.H., *Rehabilitation of the Handicapped* (Ronald, 1949).

Strong, E.K., "The Control of Propaganda as a Psychological Problem" *(Sci. Monthly*, 14, 1922).

Weinberg, J., "Mental Health Needs of the Aged" *(Proc. Nat. Conf. Soc Wk.*, 16, 1949).

Werner, E.M., *Work Music by Muzak* (Muzak, Corp., 1948).

7

THE PSYCHOLOGY OF THE PUBLIC PLATFORM

Because of the widespread dissemination of information through the press, magazines, and books we tend to overlook the fact that public speakers are still the persons who teach all of our school children for at least ten years. Moreover, the clergymen of America are each week giving speeches before millions of men and women. Since the advent of the radio it is now even possible for a single speaker to address an audience of millions, so the effectiveness of the public address is conceivably greater than ever before, and it has always been tremendous. William Jennings Bryan, an inconspicuous Congressman from Nebraska who came as simply an alternate delegate to the Democratic national convention at Chicago in 1896, stood before that great mass of delegates and, though only 36 years of age, swept them off their seats with his oratory and was immediately acclaimed their nominee for the presidency of the United States. This is one of the best examples of the power of oral speech in all history, and shows the influence of the public address in contrast to an equal exposure to print.

The person who stands before an audience either in the role of entertainer or as speaker encounters many of the same problems which are of difficulty to the salesman, and his methods of attack are also similar to the latter's in many respects. There are, however, certain differences that exist between people in a crowd and people treated singly, which warrant special consideration. We shall discuss them in the following sections of this chapter.

How to Weld a Crowd into an Audience

When the leader stands before a group, he is dealing with people who may have been thinking a thousand different thoughts. The women may be wondering if they forgot to turn off the water in the kitchen, or if the maid has started putting Johnny to bed yet, or what they are going to have for dinner the following night when guests arrive. The men may be wondering if they should not have put on the parking light when they left their automobiles, or if they locked the rear door, or what they are going to do about a business problem that is coming up for discussion the next morning. Meanwhile there is a buzzilng of conversation over the auditorium, or the turning of pages of programmer, hymn books, or leaflets.

Fortunately for the performer, he knows that the group has come together because of at least one common purpose, which may be the observation of a movie, the inspection of a play, or the hearing of a speech or musical programme. This common bond is responsible for their being present. They are, therefore, like those persons who have returned an advertiser's coupon—they have demonstrated an interest in the performance. They form a "warm" market for his ideas or entertainment. Even before the leader addresses the group, however, there are a number of devices by which he can unify the crowd into a more wieldy audience.

(1) *The lighting* – A church, theater, or lecture room should be brightly illuminated while the audience is assembling, for the mood of the audience is more cheerful as a consequence and this mental state is beneficial to the entertainer. It is easier to sway a cheerful audience than a lugubrious one. Moreover, the members have been favourably affected even before they enter the auditorium, for a birghtly lighted building suggests many people, which in turn suggests success, popularity of the idea or programme. People react with a feeling that a programme is good or bad partly on the basis of the number of others who are, or appear to be, present. Persons who visit a theater which is only half full when the curtain rises have already obtained the impression that the show must be a poor one. A well lighted auditorium also enables the spectator to view the crowd

surrounding him, and assists in creating the social unity which we shall explain under the second point.

In moving picture theaters and candle-lighted churches the darkened auditoriums may be a mechanical or psychological aid to the type of programme being offered, but darkness has the effect of introverting people through depriving them of outside stimuli. Fear and awe are more readily developed in darkness, therefore, than in light, so programmer whose aim is to frighten and thereby coerce the audience can profitably be given with reduced illumination. A seance, a Hallowe'en party, or a lodge initiation would be much less impressive if conducted under flood lights.

Since fear tends to produce introversion with a resulting awareness of ourselves, the speaker should usually avoid attempting to frighten his audience, and, instead, keep their interest and attention fully upon himself. He may reduce the illumination in the auditorium proper without unpleasant reaction if he keeps a brilliant spotlight upon himself and the other performers, or if he throws a clear picture upon the screen. In such cases, the reduced illumination in the audience is of merit in welding the crowd into a unified and stagepolarised audience, for it prevents a continuance of the distractions of page turning and is also instrumental in causing the eyes of all present to seek the source of light in front. Stage trained audience instantly grow quiet and focus upon the front of the theater as soon as the lights grow dim. Thoughts no longer are heterogeneous, but become homogenceous. There may be such a hushed expectancy that the ticking of a watch becomes apparent. The skilful performer accentuates this tension by deferring his entrance for a few seconds.

(2) *The seating arrangement* – When people are seated in alternate chairs, or whenever there are large blocks of empty seats between individuals, the latter become more individualistic and self-conscious. They are impressed subtly or consciously with their isolation, and therefore offer a more difficult problem to the speaker than the same persons would if they were rubbing elbows. As long as they are self-conscious, they feel responsible for their actions, and are more introvertive. It is more difficult for

them to assent to propositions that are placed before them by the leader. They do not even laugh as readily at his attempts at wit. But when they feel themselves a part of a great throng, they gain an impression of strength and irresponsibility.

We think it makes little difference what we do if there are enough of us doing it, for we feel that a crowd cannot be punished. Therefore, we form snake dances down the boulevard, and *en masse* visit theaters and retail stores, demanding free entertainment and goods. As individuals we would never enter upon such action, for we would instantly sense our weakness and personal responsibility. Since we aspire to be strong, we like to feel the assurance that comes from numbers, which possibly explain why we do not want to vote for a candidate who has previously been defeated.

In a crowd, therefore, we can follow the dictates of a speaker or entertainer with little hesitation, for our sense of being one of a group renders us less fearful of consequences. We laugh and cheer and fight with more abandon in groups than when our sense of isolation makes us aware of our own weakness. We are less cautious; hence, we more readily act upon the words and suggestions given to us.

It is advisable for those in charge of the meeting to see that an adequate staff of ushers is available who are instructed to keep the people seated close together. Many attendants at public gatherings and church are timid about going forward to occupy the seats near the stage or chancel, and will slip into those near the door unless an usher is present to escort them farther to the front. When following in the wake of the usher however, many people find it difficult to endure the gaze of an audience, so fail to go beyond the half-way point.

Griffith investigated the effect of position within a classroom upon the grades obtained by students, and found that those in the front and rear rows made poorer grades than those in the middle section. These differences, he believes, are not due entirely to the distance from the speaker, but to the students' position with reference to the group. Those on the fringe of the crowd fail to feel that physical compactness and polarisation of interest and attention which hold the attention of the majority focussed upon the speaker. In smaller classes where those on the rear rows were no farther away from the instructor than the central body of students in larger rooms, he still found the lower grades obtaining. The reason for the reduced output of the students occupying the front rows is thought to be the fact that they are so close they do not fully appreciate the group spirit of the crowd behind. Moreover, their attention is likely to be caught by irrelevant details of the speaker's manner of delivery, his dress, or minor characteristics of the apparatus on the platform.

(3) *The auditorium* – Everything in the meeting hall that causes a feeling of isolation or separation sub-groups and individuals from the speaker and the other members of the audience will tend to render the group less suggestible and therefore more difficult to weld into a polarised whole. The persons sitting on the aisles do not feel the sense of social solidarity which others react to who are seated in the middle of the section. Moreover, those people who happen to be unable to see the speaker because of intervening pillars or the large hats or heads of persons seated immediately in front of them, are inclined to become restless and inattentive. A number of such persons scattered through an auditorium reduce the degree of concentration upon the stage of others who are seated in their vicinity.

A room with a low ceiling is, moreover, conducive to a greater feeling of compactness and informality. People will laugh more easily therein than when placed in an auditorium with a high vaulted dome. The speaker consequently finds it necessary to be more direct in his delivery. Flights of oratory are not only more difficult for him to make, but are not accepted so readily by his hearers. People expect talks of less majestic sweep in such rooms, and do not look for the pompus manners and oratory of the loftier type. Although a skilful speaker may captivate their attention and ultimately lead them into imagery of the latter variety, he does it at a greater effort for the suggestive influences around them do not contribute to this end.

The clergyman who has utilised a theater in holding noon Lenten meetings not only senses the change in feeling tone and the effect of the environment, but his auditors are also vaguely aware of the difference. A large part of this result is traceable to the habit of hearing religious themes discussed in churches instead of commercial auditoriums, but the suggestive effects of crucifixes, choir lofts, painted windwos, and hymn books are also lost in the theater setting. It requires a better speaker to influence a group religiously when outside of a church than when inside. Indeed, many clergymen when they grow older and less inclined to do the difficult work of planning and preparing an effective address are disposed to rely on more painted windows carvings, crucifixes, music, candles, black clerical vestments and semi-darkness as aids in impressing their hearers, and consequently let the excellence of their sermons degenerate. They do not fully appreciate this fact until they give and address in a radio studio where they are deprived of all these crutches, or chance to deliver a sermon in some bare little chapel at a summer resort.

Chautauqua lecturers found that crowds housed in a large tent were rather easy to influence, especially in regard to political, educational, and entertainment programmers. There is a general feeling of pleasure and good cheer prevalent in such a gathering. Perhaps the transitory nature of the canvas auditorium contributes largely to this result, for we know that people are more carefree when their surroundings suggest instability. The social revolts during the years subsequent to the World War are traceable to a similar effect, while the converse of this type of influence is demonstrated in the massive stone fronts of our banks and financial institutions. Tents are conducive to a feeling of social solidarity and a chummy attitude. The differences in caste system are considerably eliminated therein. For rich and poor are thrown into closer physical contact.

(4) The ritual – Whenever people begin to act together they are vividly impressed with a sense of social unity. These two factors, a sense of social unity and a community of interest, are the basic axioms of crowd psychology. Our discussion of lighting, seating, and auditoriums has been chiefly directed to showing how the social solidarity of the group can be increased through attention to these factors. The use of ritual advances a step farther in the polarisation process, for it involves common motor responses. By ritual we refer to other than just fraternal rites. The hymns and liturgy of the church, the national anthem

and other songs used to begin a political meeting, and the singing of popular verses thrown on the screen in the moving picture theater may be looked upon as ritual. Even the cheering and applause following humorous initial sallies of the speaker or chairman may be so regarded. Cheering and applause are of especial values in welding a crowd into a unified whole, for they audibly convince each member that he is surrounded by many others with the same community of interests and feelings.

(5) The speech or performance – The person who strikes at fundamental issues, hitting the bull's-eye with his appeals, is obviously going to rivet the attention of his hearers upon himself. The slow, roundabout opening will seldom polarise an audience. Description alone, without a previously created suspense and conflict, is usually monotonous. If the speaker is not going to attempt a humorous beginning, but intends launching upon his address immediately, he should be sure first to catch the attention of his group by some such devices as those to be recounted in later sections of this chapter.

The Psychological Function of the Chairman

The chairman of a meeting is not supposed to employ his position as a means of advertising his own virtues. The example of the politician who spent almost all of Bryan's time between trains discussing his own political prowess and haranguing the audience on his own desirability for re-election is the antithesis of a good chairman. Instead, the chairman must perform the following functions:

(1) Polarise the audience – This may involve telling a few humorous stories, especially if the main speaker has a serious subject which renders it difficult for him to preface his remarks with levity. In all cases, however, the chairman should remember that he should perform his function as quickly as possible so that the main speaker may begin his address. It is better to have no chairman at all than one who leaves the audience restless, bored, and fatigued when the principal speaker stands up to address it. As a rule the chairman should confer with the speaker who is to follow, so that he may learn the nature of the latter's remarks. As a result, he can make his comments relevant and pave the way for

the main address. Some chairmen carry the audience in the wrong direction during the few minutes in which they stand before it, thereby placing an additional burden upon the speaker or performer.

(2) The chairman should build up the prestige of the speaker or performer – We have previously discussed the influence of prestige in rendering people suggestible. If a man is an authority and has written books or has occupied exalted executive and political positions, he experiences less difficulty in persuading his public when the latter knows these qualifications. The chairman, therefore, should act as a publicity agent for the principal speaker, for he can tell all of the prestigebuilding facts about the speaker without making the listeners antagonistic.

(3) The chairman should act as buffer when audience and speaker are known to hold opposing views – In such delicate situations the chairman, by his dignified and fair-minded comments and behaviour, can produce greater courtesy and open-mindedness on the part of the audience. By discreetly praising the auditors upon their scientific attitude, which involves hearing both sides of every proposition, he can force the audience into politeness by causing each one to feel intellecually complimented as long as he renders courteous attention to his opponent's remarks.

(4) In parliamentary and executive meetings the chairman should expedite the passage of worthy measures before the group – To do so he must studiously avoid irrelevant discussion and keep away from demagoguery. The emotional behaviour of various members must be curbed in so far as possible by a dignified manner on the chairman's part, and by occasional humorous sallies that relieve the tension. The chairman should not degenerate into simply giving recognition to one speaker after another, as a switchboard operator, but should exercise directive influence upon the course of discussion.

One of our most successful business leaders, who functions constantly in one directors meeting after another in the role of chairman, explains his rare ability to expedite the business before the group by saying: "Whenever a man proposes a motion which I feel is irrelevant or unwise I do no criticise the motion at that time, for its propounder is so definitely tied up with his proposal that my comments would taken as a personal affront, and an emotional conflict would result, with his friends on one side and mine on the other. Instead, I tell the group that the new proposal certainly warrants a full consideration and ask that a committee be appointed to look into it more fully. During the intervening weeks or months until the ensuing meeting, I see that the fallacy of the proposal is understood. When the committee reports adversely upon the measure, therefore, its authorship is practically forgotten, and an emotional conflict is avoided. Indeed, the author of the motion may be glad that his name has tactfully been omitted when he hears an impartial listing of the pros and cons."

Professor Lew Sarett recommends another skilful manoeuvre for producing the action desired by the chairman. It consists of an appreciation of the fact that there are usually a certain number of neutral voters in every group who have little preference one way or the other. They are, however, entitled to cast their ballots. They will be influenced by what they think is the consensus of the group, and are inclined to vote on the first question put by the chairman. It is wise, therefore, for the chairman to see that the motion is propounded so that the first vote taken is on the side which is more desirable. If necessary his friends may be discreetly "planted" in the group, and by having them respond vigorously when the question is put to the crowd, he can capture the bulk of the disinterested voters. We presented Rice's data in the preceding chapter to show what a small change in vote caused defeat or victory of the Republican party during the past three-quarters of a century. In a group of 100 voters arranged equally on the two sides of a proposition, we must keep in mind that a shift of only 17 votes will give one side a two-thirds majority.

When the vote is by a show of hands the chairman can further aid the desirable cause by a vigorous and positive upward thrust of his own hand as he calls for the vote. Crowds respond to suggestion more easily than individuals. A class of students will react to the movement of their instructor's hands rather than to his words. If he tells them that at a given signal they are to drop their uplifted hands upon their desks, he may produce the desired action without giving the signal simply by dropping his own hand vigorously. Certain children's games have been based on this phenomenon.

Sometimes, too, the chairman may anticipate proposals by the opposition and have one of his friends make the opposing motion first but in such a way that it demands later amendments because of objectionable features contained therein. If the objectionable features are then attacked by the chairman's friends in a telling manner, he may discredit the opposition so greatly that neutral group swings to him. A candidate for political office may occasionally do good for his conservative cause by secretly aiding the radical opposition. If the latter" fanaticism and emotional rantings become too intense, they drive all of the conservative element and even many liberals to the polls to vote for the conservative cause.

In the preceding paragraphs we have been showing how the chairman can influence the proceedings of his group. But individual members of the organisation may utilise many of these same principles, even without the knowledge or cooperation of the chairman. They may obtain recognition from the presiding officer and put a motion which is just the opposite of what they want enacted. Realising that the conservative element is against anything proposed by radical members, one of the latter may make a dangerously phrased motion of the sort which, if it were worded a bit differently, would have been offered by the conservative element itself. Some of the conservatives who are sluggish in their reactions may vote against the measure just because of its radical sponsorship. Others who realise that the motion is fundamentally of the sort which they want enacted, may try to amend it so that it is acceptable. There is always likelihood of dissension among the conservative ranks as a consequence.

Holding the Attention by Stage Materials

There are a number of devices by which the speaker can keep the curiosity of his public aroused, apart from the actual contents of his talk itself. These should be relevant, of course, and not so dramatic as to detract from the effect which he endeavours to produce by his address. Charts, graphs, curves, and pictures which he places around the platform or hangs upon the blackboard or wall behind him all serve as attention holding instruments, at least until he has explained them. Even some long columns of numbers exercise a charm over the uninitiated listeners and spectators, although the latter may be averse to mathematics itself. Until we know what those figures mean, they hold our attention. Because the speaker placed them in front of us, we assume they must have some relationship to his address. It is this uncertainty that makes us interested. As soon as we learn that those figures are simply thermometer readings at different points around the United States on a certain July day, they have no suspense value and we may be no longer interested in them.

The chemist and physicist know how much better attention they receive during lectures when apparatus is on the platform, than when the students see nothing that holds promise of a demonstration. The use of living models or real objects and merchandise likewise helps the speaker. The fact that a stereopticon or motion picture machine is set up in the auditorium suggests a "show", so the crowd is in suspense and more attentive to the speaker's words. If costumes are worn by the performer, or queer utensils and weapons are on a table within view, the spectators are also more interested.

Indeed, the simple act of picking up a piece of chalk from the tray beneath a blackboard will instantly heighten the interest of the audience. The speaker may stand beside the blackboard as if just about ready to illustrate his words, and the crowd will wait expectantly. If he fails to justify their hope, but wanders away to the front of the platform, they may begin to grow less interested. He can immediately regain their attention by stepping back to the blackboard. It is possible for a speaker to employ this crude device throughout an entire lecture with definite aid in heightening the attention of his group, and yet never make a mark upon the blackboard. His auditors, of course, grow less responsive to the trick as it becomes repeated several time, but they never fail to react in a partial degree. If the speaker does not enlighten them at the end with a drawing, formula, or phrase they may feel disgruntled, it is true, but they will have heeded his words just the same.

Such stage tricks and materials as we have mentioned above are usually resorted to by the speaker who has not evolved a speech which is interesting in its own right. They are also almost indispensible aids to the expositional speaker. In educational addresses it is more difficult to employ emotional and rhetorical material than in the popular oration. The subject-matter is often of such a nature that it does not lend itself to poetical utterances and majestic flights of fancy. Talks about bricks and automobile tires are not as intrinsically thrilling as ardent appeals to arms in defense of liberty, or as breath-taking glimpses into eternity where eons of time are treated as lightly as an hour, and space is limitless.

A word of caution should also be sounded regarding certain actions on the part of a speaker which lesson the interest of his group. Whenever he looks at his watch, a goodly number of his listeners react to the suggestion and do likewise. Although many of these may not heed the time, reacting mechanically throughout some of the listeners will become aware of it, and thoughts which have been conditioned to 8:45 P.M., or whatever the time may be, will instantly come to mind. The women may begin to wonder about their young children and the men about the parking lights on their automobiles. Even the initial deliberate unfastening of his watch from its chain and the placing of it upon the table in front of him, partially de-polarises the speaker's audience.

Moreover, whenever the speaker coughs he utters a stimulus which is likely to cause similar coughing responses throughout the crowd. Sometimes an epidemic of such behaviour passes over the audience. Even the harsh, rasping tones of a speaker with a sore throat, or the laboured utterance in a semi-whisper of the laryngitic patient will act as suggestions for the arousal of throat tickle in the members of the audience, much as a yawn will often lead to a multitude of open mouths.

Holding the Attention by the Manner of Delivery

Since the advent of radio speeches it has become imperative that the orator spend more time studying this phase of public speaking. Over the radio, for instance, he cannot utilise the stage materials mentioned in the previous section, so he is confined to the vocal delivery of his talk and its contents as the sole methods of heightening the interest of his listeners. The matter of increasing the pleasing qualities of the voice is a subject in which we have done very little. Many of the graduates of American schools of speech go forth with voices that are loud enough to reach the listeners on the rear rows of seats, and enunciate clearly, but have very little music in their speech. There is a flat, metallic sameness to their utterances which tends to become exceedingly monotonous, and sounds "Artificial".

An interesting voice is one which can hold our attention even when it is speaking an unknown language. Alexander Moissi, the German actor, is a genius in this regard. Indeed, vocal intonation and inflection constitute one of the best ways to hold attention and stimulate interest. The trouble with most of us Americans is that we have schooled ourselves in restraint of our emotions until we are scarcely capable of demonstrating them by the nuances of our speech. Tyro actors and actresses show their amateurishness more quickly through their lack of tonal inflections than in any other quality. When told to portray hatred, they may exclaim, "I hate you! in tones which are no different from those employed in saying, "I will not go." When the director orders them to put more expression into their voices, they simply increase the intensity of their utterance, especially of the second word, "I *hate* you!" Again it sounds almost exactly as "I *will* not go!" They fail to realise that tonal inflection is what the director wants, not variations in intensity. This same error is made by radio performers every day. When the story teller during the children's hour wishes to speak as Bunny Rabbit and then as Mr. Possum, he alters the intensity of his speech but his tonal inflection is almost the same in both in-stances.

The average American, if he were confined to nonsense syllables or an extinct language, could hardly show us whether he was angry, excited, frightened, or in pain, for he has almost lost the art of expressing feelings by means of nuances of tone. When we wish to express condolence for a friend we say, "I am sorry for you." If it were not for the word "Sorry" in our sentence, he would scarcely know it, for our tonal inflection does not convey much to him. A good speaker should be able to say, Ro ro roro ro ro," and thereby show his feeling of sympathy. If a person cannot inject his emotions and personality into his oral speech, then his utterances have little more effect than if they were on a printed sheet.

The children of this country, therefore, should be encouraged to play with their voices and mimic sounds. They should be praised in their efforts to portray a happy child through the *sound* of their voices; they should be stimulated to do the same in respect to an eager child, a crying child, a brave child, a sleepy child, a grateful child. After an intensive training of this sort they will later be able to utter with adequate expressiveness soft verbal caresses, friendly condolences, tender solace, rollicking gayeties, sober admonition, and caustic diatribe.

At the present time we hear speakers and singers over the radio who may be technically perfect in their enunciation and song, but who do not arouse interest. Then a girl begins singing in a voice which may lack the power and tonal range of the dozen other singers we have just "tuned out", but who possesses what is commonly called a "sweet" voice. We hear her entire repertoire with pleasure. There is more "expression" in her voice, by which we mean the overtones and nuances of inflection are more abundant and pleasing. When she sings or says, "I love you," we are emotionally stimulated. When a dozen others say, "I love you," no responsive chord is struck within us. Voices, like people, may be drab and colourless, or rich and fascinating.

Some people are endowed with vocal organs which are superior to others for speaking and singing purposes. A tenor voice, for example, cannot show the power and ruggedness of the bass. But all voices are capable of modification and improvement. It is said that Tiberius Gracchus, the great Roman orator, kept a slave behind the stage with a pitch pipe which he sounded whenever his master's voice rose too high. During an enthusiastic presentation of his address, the speaker invariably elevates his pitch. A skilful orator can, thereby, introduce suspense and a climax into his oration by means of his delivery, even though his speech has no logical climax. A perfect arrangement, however, consists of a speech which is technically built up to a climax in thought and which is delivered so that the vocal climax coincides with it.

The performer who confronts his audience face to face may also use gesture as an aid in holding the attention of his hearers. The graceful use of his hands may be of considerable importance not only in holding attention through their frequent movements, but also in depicting scenes and in emphasising his points. The lifted arm in the peroration is a vivid symbol of the suspense of the moment, and almost hypnotises the audience while it awaits the final movement. The performer, however, must guard against the development of peculiarities of diction and of gesture, for such things may detract from his effectiveness by calling attention to themselves instead of to the ideas for whose increased emphasis or elucidation they have been employed.

Holding the Attention by the Speech Itself

Although we have devoted several pages to the two preceding methods of holding attention, the speech itself should be so constructed that it hits the bull's-eye in its appeal to the hearers. A man may have a non-musical voice and no arms at all, yet he can captivate my attention by telling me that my house is on fire, my children kidnaped, that I have won an automobile, that my stock has gained five points, or that my advice is being sought in the sales or advertising departments of some large company. Pleasing utterance, graceful gestures, and curiosity-provoking stage materials are all desirable aids in public speaking, of course, but a man should have something to say or else all this forensic machinery produces nothing fundamentally valuable.

It is well for the speaker to model his behaviour upon that of the salesman who changed his attitude from one of thinking "How can I sell my product to these people?" to that of "Why should these people buy my product?" It will be of decided value to the speaker or entertainer to think, "Why should these people spend an hour of their time listening to me?" They do not do it to pay the speaker's salary or flatter his ego. He stands before them to procure these rewards, but they sit before him in order to get what? Upon his correct diagnosis of the answer to this question will depend how accurately he can shoot his verbal shafts at the bull's–eye. He may have other purposes in mind which he expects them to support, but he must constantly keep aware of their basic desires or he will fail to enlist their cooperation.

When an audience begins to go to sleep, the speaker should not censure it for being unappreciative and ignorant. As a speaker it is his task to find out in advance the level of education, the interests, aversions, ages, sex, vocations, and hobbies of his hearers so that he may adapt his address to them in an interesting manner. If he is normally polysyllabic. He should either avoid a monosyllabic crowd, or learn how to readjust to its level of vocabulary and comprehension. He is socially maladjusted when he cannot do so. It is a good motto for every one who aspires to influence people in groups to remember that "An inattentive crowd means an inefficient speaker." There are occasional exceptions, perhaps, but the speaker must not bolster his ego with this thought.

A sleeping audience is usually an indication that the speaker has been employing third degree stimuli in his language, or has failed to show the relationship between what he has to say and the immediate needs of his people. The subject of "bricks" is of no particular interest to me, but it could be made so by showing that a new invention renders possible the production or laying of bricks at only one tenth their present cost, so the city tax rate for paving purposes could be lowered to the degree that I would save $1.13 on my fall tax bill.

The Psychology of Persuasion

It is generally better to coax than to whip people into the desired course of action, and the same principle holds for men and women in crowds. The speaker who verbally fights his listeners almost instantly antagonises them. When we are hostile to an individual we will scarcely take even his logical advice, and his prestige is so lowered that we react but slightly to suggestions from him. Another axiom to remember in connection with persuasion is that a feeling of fear, pain, or unpleasantness usually results in withdrawal behaviour on the part of the subject, while a pleasant emotional state causes expansive or approach reactions.

The speaker, therefore, should endeavour to get the crowd into a pleasant mood, and link it to himself as securely as possible. He should diligently refrain from using the pronouns "you" and "I", replacing them by the editorial "we". If he attempts to criticise, he should by all means include himself with his crowd so that there is no intimation of the "judge" versus the "Judged", no "holier than thou" inference.

In joining himself and the crowd he must not throw all formality and decorum to the winds but, like the farmer-politician, should retain his white collar and tie behind his overalls.

This is clearly demonstrated in Paul's defense of himself before the Jewish mob which was attempting to kill him. Although he was both Jew and Roman, Paul skilfully emphasises his Jewish antecedents and training, and also indicates his importance in social rank among the Jews by reference to the high priest:

Men, brethren, and fathers, hear ye my defence which I make now unto you.

(And when they heard that he spake in the Hebrew tongue to them, they kept the more silence: and he saith,)

I am verily a man which am a Jew, born in Tarsus, a city in Cilicia, yet brought up in this city at the feet of Gamaliel, and taught according to the perfect manner of the law of the fathers, and was zealous toward God, as ye all are this day.

And I persecuted this way unto the death, binding and delivering into prisons both men and women.

As also the high priest doth bear me witness, and all the estate of the elders: from whom also I received letters unto the brethren and went to Damascus, to bring them which were there bound unto Jerusalem, for to be punished.

Realising, moreover, that his listeners think in images, and images are always concrete, the speaker must employ specificity – second degree stimuli. He should also capitalise upon the emotional habits of his group, employing words with emotional colour like "home" instead of "house". In this connection Scott[19] has the following to say:

The orator who has welded his audience into a homogenous crowd

> should never be gulty of attempting to reason with them, for, by the very process of forming them into such a crowd, he has deprived them of the power of critical thinking. He should affirm reasonable things and affirm conclusions which he has come to by processes of reasoning, but he should not presume to conduct the crowd through such a process.
>
> Not only do crowds think in images, but a very striking characteristic is the part played by the emotions in awakening the images and the peculiar emotional tone which accompanies them. This might have been anticipated from a study of emotions. Human emotions are always awakened by strong forms of imagery. Logical processes of thought are practically devoid of emotional colouring, while the conclusions reached by primitive man and by crowds are the results of feeling rather than of reasoning.

We have previously discussed the ways by which action is produced. The selling points may be made to out weight the objections either by shattering the latter through reasoning, or by so concentrating the attention of the group upon the desired course of action that it is temporarily oblivious of the inhibiting ideas. Affirmation and re-affirmation of the "battle cry" or strongest appeals are not only effective in collegiate debate but also in more emotional types of audience. Both methods of producing action, however can be employed simultaneously. Opposing ideas may discreetly be demolished as the desired behaviour is praised.

In striking at the fundamental motive bases of the audience, the speaker must vividly keep in mind that self-preservation (covering, food, health, shelter, and money) and sex are scarcely stronger than the desire for ascendance. The audience's ego or vanity is always to be inflated, just as the individual's requires expansion in order for him to be friendly and co-oprative. Recalling the statement of Pope that the way to please a man is to compliment him upon the subject in which he wishes to be considered proficient, the reader will appreciate the strategy in Paul's opening words to Agrippa:

> I think myself happy, king Agrippa, because I shall answer for myself this day before thee touching all the things whereof I an accused of the Jews:
>
> Especially because I know thee to be expert in all customs and questions which are among the Jews: wherefore I beseech thee to hear me patiently.

How the Radio Tests a Speech

Too often speakers get into the habit of depending upon the predisposing influences of the church or other auditorium, and therefore allow their addresses to deteriorate. Before a radio microphone, however, the matter of speaking is reduced to a straight forward presentation of appeals through the words and the orator's tonal infiections. A shallow, emotional address is not only fully brought to its author's attention, but with equal force is made apparent to the thousands of listeners in armchairs scattered around the city and state. If the speech does not ring true and strike directly at the radio listeners' primary interests, they tune out the speaker. Since they are emotionally cold as compared with the crowd which has been wrought up to an emotional level by interestimulation and the physical presence of the speaker, the radio address must be of a superior type.

After a listener's attention has been caught, however, and if he hears the applause of a real audience, often "planted" in the studio, he may become so interested that he reacts almost as if he were present in the amphitheater. He does not entirely lose himself in the speech, nevertheless, for he seldom applauds or joins in the singing and cheering. Aside from a more dramatic opening which strikes at some basic interest of the listener, the radio speech may proceed much like the one administered face to face. The speaker should unite himself and his public and rely upon all the prestige he can muster as a means of increasing the suggestive value of his words. He must, however, curb his emotionalism for radio listeners may be tuning in at any moment in the address, in which case he may appear ridiculous. He can sincerely employ sentiment but he must be extremely cautious not to slip over the line into sentimentality. The danger of the latter is much more grave in radio speaking than in the direct address.

The Anecdotal Address

The use of anecdotes and suspense in the speech itself is a common factor of almost every address. Illustrations not only make printed and oral material more interesting but they also clarify the more general abstract enunciations. In our quotation from Scott we read that the audience is more like primitive people in that it thinks in a succession of images. As a consequence, the audience enjoys a series of stories. These should be carefully selected, of course, so they may be relevant and capable of advancing the speaker's thought a bit further toward the conclusion.

The clergyman, for example, not only reads his text but usually a passage from the Bible which is narrative in nature. Thereafter he constantly refers to this narrative and reinterprets it throughout his address. The original creation of the parables was undoubtedly in order to heighten the listeners' interest, clearly to demonstrate the more abstract ideas of justice and virtue, and to leave the people with tales which they could easily remember and with whose repetition the underlying principles would again be brought to mind.

The politician employs the same method when he recounts familiar stories about a few of our famous historical leaders. These tales are known to probably every member of the audience, but we adults sit there in almost the same degree of rapt attention demonstrated by our youngsters who are listening to the *n*th repetition of The Three Bears. Like the children, we apparently are waiting to see if the story unfolds as we have always heard it before, or if some new twist is introduced by the narrator. The new twist is never forthcoming but we seem to be possessed of perennial hope.

For the past decade the writer has been analysing public speeches with reference to the anecdotal type of address and has encountered two men who have built up entire speech out of anecdotes. These were dovetailed very neatly into a unified structure with simply a few transitional sentences interspersed between each pair. One of these two men was elected a bishop, and his successor, who practised the same method, packed the church auditorium so early that the writer missed hearing him for three Sunday. The people who formed the audience were of the upper class socially, financially, and educationally, so this form of address is apparently quite popular.

It entails considerable reading, of course, and a logical arrangement of the stories so that they form a well-knit structure, but a speech of this kind is easy to deliver, for a few story titles are all that the speaker has to hold in mind. As a general rule, however, it is probably more effective to employ fewer stories and insert more affirmation of basic truths by the speaker. The average audience must be interested and entertained, but it also must be impressed by the speaker's erudition and forensic ability. It craves a few minutes of elevated style and imaginative flights of fancy coupled with some awe-inspiring denunciatory thunder. After it is convinced thereby of the speaker's capacity, he may give them straight-forward talking and somewhat less formal subject-matter.

In employing anecdotes the speaker may whet the interest of his group by saying, "On the street yesterday I met one of our foremost citizens – I shan't mention his name, for many of you know him quite well – and he told me this curious thing about one of our leading merchants. etc." The use of the subject's name would lesson the curiosity value of the story even though it may prevent many of the listeners from going off on independent trains of thought involving the possible identification of the unnamed person. On the other hand, the giving of the right name of the hero, if the story about him is not deregatory, inflates his ego and therfore tends to make him an ardent admirer of the "New preacher". Next to seeing ourselves mentioned in print we probably desire public recognition of this kind. A speaker who tactfully introduces his parishioners' names into his weekly addresses is ingratiating himself with his constituency at no loss in the effectiveness of his sermons.

How to Manage a Hostile Audience

One of the quickest ways in which to quiet an audience which is already hooting the speaker is for him to lean upon the edge of the speaker's stand and smilingly begin speaking to the people on the front row, narrating some humorous story in a conversational tone as if entirely oblivious of the yelling crowd. Almost invariably those in front begin listening, partly because of their admiration for his lack of concern about his hooting enemies and partly because they do not want to miss anything. This circle of listeners instantly begins to widen. If a few of those in front begin to laugh, then he quickly gains the crowd's temporary attention for the rest of the audience wants to know what is happening and what it has missed.

With apparent unconcern he can slowly increase the intensity of his voice and lead the group gracefully along until he may have so captured it that he can mould it to his own wishes. Nothing angers a badgering crowd more than to be verbally chastised for being unsportsmanlike and ignorant, ill-bred and rowdy. In short, it cannot be clubbed into a courteous attitude although it can be coaxed into one.

If the speaker cannot think of anything humorous to say, he may quiet the crowd, though more slowly, simply by standing non chalantly and grinning around at his audience. Fighting cannot long continue unless active opposition is encountered. We feel foolish when our rival smiles good-naturedly at us. And those on the front row lack the coercive action of the crowd for they are meeting the speaker face to face where he can recognise them later it he sees them on the street. They feel more individaualistic in their reaction to him, therefore, and can seldom retain open hostility very long. A socially intelligent speaker can always depend upon his front rows for listeners, and a nucleus is all he needs in order to quiet his audience.

If the crowd is not yet openly hostile, then the speaker can begin his address at once but should follow practically the same procedure as that outlined above. He should open with either some good humour, and deport himself with dignified non chalance, or else commend the crowd on its good sportsmanship and scientific attitude in wishing to hear both sides of the question. Since both humour and compliments inflate the egos of the listeners, it does not make much difference which opening he employs. What he is after in both cases is quickly to make the audience feel pleasant and more intelligent. After he has established rapport with the group by a continuation of his compliments and an affirmation of basic beliefs common to himself and his audience, he can slowly begin to turn about in the direction of his talk and head for his real destination. At the outset he goes with the crowd until it feels a sense of social unity with him and drops its intellectual guard, after which he leads the group where he wishes. By employing suggestion he can get his audience to thinking certain ideas without ever putting them into words, thereby freeing himself from possible censure. One way of absolving himself from blame, yet fully presenting his ideas, is the familiar device that follows: "I am not here to try to prove that the prohibition party has given the workingman's wife an auto in place of a scrub board, nor is it my purpose to show that babies in the tenement districts are now drinking milk whereas they used to have only a little sweetened water. I do not come before this intelligent audience of thinking men and women to repeat those old chestnuts about the working men who left their pay checks at the saloon and reeled into the voting booths to reelect the brewery candidates who refused to close the saloons to children. No, nor is it my purpose to say a word against those millionaire brewers who laughed at the social worker's requests for funds with which to open milk stations for the babies of the very men whose pay checks they got on Saturday night, etc." In his eulogy of Caesar we see the same technique employed by Mark Antony. Although not permitted to day anything against Brutus and Cassius, he obtained his desired action by suggestions.

> Ant. Friends, Romans, countrymen, lend me your ears;
> I come to bury Caesar, not to praise him.
> The evil that men do lives after them,
> The good is oft interred with their bones;
> So let it be with Caesar. The noble Brutus
> Hath told you, Caesar was ambitious;
> If it were so, it was a grievous fault,
> And grievously hath Caesar answer it.
> Here, under leave of Brutus and the rest,
> (For Brutus is an honourable man,
> So are they all honorable man),
> Come I to speak in Caesar's funeral.
> He was my friend, faithful and just to me:
> But Brutus says, he was ambitious;
> And Brutus is an honourable man.
> He hath brought many captives home to Rome,
> Whose ransoms did the general coffers fill.
> Did this in Caesar seem ambitious?
> When the poor have cried, Caesar hath wept;
> Ambition should be made of sterner stuff;

Yet Brutus says, he was ambitious;
And Brutus is an honourable man.
You all did see that on the Lupercal
I thrice presented him a kingly crown,
Which he did thrice refuse. Was that ambition?
Yet Brutus says, He was ambitious;
And, sure, he is an honourable man.
I speak not to disprove what Brutus spoke,
But here I am to speak what I do know,
You all did love him onec, not without cause;
What cause withholds you, then, to mourn for him?
O judgment! Thou art fled to brutish beasts,
And men have lost their reason. – Bear with me;
My heart is in the coffin there with Caesar,
And I must pause till it come back to me.
First Cit. Methinks there is much reason in his sayings. *Second Cit.* If thou consider rightly of the matter.
Caesar hath had great wrong.
Third Cit. Has he, masters?
I fear, there will a worse come in his place.
Fourth Cit. Mark'd ye his words? He would not take the crown.
Therefore 'tis certain, he was not ambitious.
First Cit. If it be found so, some will dear abide it.
Second Cit. Poor soul, his eyes are red as fire with weeping.
Third Cit. There's not a nobler man in rome than Anthony.
Fourth Cit. Now mark him; he begins again to speak.
Ant. But yesterday, the word of Caesar might
Have stood against the world; now, lies he there,
And none so poor to do him reverence.
O masters! If I were dispos'd to stir
Your hearts and minds to mutiny and rage,
I shoud do Brutus wrong, and Cassius wrong,
Who, you all know, are honourable men.
I will not do them wrong; I rather choose
To wrong the dead, to wrong myself, and you,
Than I will wrong such honorable men, etc.

The Psychological Formula for an Effective Speech

A truly effective speech must rest upon the bed rock of a polarised crowd-conscious group which has accepted the speaker as a friend. The address itself must contain ideas that are presented with a wealth of sensory qualities by which the hearers can develop concrete imagery. These ideas must also be vital;

they must related to the fundamental motive bases of the listeners. They should be phrased in simple language and illustrated by references which are familiar to the crowd. Shakespeare is relatively unknown to the average citizen today, so references to his characters give rise to few intelligent responses. Accordingly, the speaker loses many of his hearers for the few seconds during which the strange material is cited, and some other stimulus may attract their attention. The speaker should never let his hearers slip away from his control if he can help it. The speaker should be as despotic in his domination of the audience's attention as the hypnotist is in monopolising his subject's thinking. In the list below we have offered some of the salient principles which the speaker should employ in order to obtain the maximum effect. We are presupposing that the auditorium, lighting, and seating have already been attended to.

(1) *Compliment the audience* –This method entails humour as well as direct statements containing praise. A disgruntled, offended, or "ugly" audience cannot be moulded by the speaker until he gets it into a pleasant, friendly frame of mind. Criticisms, denunciation, and badgering by the speaker are usually disastrous. If he does attempt to point out flaws, he should always identify himself with the group being reprimanded.

(2) *Link yourself to the audience* – Employ "we" , "our", and "us" whenever possible. As a general rule never utter the word "you" or "your", and seldom say "I", "my", or "mine". Let the audience know that you were born on a farm, if the group is rural, or that you attended Yale if the crowd is from New Haven. By so doing you more quickly enable your listeners to identify themselves with you, and realise that you are a friend. This result is necessary for people will not take advice or criticism from an enemy.

(3) Use specificity – Memories and emotions are originally developed by specific sensory stimuli and must be aroused by the same. Since images are definite in their structure, the speaker must use sensory adjectives and specific nouns so that his hearers have the elements for constructing mental pictures. We have discussed this subject in greater detail in previous chapters.

(4) Strike at fundamental motive bases – Keep in mind that the

crowd is only interested in your address as it fits into the basic habitual patterns of the crowd. What does it procure from your talk that meets its basic cravings and desires?

(5) Keep your speech moving steadily toward its climax – A judicious admixture of description, exposition, and narration is desirable, but do not mark time in a forensic eddy nor get lost on a conversational tangent. There should be a recurrence of emphasis upon the central idea, much as the refrain in music and verse, but the speech should march steadily onward. A speech, like a musical composition, should be an artistically balanced affair in which all the components point toward the finale.

(6) Rise to a majestic note as you approach the climax – We are not very easily thrilled nor inspired by petty things, but massiveness, eons of time, eternity, and infinity are breathtaking. A truly effective address should carry its listeners to an emotional peak where for at least a few moments their scalps will tighten and they will feel a shivery, awed sensation in which they forget selfishness and mundane things. This peculiar effect should coincide with the vocal climax in the manner of delivery.

(7) Enter the climax in rhymax in rhythm – The majority of the most thrilling speeches to which the writer has listened have used verse to gain that emotional peak described in the preceding paragraph. Poetry which is relevant, which contains the final idea to complete the superstructure of the oration, will make the difference between a good speech and a great speech. Since we are more emotionally conditioned to rhythm than to prose, verse and music suggest idealism, while prose is more matter of fact.

In conclusion, we should sound a warning regarding emotionalism and the public address. The speaker should select his words with such care that they will develop the desired feelings in the audience apart from his gesticulation, intonation, and pantomime. If he endeavours to make a shallow speech into an emotionally thrilling oration, his hearers are likely to become aware of his efforts to produce an effect, but miss the effect itself. Ideally, a good speech should be one which is also so effective when in print, that it will incite its reader to the lofty feelings of its author. Too much weeping and wailing, denunciation and shaking of fists may even become ridiculous and provoke laughter in the audience unless the speech itself has warmed them in advance. In fact, a truly effective speaker can stand with his hands in his pockets and speak in a harsh voice, yet depict pathetic scenes in such well chosen words as to force tears from the eyes of his listeners. By refraining from an undue show of his own emotions, moreover, the speaker avoids the criticism of sentimentalism, even though he may be causing a lacrimal shower from his audience.

References

Armstrong, J.W., *Public Spearing for Everyone* (Harper, 1947).

Bonnell, J.S., *Psychology for Pastor and People* (Harper, 1948).

Brieland, D.M., "Speech and Personality Factors in the Education of the Blind" (*Amer. Psychologist*, 4, 1949).

Cantril, H., *Public Opinion* (Princeton U.Press, 1951).

Carhart, R., "A Method of Using the Gault Teletactor to Teach Speech Rhythms" (*Amer.Ann. Deaf*, 80,1935).

Crane, G.W., *Radio Talks*, Vol., I., (Hopkins, 1950).

Droke, M., *How to Handle People* (Garden City, 1942).

Flesch, R., *The Art of Plain Talk* (Harper, 1950).

Garrett, H.E., *Psychology* (American Book, 1950).

Griffith, C.R., "A Comment Upon the Psychology of the Audience" *Psychol. Monogr.*, 30, 1921).

Hanna, H., *Public Speaking Without Fear and Trembling* (Macmillan, 1949).

Harsh, C.M., & Schrickel, H.G., *Personality* (Ronald, 1950).

Henneke, B.G ., *The Radio Announcer's Handbook* (Rinehart, 1948).

Miller, G.A., *Language & Communication* (McGraw-Hill, 1951).

Prochnow, H.V., *The Public Speaker's Treasure Chest* (Harper, 1942).

Robinson, O.P., & Robinson, C.H., *Successful Retail Salesmanship* (Prentice Hall, 1950).

Ruch, F.L., *Psychology and Life* (Scott, Foresman, 1948).

Sarett, L., & foster, W.T., *Basic Principles of Speech* (Houghton, 1946).

Scott, W.D., *The Psychology of Public Speaking* (Noble, 1926).

Vaughan, W.F., *Social Psychology* (Odyssey, 1948).

Webb, E.T., & Morgan, J.B., *Strategy in Handling People* (Halcyon, 1948).

Woodruff, A.D., *The Psychology of Teaching* (Longman's. 1948).

Yacorzynski, G.K., *Medical Psychology* (Ronald, 1952).

8

THE PSYCHOLOGY OF WRITING AND OF ART

The prevalence of magazines and newspapers in the modern age has led to the development of the literary profession. No longer are verses and prose penned by only a few wealthy gentlemen who dabble in fiction writing as a hobby, but tens of thousands of men and women are earning their livelihood today by playing on the keys of their "ink pianos". As newspaper reporters, magazine writers and correspondents, free lance business writers, advertising copy writers, publicists, literary contestants, poets, and authors they are devoting their entire working time to placing print symbols on paper so that readers will later be able to obtain enjoyments, education and profit from the habitual responses set off by those same ink stimuli.

To those who have not had aspirations to become a second Shakespeare it may be illuminating to learn that there are approximately 18,000 newspapers in the United States, as well as 149 book publishers. Many of these publishers each year edit over 100 books. The following list shows the output of a few of the largest firms.

The Macmillan Company...................750 titles yearly
Doubleday, Doran & Co......................300 titles yearly
Harper & Brothers.............................250 titles yearly
Oxford University Press......................250 titles yearly
Appleton & Co..................................225 titles yearly
Dutton & Co.....................................200 titles yearly
Houghton Mifflin Co...........................200 titles yearly

Longmans, Green & Co........................200 titles yearly
Scribner's Sons...................................200 titles yearly

In the realm of magazines, the *Author and Journalist* carries a quarterly market list of over 700 weeklies and monthlies which pay for the material they use. In addition, there are numerous scientific or technical journals which do not reimburse their contributors. Notice the wide variety of cash literary markets in the following tabulation of magazines published in this country:

	Magazines
List A (General periodicals, standard, literary, household, popular and non-technical, which ordinarily pay on acceptance at rates of about 1 cent a word or better).	137
List B (General periodicals which ordinarily pay less than 1 cent a word, or pay on publication, or which are chronically overstocked, or which offer a very limited market, or concerning which no definite information has been obtainable.)	145
List C (Trade, technical, religious, agricultural, business, educational, and other class publications.)	378
Agriculture, Farming, Livestock	14
Art and Photography	2
Automobile, Aviation, Boating, Transportation, Highways	13
Business, Advertising, Salesmanship	23
Building, Archtecture, Landscaping, Home Decorating	11
Educational	8
Health, Hygiene	6
Musical	8
Religious	21
Scientific, Technical, Radio, Mechanics	17
Sporting, Outdoor, Hunting, Fishing	18
Theatrical, Motion Picture, Radio, "Fan" Magazines	18
Trade Journals, Miscellaneous	219
ist D (Juvenile and Young People's Publications.)	82

In addition to the print media already mentioned we could cite as the products of writers house organs and advertising brochures, as well as all the copy that confronts the reader in newspaper and magazine advertisements. In order to give a rough indication of the widespread circulation of various types of magazines we shall quote the following data*:

Typical 1950 Circulation Figures

Christian Advocate (Methodist)	340,162
Extension Magazine (Catholic)	507,000
Boy's Life (Boy Scout)	508,356
Quick (In its first 9 months)	850,000
Popular Mechanics	1,063,694
Modern Romances	1,086,208
National Geographic	1,866,674
Coronet	2,650,759
Farm Journal	2,746,310
Look	3,041,630
Saturday Evening Post	4,034,169
Ladies Home Journal	4,473,630
Life	5,341,626
Marvel Comic Group	6499,375

The Psychological Basis of Suspense

Suspense is simply the observer's expectancy that a suggested act will be performed, plus uncertainty as to the actual outcome. We noted in the preceding chapter that a speaker could heighten the interest of a crowed simply by taking a piece of chalk from the tray of a blackboard behind him. The suspense results because the students are accustomed to seeing a man write when he stands before the blackboard with crayon in his hand. If they were Hottentots, his behaviour would not occasion suspense, unless the savages might expect him to throw it at them, in which case we would still find the teacher's simple action fraught with suspense.

When a baby picks up a straight edged razor, of course there is suspense, for we know from previous experience that the

* Directory of Newspapers and Periodicals (N.W. Ayer & Son, Inc., Philadelphia, 1950)

infant can wave its arms about and that razors are exceedingly sharp. These two facts serve as suggestions for the idea that he will cut himself, and our likelihood of witnessing the act is called suspense. When a drunken man is pictured staggering along a steel girder on the 77th floor of a skyscraper, we also undergo expectancy. Whenever an attractive young man and young woman are together, we likewise have suspense. The statements that a thief is in the crowd, or a hostile submarine in the sea, immediately creates suspense. The thief and the submarine are simple stimuli that serve as suggestions for the thought that some one will be robbed or the ship sunk.

It is evident, therefore, that suspense depends upon our habitual background and the suggestions playing upon us. If we know nothing of submarine warfare, we do not care if a dozen hostile submarines are all around our vessel. And though we may know the dangers of modern naval methods, we are likewise undisturbed until we are aware of the possible presence of the submarine. The four factors, therefore, which are indispensable for suspense are (1) the possession of habits with reference to the given situation; (2) suggestions which can set off these habits and lead to expected future action; (3) the actual operation of these suggestions upon the subject; (4) the possibility that the future action may not occur. In terms of the submarine example, we must not only be familiar with the danger of submarines, and submarines must present, but we must be aware of or reactive to those submarines. The presence of submarines, however, may not be a matter of fact but only a belief. We do not need to have seen them as long as somebody else has told us he has seen them.

When a youngster toddles over to place its hand upon the glistening head of a coiled rattlesnake we observers certainly undergo suspense but the child does not, for he has had no experience with reference to the situation. In a movie the hero who reaches into a box for an aspirin tablet is entirely clam about the procedure for he does not know what we have seen, namely, that his enemy has substituted bichloride of mercury tablets for the aspirin. In other words, the third indispensable factor for suspense is lacking in his case. The suggestion that would lead to his thinking of death is present but inoperative upon him.

Another critical thing for the writer to bear in mind is the fact that it is not our thought of the death of the toddler mentioned above or of the movie hero which causes us agony of suspense, but the waiting for it to happen or not to happen. It is the *expectancy* of a serious consequence with the possibility that it may be avoided. Some writers fail to make this distinction and slay their characters on every page but still cannot command the reader's interest. They have filled their stories with blood and thunder in response to an editor's request for more action. What the editor probably meant was more suspense. The simple pysical action of the villain in dropping one bichloride of mercury tablet into the aspirin box belonging to the handsome young hero can fill the feminine spectators with terrible suspense, and keep the masculine onlookers in almost equal perturbation.

Another significant factor in considering suspense is the fact that there are degrees of it. That a robin is hopping near a fishworm creates little suspense for me. That a tiger is stalking a Boston terrier is more emotionally arousing, and if the terrier is a pet in my household, I am quite excited. This suspense is trivial, however, compared to what I feel if I am watching the jungle beast approach my own child. Similarly, if a bucket of sand is lowered over a cliff by a rope that is becoming frayed, I may be only mildly concerned. If a valuable animal is being lowered I grow more interested, and become frantic when I learn that a human being is below. As the rope becomes increasingly worn against the rocky edge of the cliff, I become a wildman on learning that one of my own loved ones is suspended in the cage that swings above abyss.

The fundamental motive bases, therefore, must be aroused before we react with a maximum of suspense. Threatened curtailment of food, drink, wealth, health, loved ones, or prestige immediately produces suspense. The writer must aim at the bull's-eye just as necessarily as the speaker and the salesman.

Why Suspense Depends on Characterisation

In the examples just mentioned we found that the danger threatening an unknown terrior did not produce as much suspense in us as that which imperiled our family pet. The reason therefor lies in the fact that we identify ourselves and the pet dog. He is a part of us, and gives rise to memories and emotions that are pleasant to us. It is characteristic of human beings to resent the loss of that which produces gratification and pleasure. No such identification occurs in the case of the bucket of sand. The animal produces a noticeable suspense, however, because it has some attributes which we also possess, notably the capacity to suffer pain, hunger, thirst, and cold. We can identify ourselves with animals, and do so the longer we are in direct association with them. With a fellow human being, the possibility for identification is correspondingly greater. It reaches its climax in our own kin.

In characterisation the writer simply endeavours to portray his hero or heroine so that the reader quickly identifies himself with them. We cannot enjoy fiction or the movies unless this identification is made. It is imperative, therefore, for the writer to employ specificity in delineating his characters for we link ourselves only with those who do the specific things which we do and in the same way as we perform them. In the previous chapter we emphasised the necessity for the speaker to facilitate this identification process. The reason why we take sides in a debate is because we note the identity in beliefs of one speaker or he other with our own.

The necessity for good characterisation is brought out in the following statement of F.E. Blackwell, editor of several magazines belonging to the Street and Smith group.

> Recently I have been able to sum up writing in this way; Interest in a story is in proportion to interest in the characters in the story. Of course, in a detective story it's a good thing, almost a needful thing, to have a novel method of killing, stealing, etc. –something that one would remember to tell a friend – but this doesn't *make* the story. You must become interested in the characters, and the more you are interested in the characters, the better you'll like the story. Thus: I recently complained to an author that I didn't think his story had much suspense in it. This remark brought a violent protest from the author. He said that

> on the first page he had killed a gentleman; on the second page held abducted a young woman, and on and on through the story, violent action had been taken against the characters. How absurd, he said, that there could be not suspense in such a story. But I told him I didn't care about the death of the gentleman on the first page, nor did I give a rap about the abducted lady. Had he written well enough, all he would have had to do, to move me to tears, would be to have had the gentleman spill a drop of ink on his new spring suit, and the lady come down stairs to meet an admiring caller without first powdering her nose.

The chief difference between a novice and a literary master like Wilbur Daniel Steele is partly reducible to the latter's excellent characterisation. The reader easily finds himself portrayed in the characters and therefore undergoes all emotional crises and suspense which they experience. The tyro, on the contrary, quickly turns out his characters with the essential qualities of man in general, but not of man in the particular. These characters have no more distinguishing marks than a factory made dining room chair in contrast to an Italian hand carved piece of furniture. The reader, therefore, sees but little of himself in the person about whom he is reading.

Amateur writers and introverts in general fail to perceive the fine distinctions in behaviour and character which make living personalities of their paper heroes and heroines. The latter may sometimes be so unreal and artificial that they appear comical when they are supposed to be paying serious roles. The following quotation from Daisy Ashford is a striking case in point. This girl was only nine years old when she wrote her novel, so she warrants praise instead of criticism. Her narrative, nevertheless, is a good example of the point just mentioned, for many college students in the sentimental mood of midnight write love scenes scarcely more true to life than this one. The narrative quoted begins at the point where the two lovers had decided to go for a day's outing. The punctuation and spelling are retained as in the child's own version.

> They arrived at Windsor very hot from the journey and Bernard at once hired a boat to row his beloved up the river. Ethel could not row but she much enjoyed seeing the tough sunburnt arms of Bernard tugging at the oars as she lay among the rich cushons of the dainty boat. She had a rather lazy nature but Bernard did not know of this. However he soon got dog tired and suggested lunch by the mossy bank.

Oh yes said Ethel quickly opening the sparkling champaigne.
Don't spill and cried Bernard as he carved some chicken.
They eat and drank deeply of the charming viands ending up with merangs and choclates.
Let us now bask under the spreading trees said Bernard in a passiuonate tone.
Oh yes lets said Ethel and she opened her dainty parasole and sank down upon the long green grass. She closed her eyes but she was far from asleep. Bernard sat beside her in profound silence gazing at her pink face and long wavy eye lashes. He puffed at his pipe for some moments while the larks gaily caroled in the blue sky. Then he edged a trifle closer to Ethels form.
Ethel he murmured in a trembly voice.
Oh what is it said Ethel hastily sitting up.
Words fail me ejaculated Bernard horsly my passion for you is intense he added fervently. It has grown day and night since I first beheld you.
Oh said Ethel in supprise I am not prepared for this and she lent back against the trunk of the tree.
Bernard placed one arm tightly round her. When will you marry me Ethel he uttered you must be my wife it has come to that I love you so intensly that if you say no I shall perforce dash my body to the brink of you muddy river he panted wildly.
Oh don't do that implored Ethel breathing rarther hard.
Then say you love me he cried.
Oh Bernard she sighed fervently I certainly love you madly you are to me like a Heathen god she cried looking at his manly form and handsome flashing face I will indeed marry you.
How soon gasped Bernard gazing at her intensly.
As soon as possible said Ethel gently closing her eyes.
My Darling whispered Bernard and he seiezed her in his arms we will be marrid next week.
Oh Bernard muttered Ethel this is so sudden.
No no cried Bernard and taking the bull by both horns he kissed her violently on her dainty face. My bride to be he murmured several times.
Ethel trembled with joy as she heard the mistick words.
Oh Bernard she said little did I ever dream of such as this and she suddenly fainted into his out stretched arms.

"Pitching" You Opening

When a writer begins his literary composition he should usually "key" it in the opening paragraphs so that the mood typical of the story or chapter is set. It is difficult to create a single mood for such a lengthy string of situations as we find in a novel, but shorter literary works can usually employ this technique with profit. If the story is to be an artistically constructed episode with a central motif, the opening words should sound the appropriate note. A tale of horror or a rollicking narrative of carefree youth should obviously open in different keys. Observe the contrasting feeling tone embodied in the following two paragraphs.

> Like gaunt wolves slinking out of their mountain den in search of unsuspecting prey, a dozen gray-black clouds slid off the jagged peaks guarding the lone entrance to the Devil's Corral and darted across the leaden sky. Old Jed Blanton cursed beneath his breath at the ill luck which had steered him into this ominous valley with his two comely daughters. He had hoped to get through Hell County the day before, but the Evil Eye of the valley and noted the radiant beauty of Jed's older girl.

> It was an ideal spring day – just the sort which Janet had hoped for to make the picnic a success. Against the blue sky she could see many fluffy white cloudlets drifting along like so many fleecy lambs. The warm sun was taking fragrant thank offerings from woods and flowers and freshly plowed fields. Even the birds seemed on a holiday. When Bob's blue roadster swooped up the drive and sopped before the white pillared veranda, Janet was so happy she gave her mother two extra kisses before she ran down the steps.

We must also remember that young people are more energetic than their parents and grandparents, so they desire faster action. The slow tempo and lengthy descriptions of Henry James are especially unsuited to youth. Young people are in the fox trot mood. They can enjoy waltzes when they are tired or grow older. Quick, incisive characterisations with plenty of suspense resulting from muscular and love conflicts make them happy. The love interest is mot effective when tied up with athletics, warfare and similar forms of competition necessitating the expenditure of much energy. Roughly speaking, the gridiron is a popular locale for the creation of a love story for youth, while the golf links are a more appropriate setting for romance among the older generation.

The psychological explanation for these two preferences is rather simple. Whenever we become interested in the hero or heroine we, of course, identify ourselves with them. If we are in ill health, or lack energy and vitality, we must, however, hoard our strength. The combats in which our heroes engage tend to deplete our store of energy, and therefore lead to fatigue and unpleasantness. This depletion of energy is similar to that which follows when we witness a boxing match or a football game. We tense our muscles and implicitly undergo all the action which we see or about which we read. It follows, therefore, that we tend to avoid those tales in which the performances of the leading characters are too vigorous for our vicarious participation. It is conceivable that suitable objective test might show differences between the people of Florida or Alabama and those of Michigan and Maine in respect to this question, for we know the warmer southern climate produces a slower tempo of living.

How to Increase the Attention Value of the Page

Yellow journalism relies upon the attention attracting value of photographs, pictures, and headlines. An intimation of sex situations in the latter holds the attention, and produces the sale of the paper. The conservative writer, however, can utilise many psychological facts for whetting the reader's interest without blatantly employing the sex appeal. We shall list some of the more obvious ones as follows:

(1) Use short paragraphs – From habit we have associated short paragraphs with conversation, and conversation denotes human beings. We are more interested in persons than in things. It is this fact which explains why many readers skip much of the descriptive matter and follow the dialogues. Young people are prone to do so. The writer has tested children in regard to paragraph lengths and has found that they invariably will choose a page broken into short paragraphs in preference to one where the paragraphs are long.

The short paragraphs also suggest short suggest short sentences, with a resulting ease in comprehension. Magazines and novels usually have much shorter paragraphs than textbooks, so the short paragraphs connote suspense. Indeed, we have become so accustomed to associating long paragraphs with polysyllables and educational treatises that the college reader a generation ago would hardly respect a textbook which did not have paragraphs covering half of a page, and whose style was not cumbersome. William James' works were a novelty in the scientific field, therefore, because he had an interesting style and illustrated his laws with concrete cases.

Short paragraphs are also easier upon the eyes, for they produce more half lines. The last line of a paragraph usually does not extend the full width of the page, so the eye muscles do not have to do as much work. Moreover, these broken lines break the monotonous appearance of the page.

(2) Use quotation marks – These attract attention not only because of their upper case position in the line, but also because they denote human repartee with possible conflict and suspense. In a one-second exposure to a page the reader will usually observe almost all of the quotation marks. They have interest value far above that possessed by any letters of the alphabet or other punctuation marks. As a rule, the writer should change indirect discourse into direct, for the page is made more attractive to the reader in consequence. Economy of space may be violated thereby, but the material gains in interest value.

(3) Use illustrations – Many an article is sold to an editor because is contains photographs or pen sketches. Pictures attract us much more quickly than do words and they greatly simplify our comprehension of an idea. Of two stories in a magazine with equally attractive titles, the average reader will choose the one which contains an illustration. There are some qualifications to the statement, however, for a few years ago when modernistic art was in its heydey, the freakish appearance of the hero and heroine in the sketch accompanying the story repulsed many would-be readers, causing them to search for an equally promising story title with a normal type of pictured heroine or else none at all. It is frequently more pleasant for the reader to construct his own image of the leading characters from their verbal description lone than to have a sketch which violates his sense of beauty.

Advertisers have long realised the importance of cuts in selling merchandise. They have statistically proved their superiority to the straight copy advertisement. Accordingly, the yellow newspapers fill their sheets with cartoons and photographs. The widespread popularity of the Sunday comic pages and the daily cartoon strips is also ample evidence of the effectiveness of pictures.

In scientific treatises a similar heightening of interests is obtained by the employment of curves, charts and graphs. We have already pointed out the effectiveness of such material in public speaking. The trouble with many charts and curves, however, is the fact that they are not self-explanatory. To be truly effective, of course, they should readily reveal their significance. Even quoted material from which quotation marks have been omitted is often attention attracting if it is printed in a smaller size of type than the body of the treatise of article.

(4) Open your paragraphs with dynamic and attention holding words – Although it has been customary to consider the end of the sentence as the place of greatest emphasis and importance, modern advertising procedure tends to reverse positions, and begin with the most dramatic work in the sentence. In running down the page with our initial glance the opening words of the successive paragraphs are first focussed upon. The value of striking words at the start of the first sentence of each paragraph is shown in the following cases.

Womanlike she decided that her next action.
Shrieking like a madman he raced onward.
Terrified by what had happened, she.
Attacked without warning, they resolutely.
Helpless in the face of the oncoming.
Love being now impossible after what she.

Whether the reader will like the material contained within the paragraphs depends upon other things than the attractive first impression which he gains from a quick survey of the page, but a dramatic plot can be made to appear uninteresting by lack of attention to these details. A dull or poorly written narrative cannot become a best seller simply by attention to the mechanics of the page any more than a drab and colourless personality can be made the life of the party by Listerine. Lifebuoy soap, and a new suit of clothes, but an interesting framework should at least assist in rendering a story more attractive.

How to Make Your Style More Interesting

When asked for a definition of literary style Dean Swift replied that it is simply "paper words in proper places." The task of putting proper words into proper places, however, is a very difficult one, involving a thorough knowledge of human motivation and control, as well as the technical and less important factors such as punctuation and diction. One of the greatest masters of English style, Stevenson, writes: "From the arrangement of according letters, which is altogether arabesque and sensual, up to the architecture of the elegant and pregnant sentence, which is a vigorous act of the pure intellect, there is scarce a faculty in man but has been exercised. We need not wonder, then, if perfect sentences are rare, and perfect pages rarer."

When the young poet Racine wrote to Boileau for criticism and advice, he said of himself, "I ought to tell you that I write with great facility." Boiliau's response was, "I hope to teach you to write with great difficulty." In a similar vein Byron is reputed to have once said, "Easy writing's damned hard reading."

Fundamentally, therefore, it is not agility in bandying words about which makes us skilful writers, but the structural patterns in which those words are arranged. A mason could lay bricks with great facility without ever knowing anything about architecture. It is not the bricks themselves, therefore, which make a great cathedral but their arrangement. The same brick might be employed with equal ease in the construction of a dog kennel, a garage, or a house. In like manner the facile speech of the college major in English does not enable him to write interesting stories. In fact, one of the most successful story writers in America knows very little about grammar or punctuation. He simply scribbles his tale with entire disregard for the English language and its rules of usage. A college girl in the editorial office of the magazine rewrites this author's stuff as soon as it arrives. The curious thing about the situation is the fact that the college girl with a superior knowledge of English cannot create the story itself. She may contribute the vocabulary but the man fills his plot with its drama and suspense.

We have presented this example to show that the psychological appreciation of human nature is the principal factor in effective writing. Any intelligent person with a few years' study of Webster and an English grammar has the verbal "bricks" for literary masonry, but few can thereupon duplicate Conrad's psychological technique in laying these "bricks" so they produce a dramatic structure.

Dean Swift's definition of literary style includes both the basic understanding of human nature plus the knowledge of the mechanics of the writing process. Often, however, the meaning of literary style tends to be associated with the melodious combination of words, involving the avoidance of redundancy and tautology. As a matter of fact, it is about as difficult to separate literary style from literary content as for the cartoonist to separate the black lines which delineate his pen characters from the characters so circumscribed. Whether he uses a fine black line or a heavy one is of relatively slight importance as long as his characters themselves are interesting.

There are a few general comments, however, which we shall make concerning the mechanics of style in contradistinction to the content of the literary product. We shall present them in the following paragraphs:

(1) Avoid repetition of the same words and sounds whenever possible – This simply involves the employment of synonyms, and is advisable in order to eliminate monotony.

(2) Avoid redundancy of the use of superfluous words, as in "Raise up the window."

(3) Avoid tautology or the needless repetition of the same idea in different words, as in "audible to the ear."

(4) Avoid triteness in words and analogies – This admonition covers not only the hackneyed words and phrases which have become so overworked that they possess little intrinsic interest, but also those proverbs, similes, and metaphors which are equally threadbare. Writers who scintillate in their literary style are seldom guilty of such phrases as "marble brow", "iron willed", "ship of state", "in the blink of an eye", and "like water off a duck's back."

In trying to be different, however, the writer must be discreet, for it is possible to re-phrase so many old ideas and analogies that the reader becomes more conscious of the writer's attempt at cleverness than of the cleverness itself. Three or four new twists to old phraseology in a single short story will usually be sufficient to impress the reader with the freshness of the author's style.

(5) Maintain a consistent feeling tone whenever possible – For example, it is not wise, as a general rule, to mix slang and colloquialisms with elegant diction. Colloquialisms may be unknown in another region of the country; hence, the readers there will react as if blank spaces were in the sentences. The writer, like the public speaker, should endeavour to hold his public throughout his entire contact with it. It is also advisable to let others read your writings before they go to press, for words which are quite proper and pleasant according to your own environment and experience may have unpleasant connotations for persons not similarly trained. The subject of feeling tone has been treated more exhaustively in earlier chapters.

(6) Read your work aloud in order to catch phonetic harshness and unmusical combinations of vowels and consonants – A story or article which reads easily aloud, will flow along well when read silently.

(7) Use specificity in your description – Sensory qualities enrich any object, making it appear less barren and uninteresting. In fact, the reason old phrases and apothegms are threadbare is simply because their sensory qualities have "worn off" as stimuli to our conscious attention. The word "Ivory" connotes richness, African elephant tusks, Steinway piano keys importation, and luxury, but it is now almost threadbare of such qualities in the phrase "Ivory Soap". We have simply employed it so frequently that the muscular (kinesthetic) quality of the word far overshadows its other sensory attributes, and it is no longer attended to consciously.

In shunning hackneyed epithets, we must create new ones which still possess sensory attributes over and above, the kinesthetic qualities involved in their pronunciation. Accordingly, these adjectives will create mental images, for they will lie in the focal circle of our attention. Three years ago the writer read the following sentence which is possibly not a verbatim reproduction, but at least closely approximates the original, "The wind in the pines sounded like a cello in a gloomy temple." The simile is specific and novel. The fact that it has remained in memory when the story containing it has faded, augurs well for it.

How to Write Interesting Exposition

Descriptive or informative material is uninteresting until it is tied up to some fundamental motive base of the human being. The art of making the educational process interesting, therefore, is principally one of showing the relationship of the new object or idea to a basic need of the reader. Boys are not much interested in social etiquette until they are to take their best girls to a formal party. Then they may become omnivorous readers of Emily Post.

The reason that Emily Post's writings then become popular with them is simply the fact that they have become acutely aware of the functional relationship of her advice to their immediate needs. They desire to be considered sophisticated and retain the respect of their sweethearts. Formerly uninteresting rules of etiquette may now transcend the sport page in interest value.

It is well to crystallise the attention of the readers upon the subject to be explained, by means of an effective headline or a question. Both of these should strike at the bull's-eye by arousing basic habit patterns possessed by the reader. Correspondence schools have employed the question method in much of their advertising. "When are you going to sit behind a mahogany desk?" "Are you prepared for the bigger job?" "Where will you be ten years from now?"

After the initial appeal to a fundamental desire of the reader, the writer should quickly state how his measure or idea enables the reader to satisfy his want. This may consist of no more than a blunt affirmation of the practical value of the measure. Then a parade of exposition may follow. Such a procedure introduces suspense into the situation. The reader has been told that he will profit greatly by the new product of idea. He awaits with interest the further details.

All the previously mentioned devices of the writer may then be utilised. Cleverness of style, the inclusion of narration, and the numerous methods of increasing the interest value of the page help sustain attention. Always, however, the intimate connection between the idea and the reader's basic need must be kept fresh in his mind. The teacher who fails to emphasize this connection finds that her students are less interested than those of another instructor who does make the tie-up between education and life's needs.

Much of the spectator's attention during a moving picture show is really taken up with exposition. The suspense is first created by showing us the hero, the heroine, and the villain. Thereafter we watch with considerable interest the machinations of the latter. The same type of thing is shown upon the pages of a novel. After the development of suspense, the writer inserts description – pages of it. We follow the heroine through the routine affairs of her life for perhaps an entire chapter before she and the hero or the villain are again brought together. But we are willing to read description because of the underlying suspense. The writer of exposition, therefore, must also develop suspense if he is going to hold his readers until the end of his article.

Writing Effective Advertising Copy

Advertising copy is chiefly expositional. It contains descriptions of a piece of merchandise, and a cataloguing of its uses. But it can retain the reader's interest by the same methods which we have described in the previous section. It must first of all strike at a fundamental need. Utility is the first asset of any product. The merchandise must serve some want, and the more basic the need, the more we are capable of becoming interested in it. Listerine advertisements illustrated an appreciation of this fact by making their appeal to the sex vanity and business ambition of people.

In order to illustrate the importance of making the tie-up between the need and the product, as well as to point out once more the absolute necessity of being definite, concrete, in motivating human beings, we shall cite the case of a young man who built a large garage featuring the mechanical department and the overhauling of cars. He sent out a neat form letter saying that he employed only competent mechanics, and that he would be open for business on the first of the week. Not ten letters were received in reply. His direct-mail venture was an advertising failure. But one of his few patrons, an advertising man, had received a copy of the letter. He came to the young garage owner and offered to write him another one. His offer was accepted, and here is what went out on the second direct-mail attempt:

> "We make an interesting offer. When repairing your car we invite you to come around and see how it is done. Allow us to explain some of the mysteries of the inside of that power plant.
>
> There are parts of your car that you know little about. There are intricacies that mean trouble on the road. We will gladly explain these points to you and initiate you into some of the little-known engine problems."

This letter brought 70 per cent of replies and the garage was quickly booked with work throughout the entire winter. The letter was effective because it corroborated the garage owner's statement that he had only competent mechanics. It acted much as a guarantee, for he offered his patrons a chance to watch his men work. Men who knew gasoline motors could therefore see if his mechanics were skilled. Moreover, many patrons, particularly women, would be pleased to be taught some of the mechanical details concerning their own automobiles. His letter met the need of these women for information.

We have already explained the method by which a public speaker can profitably disclaim his intention of criticising his opponent or of trying to influence his hearers to his own cause. It can also be employed in writing advertising copy, as the following first paragraph of one such letter well indicates.

> Dear Friend:
>
> There's no use trying. I've tried and tried to tell people about my fish. But I wasn't rigged out to be a letter writer, an I can't do it. I can close-haul a sail with the best of them. I know how to pick out the best fish of the catch, I know just which fish will make the fastiest mouthfuls, but I'll never learn the knack of writing a letter that will tell people why my kind of fish – fresh-caught prime-grades, right off the fishing boats with the deep-sea tang still in it – is lots better than the ordinary store kind.

An attention to feeling tone is also imperative in writing advertising copy. Our copy concerning the Snuggle Sweater, demonstrates the influence of specific sensory adjectives in creating pleasant feeling tone. It is just as essential for the writer as for the salesman to remember that habits are developed because of definite stimuli in the environment, and consequently they must be re-aroused by specific stimuli, either actual or symbolic.

Figure 8.1

A good direct-mail piece of advertising. Note how it "sells them the holes" Observe the opening words of the paragraphs. They are a bit weak in dramatic value.

UNION PACIFIC SYSTEM

The Overland Route

J.P. CUMMINS
General Passenger Agent

DEPARTMENT OF TRAFFIC
Omaha, Nebraska

Mark Twain
writes of his disappointment
when his first balloon ride revealed that the States were all the same colour. He had always believed, from a study of maps, that Ohio was red and Indiana was blue.

Just one of the great humorist's many witticisms, to be sure. But you and I know that there are regions, especially in the West, where Nature has been most generous in conferring her treasures of form and colour. There is a region in Southern Utah and Northern Arizona called Zion, Bryce Canyon and Grand Canyon – three national parks – so colourful that it almost defies description.

Then there are other regions of colourful beauty, such as Yellowstone, Rocky Mountain-Estes, Yosemite, Rainier and a host of others, any one of which offers a delightful vacation in the out-of-doors. Possibly you have visited some of these places, but since railroad fares will be lower this summary than ever before, why not plan to see more of our national playgrounds?

Perhaps California, the scene of the Tenth Olympiad, will be your goal this summer, as it will be the goal of thousands of others. President Hoover will officially open the Olympic Games in Los Angeles on July 30. Athletes of fifty nations, led by their national colours, will take part in the great "Parade of Nations". What a colorful and never to be forgotten spectacle that will be!

No matter what part of the West you plan to visit, the Union Pacific can take you, for it serves more of the West than any other railroad. Along its lines are located the finest dude ranches in the West. An easy and inexpensive side trip en route to or from California will take you to Hoover (Boulder) Dam, where operations are now on in full swing.

We will gladly give you complete information and literature about the trip you have in mind. There is real economy in planning your trip well in advance, and that is just the service you can receive by returning the enclosed card. We invite you to do so.

Cordially yours,
J.P. Cummins

The advertiser may also frequently inject suspense into his copy to increase its interest value. In the following part of one of the Grinnell Company's advertisements we have annotated the copy, and appended explanatory footnotes below it.

"Oh, that's the same old idea you sprang five years ago, Tom," said the president as he laid a friendly hand on the old engineer's shoulder. "I'm sorry, but the prize money for coal-saving suggestions *must* go to those whose ideas are more practical."

"But –" the old man started falteringly to explain, when the production manager cut in with, "Why, that idea came from his boy the year he was getting through Tech. That waste heat would not generate an ounce of stream. The boy himself would laugh at it today."

"But my boy. . ." began the old man again.

"What was the college boy's idea?" interrupted the consulting engineer, who had consented to help in awarding the prize money.

1. President versus employee, therefore conflict indicated.
2. Employee is an *old* engineer, therefore probably the under dog as regards the young president, so we side with him.
3. Prize money increases the suspense by denoting competition, conflict.
4. The conjunction "but" denotes the old engineer is still battling.
5. "Falteringly" shows another bid to gain our sympathy for the under dog.
6. Another indication that the old man is still fighting and not for himself alone but for his son, also.
7. At last! Somebody is at least impartial enough to give him a hearing.
8. Aha! This last interrogator is one of the judges who award the prize money, too. May be we'll see justice win out after all.

How to Write Credit Letters That Collect

The need for the use of applied psychology in credit work is being realised more fully today than ever before. Credit managers must be familiar with the methods of motivating human beings, and must appreciate that people can be coaxed into the desired payment of their bills more successfully than they can be clubbed. We do not imprison men in America, as was done in England a century ago, for their business debts, although they are still incarcerated for lack of alimony payments.

An intimation in a collection letter that the writer needs the money owed him to meet his own obligations nearly always gets a check out of the debtor, provided the latter is solvent. When a credit manager threatens his debtors, however, they grow hostile. A characteristic of hostility is the fact that cooperation between the warring factions is reduced to nil. "Let him go to court, if he wants to," we say or think, even though we may finally grudgingly meet his demands. And if we cannot pay all of our outstanding obligations, we prefer to remit to those who have been fair and considerate of us, leaving the bills of our enemies on the bottom of the pile.

Many times some unusual device will make a credit letter stand out from the "please remit by return mail" variety, and it is often far superior to the "we shall be forced to turn the account over for collection" kind of missive. A very effective type of credit letter which has been cited by McCuaig is the one following:

> "When I was a kid my mother taught me to remember things by tying a piece of string around may thumb. This worked fine.
>
> I am enclosing a piece of the kind she used, of proper length for you, and I am going to ask you as a favour just to tie it around the middle of the thumb on your right hand. You will soon see how conveniently and reliably it operates.
>
> Presently your book keeper will come in about some other matter. You will take the paper which he gives you in your right hand. You will at once see the string! Then you will say: 'Oh, yes, Smith, I wish you would make out a check for the Packard Electric Company and let me sign it right away. There is a balance overdue.'
>
> You will be glad to have the matter settled. We will much appreciate getting the money to pass along to the people *we* owe. The string you can keep and use again for all sorts of things – possibly to remind you to send your next order our way."

The reader will observe that the final sentence in the above letter attempts to take any sting out of the credit manager's words by showing that the debtor's friendship and continued patronage is desired and hoped for. There is no intimation that a conflict or legal suit is at all contemplated. It also dispels the possible thought in the recipient's mind that the credit manager is unpleasantly sarcastic. That one sentence just goes to show the importance of "proper words in proper place".

Sometimes, of course, credit men may have to write very straightforward letters. But they should never stoop to emotionalism. It is always a good thing to leave an opening so that a later reconciliation is not too difficult, nor to demeaning to the pride of the present debtor. One large firm manufacturing mattresses let a certain dealer act as its representative in a large mid-western city. The dealer did not push this company's goods and was very slow about remitting, being six months in arrears. The company finally wrote him a very honest letter stating that they felt he was not doing their line of mattresses justice, and that they thought he was not treating them fairly in regard to prompt payment of bills.

On the return mail they obtained an angry letter in which the dealer told them they could take their old mattresses out of his store, for he did not want to have anything more to do with them. The credit manager, however, sent another letter in which he stated that they did not wish to discontinue business with him, but simply wanted a fairer treatment in regard to settlement of bills. He further stated that it would be unpleasant for the mattress company as well as for the dealer if a change were made. If the company turned their account to another dealer in his city they would feel compelled to tell the new dealer the full facts. They would have to say that the present dealer was careless about keeping up a first class credit rating, that he fell six months in arrears, and that he did not push the line of goods which he was supposed to sell. The mattress company did not want to make any such statements because they would lower his standing among his fellow merchants and would be an admission that the mattress company had misjudged their man originally. Moreover, their goods had long been advertised as being on sale in his store, and they would lose some trade if the change were made. However, they left it up to his good judgment, being entirely willing to continue amicable relationships if he would change his methods in their regard.

In a week a letter came from their dealer in which he apologised, and paid up his accounts. Thenceforth he vigorously pushed their line of merchandise. They never had any more trouble with this man. The reader will have observed the credit manager's clever stimulation of fundamental motive bases possessed by the dealer. The latter had to acknowledge that the company was right, that they had treated him more than fairly, and *that he would lose in social prestige as well as financial standing* if the company changed their account to one of his rivals. Since the credit manager had not become emotional and made it impossible for the dealer to restore friendly relationships without a tremendous cost to his self-esteem and pride, the retailer came back. The credit manager had left the door open for just this possibility.

The Psychological Aspects of Art

Such problems as balancing objects upon the page are not solved by simply using a ruler and a compass and geometrically bisecting the space. The psychological center of the page, for instance, is above the geometrical center. A line crossing at a point approximately 60 per cent of the distance from the bottom of th page (the golden section) appears to divide the space into equal parts. Perspective as employed in art depends on habit. Indeed, space perception in general is developed by the infant through his experiences with his environment. He reaches for the moon, not realising the differences in the distance of objects surrounding him. He therefore lacks perspective and could not appreciate landscapes portrayed in the art galleries. Only as he gains the power of self locomotion does he fully realise those psychological elements which enable accurate special perception. He then finally becomes aware of the fact that in general the less distinct an object appears, the farther it is from him; that the seemingly smaller of two like objects is farther away; that the object which he sees in entirety is between himself and the object which it overshadows. These and other visual habits have already been fully presented to the student in his course in general psychology.

Without having been conscious of the learning process underlying the phenomenon, we have become conditioned to the fact that the more strain upon the rectus medialis muscle of each eyeball, the nearer is the object upon which we are focussing. Vertical distances appear greater than equal horizontal ones because of the greater strain upon the superior rectus muscles. In short, we project into our environment as distances those sensations of effort entailed by the muscles of the eyeball. In a similar manner we project upon a stone more weight than upon a feather, when our bases for such comparisons really lie in the greater strain in the arm muscles while lifting the stone. This is psychological weight in contrast to physical weight as measured by specific gravities.

The balance of a picture depends upon both its physical measurements and its psychological attributes. A little dog pictured on one side of the middle of the page overbalances many times his actual area on the other side providing the latter space is filled with a boulder or other less attractive object. Our interest in a thing renders it psychologically heavier. In advertising, for example, a cut more than balances an equal area devoted to copy. A very striking headline for the copy may help offset this difference, and the whole situation is also influenced by the interest value of the scene depicted in the illustration.

An unbalanced scene is vaguely unpleasant because we either identify ourselves with the pictured characters and feel implicit muscle strains arising in consequence, or else the prolonged suspense resulting from our expectancy that an object will fall, becomes fatiguing. The suggestive value of unbalanced figures, however, is utilised in denoting movement, as in the case of the winged Mercury. The human figure itself may be represented in an unbalanced posture to create the illusion of running, but the entire piece of sculpture retains a balanced effect by having streamers extend behind the runner, or by some object in the hand behind him which is of interest value.

The employment of colour also involves psychological factors, dependent largely upon our early experiences. Blue is considered cool, probably because water has often had this appearance. Red, being the colour of fire, denotes warmth, and yellow-orange is cheery because of its association with sunlight. Green, being the principal hue of all vegetation, suggests those qualities that are experienced in the outdoors, namely, relaxation and relief. It is therefore regarded as a restful colour. White denotes both coolness, cleanliness, and purity, for reasons that are self-evident. It also conveys a suggestion of spaciousness, which party explains the fact that light coloured clothing enhances its wearer's appearance of corpulence. White paint makes a house or other building appear larger. The ceilings of rooms are usually lighter than the walls in order to increase the apparent size of the room. A black or dark brown ceiling makes a room seem small and oppressive. Black and very dark blues are forbidding colours because of their association with storms and nightfall. Fear lurks in darkness, not in brightly lighted regions. Light shades and tints, and bright hues like yellow, tend to be extrovertive in their influence, whereas dark colours tend to produce introversion.

We have previously discussed such matters as the colour preferences of males and of females, and have pointed out the resultant effect of simultaneous colour contrasts, and the fact that complementary hues increase each other's apparent richness. In addition to colours, moreover, we find that certain distinctive feeling tones attach to lines. Hollingworth states that delicacy of texture is denoted by the fine gray line, while the fine black line suggests precision and hardness. Homeliness and solidity are conneted by a broad rough line.

Beauty and grace are so dependent on psychological interpretation, however, that it is almost impossible to define them arbitrarily. A beautiful female figure in one generation may be too fat or too slender to be so considered by another generation or a different race. Since such mechanics as line, colour, and perspective are so dependent upon the previous conditioning to environments of both artist and critic, it is little wonder that the more fundamental aspects of the subject are so frequently debated. The items which we have just been discussing are comparable to the popular interpretation of literary style, namely, the mechanics of putting the material into lasting shape. There are thousands of artists who understand these facts, but they still do not become famous. They are like the college majors in English who possess the knowledge of vocabulary, punctuation, and grammar, but cannot write an effective short story.

Why Some Artists Succeed While Others Fail

Although many artists and sculptors fail financially because they have not attained sufficient knowledge of the mechanics of their craft, the majority of them never rise above mediocrity because they do not choose scenes and themes which have dramatic value. They may be hired by Gutzon Borglum or Lorado Taft to do much of the work of the latter but they themselves lack the ability to conceive ideas which are of interest or suspense value when crystallised in marble or bronze. They may be skilful enough in laying the "bricks" as long as some artistic genius creates the blue prints for them.

To illustrate this point more clearly, we may mention the cases of two young people starting out on a pleasure trip, each equipped with a camera and plenty of films. One of them "snaps" everything that has any appeal whatever to him. The other waits until he sees especially intriguing combinations of wood and sea and sky. Both persons have the same technical equipment, namely, their cameras and films, but one has the ability to select scenes which will interest the folks back home, whereas the other's prints will scarcely hold the glance of any but himself. The one can probably sell some of his photographs to travel magazines because the scenes have general interest. The other may not be able to give his away.

The psychological test of a promising young artist would be his skill in the use of a camera. If he could not bring back photographs of human interest value, then he certainly could hope for little success on the end of a paint brush, for he would not be greater than his technical ability, whereas a great artist, like the writer, depends on a combination of technique and interesting subject matter. In the realm of cartooning, for instance, many of the skilled technicians depend upon other people for ideas. They can illustrate your mental picture provided you tell them just what you have in mind. They are simply pen photographers. Too many artists are of the same class. They can paint well enough if they can be given a thrilling scene. After all, a great artist, sculptor, speaker, writer, salesman and advertising man have much in common, namely, an understanding of human motivation.

A pastoral scene, 'especially a landscape, is about as interesting as its homologue in the literary field, namely, exposition. The artist's technique may be very good and he may at times inject a reasonable amount of suspense, but he cannot hope to compete in interest value with the painting which, like the short story, strikes at more fundamental motive bases of human behaviour. Since human beings are usually more interesting than trees, other things being equal we shall look at and purchase scenes depicting men and women, girls and boys, in preference to the technically clever, but less interesting inanimate objects. The skilful artist, like the understanding writer, of course, can intertwine description and exposition with conflict and suspense.

A final comment concerning financial success in art involves the matter of salesmanship, not only of the producer's creations but also of himself. It has not been an exceptional thing for a great artist, musician, or writer to live in poverty for years until some society leader, connoisseur, or social pacemaker "discovered" him, whereupon work which he had done years before suddenly becomes great. Critics who would not look at it previously, now proclaim it remarkable. Even Michelangelo deliberately tinted one of his paintings to give it the impression of an antique after which it was sold at a large sum to Raffaelle Riario, Cardinal di San Giorgio.

We may conclude by stating that the reason why some artists succeed while others fail is owing to the fact that the successful persons have acquired not only the mechanical technique of their craft, but also a basic understanding of human nature so they can select scenes and situations which have greater human interest value. In addition to these two necessary qualifications, the artist who hopes to earn a livelihood needs to be a good salesman or else enlist the cooperation of some one who will care for the publicity and merchandising of his products.

References

Archer, J., *I Sell What I Write* (Fell, 1950).
Ashford, Daisy, *The Young Visiters* (Doubleday, 1919).
Author and Journalist Magazine (Monthly, 250, Boulder, Colo).
Barnouw, E., *Handbook of Radio Writing* (Little, 1948)
Burack, A.S., *The Writer's Handbook* (Writer, 1949).

Burack, A.S., *Writing Detective and Mystery Fiction* (Writer, 1945).
Contest Magazine (Monthly, 250, Upland, Indiana).
Cousins, N., *Writing for Love or Money* (Longman's, 1949).
DeVoto, B., *The World of Fiction* (Houghton, 1950).
Henneke, B.G., *The Radio Announcer's Handbook* (Rinehart, 1948).
Hull, H., *The Writer's Book* (Authors' League, 1950).
King, H. *Prize Contests* (Freese, Upland, Indiana, 1950).
Lichtblau, J., "Pet Peeves' of Editors" (*Author and Journalist,* July, 1932).
McCuaig, C.B., "The Human Inerest Angle the Credit Man Needs" *(Printers' Ink,* June 17, 1920).
Meier, N.C., "Studies in Psychology of Art" (*Psychol, Monog.,* 18, 1934).
Millett, F.B., *Reading Drama* (Harper, 1950).
Neal, M.B., *Writing and Selling Fact and Fiction* (Funk, 1949).
Orvis, M.B., *The Art of Writing, Fiction* (Prentice-Hall, 1949).
Printers' Ink (Dec. 15, 1921).
Reynolds, P.R., *The Writing Trade* (Writer, 1940).
The Writer (Monthly, 250, Boston, Mass.)
Van O'Connor, W., *Forms of Modern Fiction* (Colwell, 1948).
Writer's Digest (Monthly, 250, Cincinnati, O.).
Writer's Monthly (Monthly, 250, Springfield, Mass).

9

CHILD PSYCHOLOGY

The modern trend in child psychology is to look to the environment of the youngester instead of to his heredity for those determining factors which will make him good or bad, introvertive or extrovertive, confident or afraid. If a choice were to be made between heredity and environment, the latter would be the more dynamic selcetion since it enables people to build personalities of the short which they desire, whereas their own heredity is beyond their control.

A complete discussion of the child must, nevertheless, involve his inherited traits as well as the environment in which those traits are being expressed. A good environment somewhat offsets a poor inheritance, while a poor environment stunts to some degree the talents of a rich inheritance. Ideally, the optimum heritable traits in the most favourable milieu would produce the best results. In stating that a favourable environment partly offsets a meager inheritance, one must not forget that there are limitations to the interaction of heredity and environment. A moron cannot become a college graduate despite a wealth of music, books, and tutors with which he may be surrounded. Indeed, the parable of the talents may fittingly be applied to human inheritance. Some children receive five mental talents, whereas others receive only two or but one.

This fact is illustrated indirectly by Hollingworth in the Table 9.1. The reader will note the earlier maturity of those children who possess high intelligence quotients, and the significant delay in walking and talking of the subnormal youngsters. Throughout the remainder of this chapter, however, we shall emphasise chiefly the influence of the child's environment upon him.

Table 9.1
The different average ages of walking and talking of superior, normal, and subnormal children.

Intelligence level	*Average age and measure of variability*	
	Walking	*Talking*
Gifted (600 Cases)	12.8 months S. D. 2.5 mo.	11.2 months S. D. 2.8 Mo.
Normal, or somewhat Higher (50 Cases)	13.9 months A. D. 1.6 mo.	15.3 months A. D. 3.0 mo.
Feeble-minded (144 Cases)	25.1 months A.D. 9.6 mo.	38.5 months A. D. 16.8 mo.

The Child's Struggle for Individuality

In order to imagine more accurately the attitude of children regarding their adult surroundings, it is well to remember that chairs, tables, and other items of furniture are almost all built for persons who are giants in the eyes of their youngsters. We can comprehend this fact more readily if we suppose as adults we were placed in a world where all those who arbitrarily commanded us were at least 10 feet tall, weighed 400 pounds, and mysteriously possessed the ability to know what we were doing in their absence. The pre-kindergarten youngster, for instance, may have a father who is twice his height, and five times as heavy.

During childhood, therefore, the boy and girl are vividly aware of their dependence. "Don'ts" and "mustn'ts" are frequently heard, each of which deflates the child's ego. For twelve to fifteen years he does the will of his parents and teachers, with only occasional revolts. As he enters puberty, however, the size difference between himself and his parents has become lessened. He may even be as tall as his mother and the schooll teacher. He begins to taste some of those choice pleasures that follow partial independence. He goes to the scout camp alone, and has his own friends.

Meanwhile, in order to bolster his sense of importance he tries to impress his playmates in various ways, one of which is the creation of secret societies. May be these are fore his own sex alone, girls being entirely tabnoo, although often they are heterosexual in personnel. By such a method he arbitrarily separates himself from the hoi polloi and with elaborate ceremonies as well as the use of the blackball he indirectly inflates his own ego. The following college girl's paper describes a fairly typical instance of this sort.*

> The ROYAL ORDER OF WHAT we called it, and our pins were gold question-marks. Ours was a very exclusive organisation, since it would not admit anyone under twelve years of age and then only on the very highest recommendation and after a rigid examination. Those who did not belong to our club delighted us by asking the name of the club. "We belong to the royal order", we'd respond. That was their cue for "The royal order of what?" Then we would beam with the snappy comeback: "Theat's just it – THAT ROYAL ORDER OF WHAT? So great was the curiosity of those not admitted to our club that those under twelve counted the days to their twelfth birthday, and those over twelve but not admitted formed counter-organisations of their own. These, however, never attained the status of our club and were not very long lived.
>
> Both boys and girls belonged to our club, and nationality was something we never thought of. Most of us went to the same church, but there was no connection between the club and the church, except that we found Sunday School a very fertile field for deeds of curiosity, on which we fed with relish.
>
> Because so much eagerness to join was displayed by the initiates, we made the initiation quite difficult, "a test of character" we called it. Each initiate was subjected to three tests: the mock initiation, which consisted of the usual pranks and foolishnesses, but perhaps a little more foolish: the intelligence test, which consisted of answers to as many questions as we could think of, with a good deal of our own homework thrown in: and, finally, the solemn initiation, which we all attended in our long black robes and masks. At the solemn initiation, 'the constitution was read by candle light, and every initiate had to sign to sign it in blood, a rather severe test and somewhat of a shock. We never experienced any difficulty, however, in getting the victims to conform with the requirements.
>
> The election of officers was also a serious business surrounded with a great deal of formality. The most coveted office was that of "High Monkey-Monk". He was assisted by numerous royal officers, so that

* Paper by Marv Campbell

almost everyone had some fancy title. The vote was by secret ballot, in keeping with the spirit of the Royal Order.

However, the high position was usually held by the same boy every time. This is not hard to understand as he was an extremely capable leader with a powerful imagination, of which most of our ritual was a product, and he wore his ceremonial robes with a majesty which suited us all. In addition, he was a great diplomat, with a gift for eloquence which kept everybody happy.

At his suggestion, we held our most important meetings in his attic, which he furnished to suit the majesty of the occasions. However, we considered our homes good enough for ordinary meetings and took turns as hosts. Although everyone knew when and where the meetings were to be held, we had a Grand Scribe whose duty it was to send mysterious notices to the members.

Although the secretiveness formed a very important part of our activities, we were primarily a social group. Parties, picnics, beach parties, and grand tournaments (with much ceremony) helped to make us a self-satisfied organisation.

However, this was not to last forever. One day the minister of our church, probably on the theory that too much self-satisfaction is bad for the soul, told our High Monk that we really should be more democratic and let any young people of the church join our club. At the next meeting an atmosphere of tragedy prevailed for we were to decide how to reply to the minister's request. We finally decided on "Give us liberty or give us death", and so as a club we broke up, but many long friendship have grown out of the old

Royal Order of What

I should like to tell WHAT it was THE ROYAL ORDER OF but I promised I wouldn't and signed my name in blood!

The badges or pins of secret organisations are invaluable insignia without which the parent societies would probably disintegrate, for a part of the ego inflation of their members results from the envy of those with whom they associate. Other insignia prized by the child are those items of apparel or profession which pertain to adults. Thus children like to dress like their fathers or mothers. Long trousers, silk stockings, the father's old pocketknife, or the mother's discarded purse – these are cherished possessions of youngsters. Indeed, games in which they "play house" and assume parental roles are quite popular even with tots.

The child's struggle for individuality, therefore, consists of an attempt to throw off the bonds of serfdom and gain the social freedom of adults. His ego is deflated so constantly by his subservient position that he prizes anything which will bolster his individuality. The intelligent parent and teacher endeavours to give the child a reasonable amount of ego inflation by granting him possessions and praise and by making him class monitor, a juvenile traffic policeman, a member of the boy or girl scouts, or disburser of his own money. Those children who do not receive such treatment, moreover, are usually the one who get into trouble when they go to college or otherwise attain independence. Many adults go through life always struggling to make up for a childhood which was too repressed. They form the nuclei for the "anti" groups in society and compensate so far that their behaviour becomes almost atypical. We shall develop this topic more fully in the ensuing section.

Why we Sympathise with the Under Dog

Because the child himself has been the under dog for almost a score of year it is easier for him to identify himself with those who are being victimised or abused than with their tyrants and taskmasters. Even after the child reaches adulthood he still reacts with feelings of sympathy for the weaker party. It is possible that the maternal instinct, if there is one, explains in part the sympathy of women for the unfortunate folks around them, but the former explanation alone is adequate.

The successful person is envied by all and imitated by many, but is seldom sympathised with, for success and superiority have so long been identified with adulthood that it is difficult for us grown men and women to avoid slipping into the childhood attitude of resentment toward such persons. Other things being equal, the challenger has more friends among the spectators than does the champion, and the independent grocer gains sympathy in contrast to the chain store, even though people may patronise the latter.

Such behaviour illustrates not only our identification with the weaker individual or business organisation, but demonstrates the "negative protest" of youth. It is this protest against authority, which explains in part the desirability of avoiding direct statements in salesmanship and the effectiveness of suggestion. The popular belief that youth must have its fling expresses an appreciation of the tendency toward radicalism on the part of young people and their desire to break conventions and restrictions. Some of those children who have been ordered about most autocratically during childhood become the violators of laws and conventions when they do have their fling. We have mentioned in the previous section the chronic "antis". For fifty years of adult life these individuals may continue their protest against those forces and ideas connected with the adults who robbed them so completely of their youthful self-respect. That college men and women often flaunt the religious tenets of their parents, and choose an vocation except that of their fathers show evidences of simply a negative protest which has not expended itself.

For the average adult, however, the pendulum ultimately swings nearer the vertical, although few persons ever lose their sympathy for the under dog, since memories and attitudes of childhood are so lasting and dominant. The typical plot for a story or novel accordingly carries the hero or heroine along in an under dog role until the final chapter. Villains must be in the dominant position or be actively attempting to hold such authority. Even Cinderella would not elicit much interest if she were always a princess. But as a scullion who was ordered about by her cruel stepmother and stepsisters she obtains our support, for although we may not have been scullions we can readily identify phases of our childhood with her subservient position. If human beings sprang, like Athena, fully developed from their parents, it is quite likely they would feel less sympathy for the under dog, so the appeal of much current popular fiction would be considerably reduced.

From the psychological aspect, therefore, the adult's sympathy for the oppressed individual results from his ready identification with the latter, an identification which is a direct outgrowth of his many years of childhood wherein he himself was dependent and weak. In the following section we shall see how the child's intellectual immaturity leads to his belief in the supernatural and mysterious.

Why Children Believe in Magic

The child differ from the adult not only in his more limited experiences with life but also in his nervous immaturity which renders him incapable of the involved thought processes of the intelligent grown person. A little girl asks, "I bet you can't guess who drove the horses this morning?" An older girl replies bluntly, "You did." The younger child then inquires in mingled wonder and disappointment, "How did you know?"

In a similar manner the child who has been left at home alone by his parent and who knocks over the fish bowl or breaks a window, may reply to his mother's accusation, that he did not commit these errors. When his parent punishes him, he is nonplussed at her psychic power. How did she know he did it, for she was not there at the time? The "little bird" which tells mothers such things amounts to simply the five to ten years of additional mental age which the mothers possess beyond that of their children.

The child cannot reason, as does his parent, that inasmuch as he was the only occupant of the room or dwelling during her absence he is the one who must be responsible for any changes occurring therein. Because he sees evidences of apparent ominiscience on the part of his father and mother, therefore, he is inclined to believe in magic.

Among the phantom creatures with which he peoples his childhood milieu are, of course, giants and ogres, but his usual favourite is the elf or fairy, for the latter is a little fellow who can defeat a big fellow. He can identify himself with the fairy on the basis of size and apparent inability to defend himself against superiors. The success of the tiny magical creature becomes his own success, experienced vicariously. The elf or fairy shares the hero or heroine role with little boys and girls in childrens' tales, and helps the latter out of difficulties.

In conclusion, therefore, we may state that the youngster's predilection for fairy tales results from his contact with adult reactions which are magical to him. Since his parents are apparently psychic, he finds no difficulty in granting reality to additional supernatural phenomena. His faith in fairies is not dispelled simply because he is unable to see them, for he cannot see how his mother knows his actions in her absence, but he must admit that she knows them. When his memory span and ability to handle longer and more involved ideas become greater, he can understand those mysterious inferences which his parents now make. His belief in fairies and a Santa Claus will then wane.

The Effect of Siblings on the Child's Personality

Because children are born of the same parents, develop in the same home, and have the tutelage of the same school teachers, people are inclined to state that their environment is the same. But such is not the case. The first child, for example, monopolises the attention of both parents, and may be the grandparents. His whims are the laws of the household. The people with whom he mingles are all adults. He finds that his is on the receiving end of almost all the parent-child reactions which ensue. He is the center of attention and occupies the spotlight on his domestic stage.

Then a younger brother or sister arrives, and for the first time in his life he becomes aware of real competition. His parents may hardly realise the shift in their interest to the newborn, but the older child instantly feels the change, and resents it. He dislikes the newcomer, and wishes for its removal. Since it cannot be removed, he must readjust his outlook upon life and try to effect a fairly satisfactory compromise. As the younger child grows older, the pleasure which the older youngster obtains from games in which the two engage begins to offset the dislike and antagonism which previously existed. But the elder child is inclined to be more domineering and blunt, relying upon his superior strength to procure the toys which he desires. However, his introvertive tendencies which developed prior to the second child's birth are somewhat modified by the extrovertive influences of the latter's presence, and his parents' insistence that he share his pleasures and property with the baby.

As for the second child's environment, we may begin by stating that he does not monopolise the family stage at any time, even though for the first few weeks he obtains the major portion of the parental attention. As soon as he is old enough to take note of his surroundings, he sees another youngster present much like himself but stronger. Thenceforth he finds himself in competition with the older child, and is compelled to rely on his wits to satisfy his wants, since he is physically weaker than the first-born. He starts out in life with a tendency to extroversion, therefore, and soon begins to utilise his mother as a defense against his older sibling. He quickly learns that if he cries, the mother on general principles will assume that the older child has taken something away from him, and especially if she is weary or ill she will be inclined to make the elder youngster surrender any desired possession to the baby. When they are out of her sight, however, the stronger child usually regains his toys.

Another difference is the fact that the first child obtains new playthings, new clothes, new books, while the younger sibling frequently has only secondhand toys, "made-over" clothes, and used schoolbooks. The second child, moreover, tends to be more bold and irresponsible than the older, for he always feels that he can rely on the greater strength of his elder brother or sister, and his tendency toward extroversion renders him more socially curious and explorative. In previous chapters we have mentioned in this connection how the intuition of women tends to develop because they are physically weaker than their masculine playmates, and how younger children seem to be relatively more prevalent than first-borns among salesmen.

Let us suppose, moreover, that a third child enters the family. The effect upon the oldest youngster is not very great, since he must share with simply an additional sibling. But note the dilemma in which the second child finds himself. He neither has the prerogatives of the firs-born with the consolation of probably being his grandparents' favourite, nor can he maintain his former special rights which belonged to being the baby. He finds himself confronted with the difficult situation of using his wits to deal with his stronger elder sibling, and using his greater muscular power in taking what he desires away from the new baby, which in its turn soon learns to utilise its lungs in gaining its mother's favour and partiality. The middle child, therefore, is in an environment which is most conducive to extroversion, while the youngest probably is next most extrovertive, whereas the first-born still lends toward introversion. The introvertive tendency of the eldest comes chiefly from the fact that he was an only child for a while. The manner in which introvertive personalities militate against successful social adjustments is brought out in the next section.

We may conclude our survey of the effect of siblings upon the child's personality, therefore, by saying that additional brothers and sisters tend to extrovert him. If only a year or two separate the ages of the first-born and the next youngster, this extrovertive influence has a greater effect upon the elder child's personality. If the latter is five or ten years old before the younger sibling arrives, he more nearly resembles the only child in his tendencies toward introversion.

How to Lesson the Child's Divorce Hazard

It is well to keep in mind that the majority of factors which occasion divorce do not develop only within the duration of the couple's marriage, but antedate it by almost a score of years, for they originate in the childhood experiences and training to which the husband and wife have been subjected. Such essential social virtues as a spirit of fair play, a willingness to compromise, an appreciation of the feelings and interests of others, and a realisation that money is simply minted energy, these and many others are taught the child who develops in an auspicious milieu, or are lacking to the youngster in a less favourable environment.

Despite certain sentimentalists who emotionally look upon youth as "that sweet period of irresponsibility and earthly paradise," and who aver that it is wrong to "shackle the life of a carefree child with the fetters of adult society." We know that the youngster develops wholesome character only by grappling with the problems of his own little word as they arise. Experience is the bedrock on which the young as well as old construct personalities which will withstand the temporary squalls of emotional discord. Ad for later social contacts, particularly of the strenuous sort involved in marriage, the child deserves all the intelligent training and preparation which parents and teachers can offer him.

A child in a totally carefree environment cannot be expected to blossom into a responsible and responsive husband or wife through the magic ritual of a marriage ceremony. But the youngster who has grown up with a sense of some responsibilities intermixed with his play, and with the extrovertive influences of other children to produce unselfishness in him, will be a good marriage risk. In the preceding section we have discussed the different types of personality which tend to develop in siblings from such similar surroundings as the same home. In the Table 9.2 we shall show the divorce hazards of husbands and wives who came from home in which they grew up as the only child, the oldest, the middle, or the youngest. By "middle" child we refer simply to a youngster who has at least one older and one younger sibling. These data are based on 2534 divorced men and their 2634 divorced wives, the family histories of whom were procured from college students who knew the participants in the divorces.

Table 9.2
Percentage of various types of children who as adults procure divorces.

Husbands			*Wives*			
			Only	*Oldest*	*Middle*	*Youngest*
		(%)				
Only	754	(28.6)	191	236	147	180
Oldest	655	(24.9)	153	158	176	168
Middle	638	(24.2)	132	155	207	144
Youngest	587	(22.3)	74	158	181	174
Totals	2,634		550	707	711	666
(%)			(20.9)	(26.8)	(27.0)	(25.3)

To fully understand the significance of children's order of position in the family and its relationship to their divorce hazard. We must obtain an index of the percentage of only children, oldest, youngest, and middle children among the adult population. Since the United States Census Bureau has informed the writer that no such tabulation has been made heretofore, he selected at random 100 families with children. Since the majority of the participants in divorces listed in the table 9.2 were from 20 to 40 years of age, the writer chose his 100 families so that offspring thereof would now be within the age range mentioned. In these 100 families were 16 only children, 84 oldest, 84 youngest, and 132 middle children, making a total of 316. On the basis of these figures, therfore, there are in the present adult population falling between 20 ad 40 years of age the following percentages: Only children, 5.0 per cent; oldest, 26.6; youngest, 26.6 per cent; and middle, 41.8 per cent. The Table 9.3 will show the difference between the percentages of various types of child in the adult population and the incidence of divorce in such groups.

Table 9.3
The divorce hazard of men and women occupying different postions in the sequence of children. Hazards are computed by dividing divorce percentage by the percentage in adult population

Types of Children	*% in adult population*	*%divorced husbands*	*% divorce wives*	*husbands' hazard*	*wives' hazard*
Only	5.0	28.6	20.9	5.72	4.18
Oldest	26.6	24.9	26.8	.94	1.01
Yongest	26.6	22.3	25.3	.84	.95
Middle	41.8	24.2	27.0	.58	.65

From the Table 9.3 it will be seen that an only child of the male sex has 5.72 times as great a likelihood of divorce as should be warranted by the percentage of only children in the adult population, and for only children of the female sex the ratio is 4.18. The middle child, with his greater extroversion which we have previously mentioned, is the best marriage risk for both sexes. Indeed, among men an only child is approximately ten times as likely to enter divorce as is a middle child.

Such ostensible causes for divorce as differences between husband and wife in race, religion, education, and social position, or the effects of alcohol and sexual maladjustment are probably spread uniformly throughout the various classifications of children, for there seems no *a priori* reason why only children should be especially prone to cross religious or racial lines, or be any more addicted to liquor than oldest, youngest, or middle children.

Since in these 5,268 cases the only child is such a great

divorce hazard in contrast to children who have grown up with at least one sibling, it behooves educators and parents to adopt every ameliorative measure which will reduce his danger of marital unhappiness. Among such instruments we can cite the presence of living playmates in the home, such as kittens or puppies, in case the parents are resistant to having an additional youngster.

Moreover, the early contact of the only child with human companion of approximately his own age will help reduce his hazard. The nursery school is especially valuable in this regard. Indeed, it might be wise to reduce the age of entrance to kindergarten to three years instead of the present five years. Such a change would seem to be advisable, since the increasing economic competition is reducing the size of families, and as the number of one-child families increases, it seems probable that the incidence of divorce will correspondingly be accelerated. There seems to be a marked negative correlation, therefore, between the size of the average American family and the divorce rate.

In subsequent sections of this chapter we shall describe additional methods of lessening the child's divorce hazard. It is sufficient to conclude here that the chief method of insuring children a later marital happiness lies in extroverting the youngsters by means of such available instruments as animal playmates, other children either of the neighborhood or nursery school, and, as we shall later discuss, by developing self-reliance in them. Since the integrity of the home is one of the principal bulwarks of the nation, and since the divorce rate in the United States in now about one to six, it is apparent that the divorce problem is of national is of national as well as of moral significance.

The "Reversible Why" in Child Training

Everybody who has dealt with young children is familiar with the incessant barrage of questions which they can fire upon the adults in their vicinity. Many of these queries are rater profound, or at least demand a keener insight into science and religion than the average person possesses. And because of their constant recurrence many parents become irritated at the child and send him forth to play.

As a matter of fact, it is quite likely that the more questions a child asks, the more intelligence he possesses. Since his queries are mental hooks with which the youngster goes fishing for information about the mysterious universe in which he finds himself, it is wise for parents and teachers to satisfy his curiosity as long as their patience will last. In so doing, however, they must not only phrase their replies in language which the youngster can understand, always remembering that his mental age is far below the adult level, but they should also recall that active learning is superior to passive. They should, therefore, endeavour to reverse the child's query so that he utilises all his present fund of knowledge in regard to his own question. Then if he cannot evolve a solution, they must add their comments.

The "reversible why" is an excellent habit for adults to acquire, as we have previously mentioned in our discussion of salesmanship, for it quickly places the mental effort upon the other party, thereby freeing its propounder for a moment's respite in which to collect his thoughts or survey his comrade. In dealing with children the teacher and parent can also profitably employ it, thereby keeping on the offensive and giving the youngester more cerebral exercise. The following excerpt will demonstrate the method more clearly, although in dealing with adults a little more finesse should be shown in reversing their queries.

> "Why do you put that stuff on your face?" Junior asked on the first morning of my visit, while I was going through the drudgery of my daily shave.
>
> "Why do you think I put this on my face?" I countered.
>
> He stopped for a moment, probably dumbfounded at this sudden offensive on my part.
>
> "I don't know," he replied, but I refused to let him off with such an easy answer.
>
> "What does it look like?" I continued, glad of the chance to keep on the offensive.
>
> "Like cream when Mother whips it," came his immediate response.
>
> "All right," I agreed, "but what else does it look like — something you use when you take your bath?"
>
> "Oh, I know. It's soap."
>
> "Righto," I answered. "Now why do you think I am putting soap on my face?"

"So you can wash it."
"But I'm not putting it all over my face. I rub it just on the hairs on my chin and jaws. Why do I do that?"
"So they'll get clean," he replied.
"All right," I said, "but how does your hair feel when Mother puts soap on it and gives you a shampoo? Is it soft or is it hard?"
"It's soft and wet," he answered.
"That's the way my beard is. The soap makes it soft and it's easier to cut the hairs when they are soft. They don't pull so much and hurt me while I am shaving."
"Then why doesn't the barber put soap on my hairs? He didn't do it when I got my hair cut."
Fortunately his mother called us to breakfast and I deemed this an opportune moment to drop the conversation.

A few years ago the writer tested this method with five children ranging images from four to seven. They were with him at various times and of course wanted to know this and that. The writer made notations of the first forty questions each child asked. In the first twenty of these he made a careful reply, which was entered upon his data sheet. On the second twenty questions of each child, the writer employed the reversible why, holding the youngster to his query until he had answered it himself in as complete a fashion as he could, after which, if he was not then successful, the correct information was given to him.

Ten days later the writer took each of the youngsters in turn and put to him the same forty questions which the child had previously asked. On the twenty questions which the writer had carefully answered as soon as the child had originally asked them, the five youngsters averaged twelve correct replies each, but on the twenty where the reversible why had been employed, they averaged eighteen correct responses apiece. In this experiment, therefore, the reversible why apparently led to a 50 per cent greater retention of the information which was presented to them. This occurred not because the writer had not fully replied to their first twenty inquiries on the initial day of the test, but because the answers to the second set of queries made a deeper impression upon them, due in part to the fact that they themselves had helped work them out.

From the psychological standpoint, therefore, the reversible why enables the adult to remain on the offensive and compels the child to cerebrate in response to his own question. Since he takes an active role in evolving the solution to his query, he is much more likely to retain the information thus arrived at. The reader will recall the statement from William James regarding the fact that children whet their wits on each other's. In the employment of the reversible why, moreover, the child has an opportunity to whet his wits upon problems turned back upon him by the skilful adult interrogator. The netresult of this procedure is beneficial to the youngster both in respect to the greater retention of material which he encounters, and also in the mental exercise engendered in the process.

How Children Educate Children.

We have previously mentioned the extrovertive influence which children have upon each other, and the value of such training as it relates to their later marriage risks. But there are other aspects to this problem which should be noted. The first-born, for example, tends to be slower in his development of speech than do his younger siblings, owing largely to the lack of oral stimuli with which he is surrounded. Adults may think that they converse freely with the only child, but they do not equal the talkativeness of an equal number of youngsters.

Playmates are stimulating in other respects, moreover, than simply the acquisition of oral language, for they bring to bear upon each other the combined knowledge of all members of the group. Probably no one parent takes the time to answer all his son's queries, or to explain every aspect of a new situation or object. But if each of a dozen parents gives his child one different idea regarding the operation of a toy or machine, when these twelve youngsters get together they soon gain eleven additional viewpoints, and go home to lunch with twelve ideas instead of the original one.

This result is especially true in the realm of sex where, despite the franker discussion of the subject by parents and teachers of the present generation, the youngsters still gain most of their knowledge from their playmates. Just one of the latter who possesses some first-hand information may enlighten the children of the entire neighborhood or school. The avoidance of sex topics by some parents of course whets their children's curiosity, rendering them more ready listeners to their playmates' ideas on the topic. In the quotation which follows the reader will see how Professor Katz's older son casually discussed the matter of human births with his mother, and then probably dismissed it from his mind. The reader may be interested to know that the child, named Theodor, had a chronological age of not quite five years and two months at the time of this conversation. His parents have obviously already enlightened him concerning the origin of human infants.

> Conversation: December 29, 1925. Evening, in bed.
> T. "Why did you stay in Berlin and not go back to that school? (A school in which Mother had been a teacher.)
> M. "The war came, so I couldn't go back again."
> T. "Why couldn't you go back?"
> M. "The railway, were being used by the soldiers, so I couldn't get a train."
> T. "Was there a lot to eat then?"
> M. "No, there wasn't much to eat."
> T. "But Papa had enough to eat, didn't he?"
> M. "Yes, Papa was a soldier and the soldiers had enough to eat."
> T. "Why did the soldiers have enough to eat?"
> M. "If the soldiers hadn't had enough to eat, they couldn't have fought."
> T. "And the other people didn't have enough to eat?"
> M. "No, they were all hungry, even the little children."
> T. "Mama, the little babies who hadn't been born yet had the best of it, didn't they? They were lying nice and warm inside their mamas."
> M. "Yes."
> T. "Mama, when the babies crawl out, have they anything on?"
> M. "No, they are naked."
> T. "Aren't they cold, when they're naked?"
> M. "No, because they're dressed immediately."
> T. "Why don't the children come out together?"
> M. "What do you mean?"
> T. "I mean, why didn't Baby and I come together?"
> M. "Babies do sometimes. Then we call them twins."
> T. "Then they would have to be smaller, or else they couldn't come out easily."

The above conversation also illustrates the fact that children cannot be looked upon as simply the uncritical recipients of information, but have the capacity to do some original or creative thinking. It is partly because of the latter function that they educate one another. As a consequence, it is well that they be given correct advice at the outset, else they may later develop resentment toward the parent or teacher who misinformed them, particularly when some other child in the neighborhood challenges their statements, and proves them in error.

The methods by which children educate children consist primarily, therefore, in their extroversion of one another, but they also serve as stimulants to each other's thinking by means of their frequent challenges of one another's statements, thereby whetting their wits after the fashion described by William James. They also bring to bear upon a given problem their combined knowledge and consequently play respectively the roles of teacher as well as pupil. Since the formulation of ideas for their presentation to others is likewise beneficial to the instructor, these youngsters not only gain information from each other, but they obtain the profit which results from organising facts. The older children, moreover, repeat the admonitions of parents and instructors to their younger siblings and serve as models after whom the younger children can pattern their behavior. Both of these functions relieve adults of a part of their teaching load, yet further increase the enlightenment of the children. In the next section we shall consider an additional important educational function of youngsters.

How Children Educate Adults

The classic instance in literature of the remarkable transformation in Silas Marner when he became the guardian of a child demonstrates one of the principal educative effects of children upon men and women. Childless adults tend to grow more and more introvertive with age. Indeed, all adults approach extreme introversion at senescence but the presence of children and grandchildren greatly retards the process. At the age of sixty people could probably be classified in four general groups as regards their degree of introversion; first, the bachelor or spinster; second, the childless married person; third, the married person with children; fourth, the married person with children and grandchildren.

Parents are usually compelled to become somewhat conversant with current educational methods, at least as long as their youngsters are of school age. They even follow the athletic successes of the teams representing their children's school or university. In fact, vicariously they gain many of the advantages of a college education through the letters and oral descriptions of their offspring, often possessing information concerning campus matters which is unknown to the professors at the university.

With current amusements of young people they also are in touch, and become attentive to styles and fashions in the apparel of youth. Their active participation in religious affairs is frequently a direct result of their desire to set an example to their youngsters, and they are usually active sponsors of the boy and girl scout organisations, and similar societies which will exert wholesome influences upon their progeny.

After a quarter of a century they again go through a part of this extrovertive process when their grandchildren are born. They do not follow the school curricula so closely, nor are they in such daily contact with the children, but they find many more outside interests than other elderly persons who lack the interrogations of youngsters.

But in extrovertive influence of children is not their only means of benefiting the adults in their environment. The frequent queries of the youngsters force their parents into cerebral activity, often of a sort which is severe. Moreover, the candor and naivete of children is often refreshing as well as informative. To answer the demands made upon them by their offspring, many adults find it necessary to engage in more reading and study. Parent teacher organisations and books on child psychology become popular with mothers. Several magazines in the United States are maintained chiefly by parents who wish advice concerning the rearing of boys and girls.

Parents also become aware of the need for better pictures and music with which to stimulate their children's imagination. Encyclopedias and reference volumes of different sorts also begin to make their appearance in the home, and are used by the adults as well as the children. Meanwhile the fathers and mothers find themselves going through a change of attitude regarding international politics, for those who have severeal sons are not so prone to telegraph their senators at Washington to vote for war.

The principal educative value of children upon adults, therefore, consists of the extroversion of the latter with its attendant advantages of keeping the adults in touch with current phases of business, science, and the arts. Additional benefits which accrue to parents are their increased participation in worthy school, civic, and religious activities as well as their greater patronage of music and literature. Such activities also are frequently of value to the community as a whole so that the state gains a more responsible type of citizenry thereby. The adults themselves profit by the wider range of interests which they develop and their greater capacity for social enjoyment.

Developing Self-reliance in the Child

Whether or not the child will be able to face the responsibilities and defeats of adulthood will depend very largely on the training which his parents give him. If they constantly act as buffers between him and the hard knocks of life he will find adult problems too fierce or rigorous for his temperament, and may lean upon his parents for comfort and assistance as long as they live. Every reader is doubtless familiar with many such individuals who may have remained bachelors and spinsters because of mother – and father-fixations, coupled with an inability to fend for themselves. Others may attempt marriage and economic independence only to make miserable failures of both, after which they return to the parental roof.

In our discussion of the development of confidence and aggressiveness in the child we pointed out the fact that the tasks assigned to him must not be too great for his capacity, nor must they be permitted to remain unfinished, else he develops a defeatism complex similar to that illustrated by Half-Way Hurley. Since confidence is really the habit of success, parents and teachers must be careful to motivate the youngster adequately, and adjust his duties to fit his present capacities.

Since life cannot satisfactorily be met by an individual who is always carefree, it becomes advisable to temper the youngster's play with a judicious admixture of tasks or "chores". These may begin as soon as he is old enough to walk. He should learn to put his playthings away after he is through with them, and thereafter should be taught the various responsibilities which he is supposed to assume in life.

In this connection it is well for him to gain an impression of the meaning of money, for when he realises that it stands not only for ice cream sodas and candy but also for human energy expended in its acquisition, he is able to disburse his funds wisely. Children who are dependent upon coaxing and cajolery and their parents' largess in order to have spending money are losing one of the best means of gaining self-reliance, namely, the earning of their own nickels, dimes and quarters. When a child earns his money his ego is inflated, for he feels more independent and competent. In order to illustrate an ingenious method by which a father not only changed his twelve-year-old boy's attitude concerning mathematics, but also made him much more self-reliant, we shall offer the following paragraphs.

> "He told the lad that he might act as purchasing agent for the family's groceries. Under the new arrangement the boy bought at cash and carry stores, whereas formerly the father had patronised a store nearer home from which goods had been delivered. The prices had been slightly higher at the latter store, and these prices were used as the basis on which the youth was permitted to operate.
>
> If, for instance, he purchased butter at fifty-two cents a pound at the cast and carry store, when the other grocer was charging fifty-four, the boy received two cents for his foresightedness and effort in carrying the goods home. Soon he became so interested in this financial game that the page of the evening paper to which he turned first was that on which the grocers' advertisements were displayed. Arithmetical figures no longer remained only stupid black marks to be juggled according to some stereotyped rule, but were changed into useful tools. Without being aware of what had brought about his new attitude, the boy presently found himself taking an interest in arithmetic, and soon he was the most proficient mathematician in his class.
>
> His parents had not scolded him. He had, therefore, been saved from developing a defense reaction. And by the father's tactful plan he had also been brought to the forefront of his class, and hence developed a liking for mathematics."

In the public schools it is not unusual to find projects undertaken in which the pupils build a miniature store, and go through the action of buying and selling. Such procedures are not only of educational value, but they are pleasant to the youngsters, who feel more grown up in consequence.

Another very good method for increasing the child's self-reliance is that of letting his assume the responsibility of some living thing, such as an animal, or potted plants, a garden, or the goldfish. He attains, therefore, the feeling that some weaker being is dependent upon him, and as a result no only is complimented but also is extroverted by his duties with reference to these living objects.

In the child's play, moreover, he finds an additional opportunity to develop his self-reliance, for he discovers that compromises are a necessity if he is to retain the friendship of his mates. It is not difficult to diagnose the environmental background of the youngster who is of the I'will–take-my-ball-and-go-home-if-I-can't-be-captain type. Until puberty, however, the child is rather uncooperative and individualistic. But as he enters the teens he begins to like group games and will acquire a spirit of cooperation and fair play if he is situated in the proper environment. It is illuminating in this connection to note the words of Dr. H. D. Williams' son who, while visiting a summer camp of juvenile delinquents, entered a ball game being played between two teams of young offenders. Later he remarked to his father, "Those kids don't know how to play. They stand there and argue and fight, and hold up the game so there's no fun in it."

There is no more tragic sight among children than a youngster who wants to be included in the games of others but who has been deprived of human playmates for several years so that he is ignorant of the rules of their games, or is so awkward and inept that the other boys ignore him. When sides are being chosen for a ball game, he stands up hopefully, thinking that he may be selected next by one of the respective captains only to find that the last member of each team has been chosen without his name called. "Aw, we don't want him on our side," his associates may remark with the brutal frankness of youth, "for he can't hit the ball." If the child is very intelligent and sensitive a few such public humiliations may send him to the sidelines for the remainder of his youth, and perhaps his entire life. Thereafter he may retain his interest in social groups, but always stay on the outskirts of the crowd. "Wallflowerism" is a category which covers his social inferiority complex.

On the other hand, this disappointed child may become a misanthrope, or engage in atypical behavior in order to attain some social recognition and envy. He frequently becomes the scholar so that he can compensate intellectually for his physical inability. If, however, a child has physical strength and dexterity but lacks brilliance or polite manners, he may compensate by becoming the bully of the crowd, or the "bad" child in the school. He finds that he can gain therby a certain awed admiration and notoriety even if he cannot attain fame by the more onerous plan of study and scholastic pre-eminence.

Neither of the two types of reaction just mentioned is expressive of a well integrated personality. Because both youngsters feel their lack of self-reliance, they have adopted a compensatory form of reaction, and to explain their apparent inefficiency in the quality wherein they are inept, adopt a "sour grapes" attitude. Although it is true that some of the great works of art and or literature, of music and of science have come down to us as the fruits of compensation, as probably demonstrated by Beethoven, Byron, and Steinmetz, they have been produced at the cost of social maladjustment. Although society occasionally may profit thereby, from the standpoint of psychology such compensations as those of the two boys mentioned above are unwholesome.

As for the matter of emotional development and its relationship to the self-reliance of the child, we may state that many of the fears and doubts and emotional stresses which trouble the adult have their roots in childhood experiences. We shall treat this subject more fully in Chapter 10. Although Watson believes there are only the three primitive emotions – fear, rage, and love – these three may, like the four primary taste qualities, become so tied up with thousands of situations and stimuli as to affect a large portion of the individual's reactions. The difference between the coward and the brave man, for example, is often simply the fact that the coward is afraid, while the courageous man is afraid of being afraid.

In concluding our discussion of the development of self-reliance in the child, we should state that the aim of parents and teachers should be to add to the sum of the child's whole-some habits. The child with 1,000 habits is obviously less self-reliant than the youngster with 10,000 habits, other things being equal. Accordingly, it is imperative for adults to see that the child knows how to play the games of his age and sex, how to earn and spend money, how to care for his wants and make the mechanical and social adjustments expected of him because of the type of environment to which he will be exposed. Confidence and assurance follow the youngster who is sufficiently equipped with methods of reaction to the stimuli of his milieu so that he can make satisfactory adjustments thereto. No one is continuously successful, so the child must be schooled to meet the stimulus of defeat and know how to react successfully to it. This reaction does not involve running home to mother, or the development of a sour grapes attitude, but a close scrutiny of his own performance so that he can detect the flaws therein and avoid their repetition.

Sculpturing in Human Clay

When a Michelangelo stands before a block of marble he may sculpture a "Moses" or a group of "slaves", but in either case his product is insignificant compared to the human personality which can be produced by intelligent parents and teachers out of eight pounds of animate human clay. If the child possesses normal intellectual endowment and sensory acuity, he can be moulded into an outstanding surgeon, lawyer, artist, musician, poet, philosopher, orator, or writer. His parents, by the proper control of the stimuli playing upon him, can direct him into any one of these professions. The difficult task which they confront, however, is twofold, consisting of an understanding of what are the kinds of stimuli to employ to sculpture the child's personality, and how to procure or utilise those stimuli after they are known.

The first of these two problems is usually the more frequent cause for failure, since the intelligent parent and teacher do not need million dollar equipment and tools for the training of their Lincolns, as the following quotation from Dorothy Dix's column demonstrates.

(By Courtesy of the Philadelphia Public Leader.)

"I know now that when I was a child we were very poor. I had so few clothes that my mother used to wash at night the little shirt that I wore to school the next day, but I was always clean and neat. I had to begin earning money almost as soon as I could walk, and I delivered papers when I was so little I could hardly reach a bellpull. We had such plain food that it was a gala day to be remembered for weeks when we had pie for dinner.

But I never knew that I was poor because I never remember to have heard the subject mentioned in our family. My mother never whined and complained about what she couldn't have or because she wasn't as well off as other women or because she couldn't give us children the advantages that rich parents could give their children. She was always cheerful and made our home the happiest place in the world, and if we didn't have anything but stew and bread for supper we ate it to the accompaniment of so much laughter and good cheer that it made it a feast.

My mother never let us be sorry for ourselves. She never inoculated us with the virus of self-pity, as so many poor mothers do their children. She never let us feel that it was hard luck that we had to work when other children played. She managed somehow to make us feel that we were superior to the poor little rich children who had to ask their parents for pennies, because we were clever enough to earn money ourselves. She made us feel that we were men and women while they were still children. I can remember being actually sorry for the little boys who didn't have newspaper routes and had nothing to do but to play marbles, while I was a responsible individual with what I considered an important job.

My mother never deplored the fact that she couldn't give us college educations and that our father didn't have a bank that he could take us into as soon as we were grown. She never even intimated that poverty was a handicap to a boy.

On the contrary, she talked to us continually about the poor boys who had become millionaires, about the boys who had no schooling, but who had educated themselves by reading and study; about the boys who had gone from behind plows and the towpaths of canals, from the humblest places, to the President's chair. The names of great doctors, lawyers, merchants, men of affairs who had been poor boys were always on her lips, and it was just bred into us that we could be like them if we were man enough to do it.

I often think of my mother and other poor mothers that I have known since – mothers who make failures of their children in their very cradles by bringing them up in an atmosphere of gloom that chokes out every hopes and aspiration and makes them feel that they are the victims of a malign destiny against which it is no use to struggle.

> Mothers who break down their children's morale and weaken them by weeping over them because they have to work. Haven't you seen such mothers, time and again, wringing their hands and shedding tears because their poor little Tommies had to punch the time-clock in a factory every morning instead of lying abed or because their darling Mamies had to stand behind a counter or pound a typewriter instead of going to pink teas?
>
> And, of course, that made Tommy and Mamie feel that they were poor, persecuted martyrs when they should have been rejoicing that they had brains enough to hold down a job and were independent, self-supporting men and women who could look the world in the eye and tell it where to go."
>
> (Copyright, 1932, by Philadelphia Public Ledger.)

In summarising this matter of sculpturing in human clay, it is evident that a thorough understanding of human motivation and control must be possessed by the sculptor if he wishes to mould his clay into the desired form. In addition, he must be cognisant of the great responsibility which devolves upon him after he has attained this knowledge. The majority of parents and teachers do not wish to be held accountable for pre-determining the child's future vocation, but are content if they can only equip him adequately for whatever demands life may make of him. That goal in itself is sufficiently difficult to test the ingenuity of adult intelligence, and should occupy the attention of those who have the opportunity to sculpture in human clay.

Since such tremendous potentialities reside in the child it is no wonder, therefore, that many parents and teachers are awed by the responsibilities, which are theirs. And if an artist or sculptor in marble feels that he must spend many years mixing paints and learning the technique of wielding a chisel, how much more imperative must be the need for men and women who with youngsters to acquire adeptness in manipulating verbal stimuli and the physical elements of the milieu.

References

Anastasi, A., & Foley, J.P., Jr., *Differential Psychology* (Macmillan, 1949).

Arlitt, A. H., *Psychology of Infancy and Early Childhood* (McGraw-Hill, 1946).

Beach, F. A., *Hormones and Behaviour* (Hoeber, 1948).

Bentley, J. E., *General Psychology* (Lippincoot, 1947).

Bosselmam B. C., *Neurosis and Psychosis* (Thomas, 1950).
Breckenridge, M. E., & Vincent, E. L., *Child Development* (Saunders, 1950).
Cameron, N., & Magaret, A., *Behaviour Pathology* (Houghton Mifflin, 1951).
Cole, Luella, *Psychology of Adolescence* (Rinehart, 1948).
Crafts, L. W., *et al.*, *Recent Experiments in Psychology* (McGraw-Hill, 1950).
Crane, G. W., "The 'Reversible Why'" (*Child Welfare*, 26, 1931).
Crane, G. W., "Tact and Child Education" (*Forecast*, 35, 1928).
Crawford, J. E., *Better Ways of Growing Up* (Muhlenberg, 1948).
Educational Policies Commission, *Moral and Spiritual Values in the Public Schools* (N. Educ. Ass., 1951).
Erickson, *C. E., A Practical Handbook for School Counsellors* (Ronald, 1949).
Gesell, A., *et al. Child Development* (Harper, 1949).
Guthrie, E. R., & Powers, F. F., *Educational Psychology* (Ronald, 1950).
Havighurst, R. J., & Taba, H., *Adolescent Character and Personality* (Wiley 1949).
Hollingworth, H. L., *Mental Growth and Decline* (Appleton, 1927).
Hopkins, P., *Gone Up in Smoke* (Highland Press, 1948).
Hurlock, E. B., *Child Development* (McGraw-Hill, 1943).
Johnson, D. M., *Essentials of Psychology* (McGraw-Hill, 1943).
Kanner, L., *Child Psychiatry* (Thomas, 1949).
Katz, D., *The Vibratory Sense and Other Lectures* (U. of Maine Studies, No. 14, 1930).
Kunst, M. S., *A Study of Thumb- and finger-Sucking in Infants* (Psychol. Monog., No. 290, 1948).
Lehner, G. F. J., *Explorations in Personal Adjustment* (Prentice-Hall, 1950).
Louttit, C. M., *Clinical Psychology of Chilaren's Behaviour Problems* (Harper, 1947).
Moore, T. V., *Driving Forces of Human Nqture* (Greene, 1948).
Murphy, G., *Introduction to Psychology* (Harper, 1951).
O' Kelly, L. I., *Introduction to Psychology* (Prentice-Hall, 1949).
Olson, W.C., *Child Development* (Heath, 1949).
Schneiders, A. A., *Introductory Psychology* (Detroit, 1948).
Skenner, C. E., *Elementary Educational Psychology* (Prentice-Hall, 1950).
Skodak, M., & Skeels, H. M., "A Final follow-Up Study of One Hundred Adopted Children" (*J. Genet. Psychol.*, 75, 1949).
Wolff, W., *Threshold of the Abnormal* (Dryden, 1950).

10

PSYCHOLOGY APPLIED IN EDUCATION

The relationship between psychology and education has been a very close and cordial one. Each has profited by the data and principles of the other. The first practical applications of psychology of a systematic type were made in the field of education, where today many of the individual and group methods of the laboratory are employed under the heading, "experimental pedagogy". Indeed, both the methods of teaching and the content of the curriculum have been altered in accordance with progress made in psychology.

At an early period education was directed toward "training the mind" in which the mind was conceived of as a distinct entity which was more or less independent of the environment but could grow stronger or more powerful by contact with external stimuli. The difficulty with this conception was the confusion between intellectual development and muscular development. In the latter the same dumb-bell is just as effective in increasing the size and strength of the right biceps as are 100 equally heavy dumb-bells, so the subject needs but one to become a second Samson. In mental development, however, the very reverse of this rule holds true, for twenty years spent upon the study of Latin declensions will never stimulate mental growth like one year devoted to each of twenty different subjects.

Even yet this fallacy is not wholly understood. We send our children to high school and teach them geometry, for which the great majority will never have a single use later in life, yet fail to train them in applied psychology which is fundamental to their social and economic success. The former belief that geometry exercised the reasoning "faculty" more than salesmanship or accounting is now known to be false. A young fellow can obtain as much mental exercise trying to develop a successful campaign by which to win a girl who shows no interest in him, as he can in working any of the theorems presented to him in high school, and the relevancy of the former to his life's problems is obviously much greater. Thorndike has the following to say regarding the relative disciplinary values of various school subjects:

> By any reasonable interpretation of the results, the intellectual values of studies should be determined largely by the special information, habits, interests, attitudes, and ideals which they demonstrably produce. The expectation of any large differences in general improvement of the mind from one study rather than another seems doomed to disappointment. The chief reason why good thinkers seem superficially to have been made such by having taken certain school studies, is that good thinkers have taken such studies, becoming better by the inherent tendency of the good to gain more than the poor from any study. When the good thinkers studied Greek and Latin, these studies seemed to make good thinkers. Now that the good thinkers study Physics and Trigonometry, these seem to make good thinkers. If the abler pupils should all study Physical Education and Dramatic Art, these subjects would seem to make good thinkers. These were, indeed, a large fraction of the programme of studies for the best thinkers the world has produced, the Athenian Greeks.

Since reasoning is resorted to in the solution of any problem it makes little difference where the problem is encountered, for the effect upon the subject's thought processes, if the problems are the same in difficulty. Will be equally beneficial. As a result, the choice of the curricula for schools and colleges can be made more profitably on the basis of the practical value of various subjects as related to the child's needs. This modern viewpoint is especially significant when one realises that approximately two-thirds of all children never go beyond the eighth grade of grammar school, and 90 per cent of all the children who later become the voters of the nation, never matriculate at a college or university. The opportunity of the state to prepare its citizens for a happy and well adjusted adulthood is practically completed in the senior year of high school. Such courses as geometry, therefore, can well be considered in the light of what they contribute of merit to the 90 young people out of every 100 who immediately go into business and the home. It would seem that time devoted to music and to art would have greater value to them.

In addition to producing changes in the curriculum, however, psychology has been of considerable value to pedagogy in bringing out the definite fact of intellectual differences between pupils. Heretofore, the teacher has attempted to deal with varying degrees of mental age within her class, even though the children were all of the same chronological age. Her task has been somewhat like that of a teamster with a dozen spans of horses among which there were Arabian thoroughbreds coupled with large draft horses. As the thoroughbreds would leap at the command to go and chafe at the sluggishness of the slower animals, so the teacher's bright pupils quickly grasp the new problems, and are irked at the repetitions thereof which she must perform with the slower children.

In consequence, the more alert youngsters must be given additional material which their mates do not receive, or they may divert their idle energy into destructive channels. Some of the most brilliant of her pupils may be promoted ahead of their classmates until they get into a group more nearly matching their intellectual leave, but the majority of them do not "skip" grades. By means of the intelligence test to be described in succeeding sections it is possible to sort the youngsters who are of a given chronological age into groups with comparable intellectual endowment. For example, in one large city school where the fourth grades were divided in three sections, called "A" , "B", and "C", on the basis of their mental age, it, was found that the "A" class covered 225 pages in reading during the term against 150 pages covered by the "B" group, and 95 pages by the least alert section.

Numerous advantages result from such a preliminary selective process. In the first place, the most alert youngsters can be given new material as fast as they can assimilate it, and they will all advance at about the same rate. Competition therefore becomes keener, so the children do not "coast" throughout grammar and high school on the basis of their superior intellectual heritage, and then "flunk" out of college during their freshman year because of faulty habits of study. In the colleges, of course, the student is confronted with a very intelligent group, so he does not surpass his mates as he may have done in high school and especially in grammar school. He is compelled, therefore, to study diligently, for his fellow students are just as alert as he. If he lacks adequate habits of study, he is likely to be left behind.

Even in the least alert section of school children, moreover, there is a marked advantage because of the uniformity of ability demonstrated by the children. They no longer need feel an inferiority complex about competing with their classmates, since they all are of about equal ability. Rivalry is more fruitful of productivity since they are now more willing to compete inasmuch as they have a chance to win. The other advantages, of such a mental age classification of school children, particularly in regard to simplifying the teacher's problems, we shall not be able to consider here because of space limitations.

Intelligence and Intelligence Tests

We have previously remarked upon the intimate relationship between heredity and environment as they pertain to intelligence. Since it is impossible in the light of present scientific advancement to separate the two, as might conceivably be done by calling the number of synapses the inherited intelligence, and the number of functional synaptic linkages the acquired intelligence, the reader will understand why there has been so much difficulty in defining intelligence. Probably the most widely accepted definition is that one given by the German psychologist Stern, who says that intelligence is the ability to meet and solve novel situations.

Although people had long recognised intellectual differences between individuals there was no systematic and objective test for separating children or adults into groups with definite mental ages until the French psychologist Alfred Binet was commissioned in 1904 to survey the schools of Paris for the purpose of detecting feeble-minded pupils. With the cooperation of Theodore Simon, Binet set to work developing a scale of tests for the mental alertness of youngsters of various chronological ages. In 1905 the Binet-Simon test was first published.

Almost immediately the Binet scale established itself as the most reliable method of measuring general intellectual ability then in existence. But there were many defects in the original scale, some of which Binet himself attempted to remedy, while others were modified in America by such experimenters as Kuhlmann, Goddard Terman and Yerkes. Of these the latter two have made the most significant alterations, and Terman's *Stanford Revision of the Binet-Simon. Intelligence Scale* is now the standard intelligence test in this country for school children.

The actual standardisation of the test was as follows. First a representative group of children was obtained. Let us assume there are 100 three-years-olds, 100 four-years-olds, etc. The experimenter then administers various items of the scale to each youngster. Suppose he inquires. "Are you a little boy or a little girl?" He finds that may bc 20 per cent of two-year-olds can answer correctly; that 77 per cent of two-years-olds are correct; and that 98 per cent of four-year-olds give the proper answer. As a result, he places the ability to give one's sex as an item which should be characteristic of the normal three-year-old, using the attainment of 75 per cent of the children at any given age as the standard. If, however, 95 per cent of three-year-olds could give their right sex, this question would not be a desirable one for any age group. Not only must 75 per cent be able to answer the query correctly, but not much over 75 per cent must be able to do so.

Following such a plan Terman re-standardised Binet's scale upon American children. Some of the items for different ages will be found below.

Three years

Points to nose, eyes, and mouth.
Enumerates objects in a picture.
Gives family name.
Repeats a sentence of six syllables.

Four years

Compares lines regarding length.
Counts four pennies.
Copies a square.
Repeats four digits.

Six Years

Distinguishes between right and left.
Counts thirteen pennies.
Names missing parts of mutilated pictures.
Distinguishes between morning and afternoon.

When the scale is actually administered to a child, the psychologist first endeavours to establish friendly relations and gain the cooperation of the youngster, after which the test items are regarded as a game. The highest age at which the child passes all tests is termed his basal age. For example, a four-year-old youngster might be able to answer all the items under the THREE YEARS test above, but not perform but three items under FOUR YEARS. His basal age would therefore be three years, or thirty-six months, For each of the items under FOUR YEARS he gets a credit of three months, if it is correctly answered. The child receives a total of nine months from the FOUR YEARS, for which he obtains an additional three months. His total mental age is 36 plus 9 plus 3 months, or 48 months. Since his chronological age was stated as being four years, or 48 months, the child is normal and has an intelligence quotient of 100. We have previously discussed the fact that Terman, following the idea of Stern, has introduced the I. Q. or Intelligence Quotient as a means of expressing the relationship between a child's mental and chronological ages. The I. Q. equals the mental age divided by the chronological age.

The Intelligence Quotient is fairly constant, varying scarcely at all when the child remains in the same type of environment throughout his development to maturity. Thus, the youngster who at the age of four is given a Binet test which shows him to have an I. Q. of 120, will also be found to have approximately 120 for an I. Q. when he is tested at ten or fifteen years of age. If, however, he has visual or hearing defects at the age of four, or if he is undernourished or convalescing from a protracted illness, his decreased energy and lessened sensory acuity may cause him to obtain lower I. Q. than he will later demonstrate when these errors are corrected.

The I. Q. has also been found to change somewhat when children are adopted into homes where the educational influences are more pronounced than in the child's orphanage or tenement environment. Freeman has shown that the greater the change in the conditions of the home, the more likely will be the alternation in I. Q. In a few cases, after several years' exposure to the superior milieu children gained as many as fifteen to twenty points. In this connection Terman states that children of the same native ability but located in superior and inferior homes may show a difference of about ten points in favour of the youngsters from the better type of environment.

In addition to the Binet test, the Army Alpha examination is another famous mental scale noted for its widespread use in measuring the intellectual differences of adults. During World War I this examination was devised by a group of psychologists appointed by the American Psychological Association and administered to 1,750,000 men. Since then it has been used extensively in college and the business world, although a number of somewhat similar examinations superseded it during World War II.

The Army Alpha is a battery of eight sub-tests, of which the first is intended to measure the subject's ability to follow oral instructions and contains twelve items. The second sub-test consists of 20 problems in arithmetic running from very simple addition to rather complex problems. The third sub-test of 16 problems endeavours to measure common sense, and is of the multiple-choice type with three answers given to each question. The fourth is a synonym-antonym test in which the student determines whether two words mean the same or the opposite. There are 40 such pairs in the list. The fifth sub-test consists of disarranged sentences which must be mentally re-arranged into sensible statements, and then answered with the words "true" or "false". It contains 24 items.

The sixth sub-test consists of 20 sequences of numbers which must be completed, as 2 2 4 4 6 6 — —. The seventh sub-test involves a somewhat similar recognition of logical relationships among words, as Hand : Arm : : Foot : - EAR TRUNK LEG HEAD. The student underlines one of the four capitalised words which has the same relationship to "foot" as "arm" has to "hand". There are 40 items in this sub-test, and 40 in the eighth, which is a range of information test. In the latter the student completes a sentence by underlining one of four words, as BRIDGE is played with RACKETS PINS CARDS MARBLES.

The total score possible is 212, which is practically impossible of attainment, while that made by the average person is probably around 70. The median score for college students falls at 150, and practical experience has shown that those who make below 110 are not very likely to succeed in college. In this connection it is well to remember that the possession of a high I. Q. or a remarkable score on Army Alpha is not an invariable prognosis of business or scholastic success, for studious habits and the adequate motivation for hard work are also important correlates. A person with a low I. Q. cannot graduate from college, but one having a high I. Q. may not do so, either.

The Army Beta was developed at the same time as Army Alpha but for us with those recruits who were either illiterate or non-English readers. It is a non-langauge examination and is akin to the usual performance tests except that it involves the use of pencil and paper, and was employed chiefly with adults. Performance tests were given considerable impetus by Pintner and Paterson, who had to perfect some scale for testing the alertness of deaf children. They employed fifteen tests derived from various sources, among which the following three are representative.

(1) The Seguin-Goddard form board which has also been extensively used by Sylvester with children of various ages. In this test the task confronting the child consists of laying a wooden block in the form of a cross, a square, a circle, a triangle, etc into its appropriate indented place in the form board, in a minimal time and with no errors. The time limit for placing the ten blocks in their proper positions in five minutes. A common error of the feeble-minded youngster is his attempt to place a

triangular block into the indenture for the star, or the rectangular block into the space for the square. Even normal youngsters of limited years are liable to the same confusions.

(2) Healy's pictorial-completion test, in which the child is to complete a picture by inserting the proper cut-out portions. This test is somewhat similar to many games sold on the market except that here the child has a great many choices from which to select the appropriate cut-out pieces, and is scored on the basis of the relevancy of each insert.

(3) The Knox cube test - There are five of these small cubes of which four are placed in a row before the child while the fifth is held by the experimenter. The latter then taps the other cubes with the one which he holds, varying the order to form a more difficult sequence on succeeding trials, as 1-2-3-4, 1-2-3-4-3, 1-3-2-4-3. At the conclusion of each series the experimenter hands the cube to the child who is told to tap likewise. A definite, unchanged series of numbers is used with all subjects tested. Pintner and Paterson offer tables based on the extensive examinations made by themselves and other researchers. In them one finds that both the time consumed and the errors made in the test decrease with the increasing age of the subject examined.

In summarising our discussion of intelligence and intelligence tests, we may state that Stern's conception of intelligence as the ability to meet and solve novel situations furnished the incentive for an attempt to create an objective scale for measuring this capacity. Such scales involve a number of sub-tests on which measures are taken, the sum of which constitutes the person's score. Some of the sub-tests may be weighted, as numbers 4, 7 and 8 on Army Alpha where there are 40 items each, instead of 12, 16, 20 or 24 as in the other sub-tests of that scale. As for the types of mental tests developed, there is the Biner-Simon for children the Army Alpha for literate adults, the Army Beta for illiterate adults and children, and the performance scales usually for children. Among these tests the Binet-Simon is strictly an individual examination wherein the administrator takes but one child at a time. The same procedure is true of most of the performance scales, but Army Alpha is a group test, being given to as many as a hundred or more simultaneously. Other intelligence tests are usually based on these general principles, and employ a number of sub-tests, the sum of whose scores becomes the subject's final index. In order of interpret the latter, of course, norms or the known performances of large goups of persons must be available. A score of 106 is only half the possible score on Army Alpha, but it is decidedly above the median for the American population, for only about 20 per cent can attain it.

The Uses of Intelligence Tests

During the years immediately following the World War psychological tests were employed more or less indiscriminately in the hope that a paanacea of industrial and educational problems had been obtained. But mental and vocational testing requires a rigid technique and a scientific training for the adequate interpretation of the records procured. Many persons were lacking in at least one of these respects, so their results were often disappointing. Moreover, there are usually so many additional factors involved in both scholarship and industrial ability that the intelligence test score must be supplemented by other data. When rightly used and modified by additional measures, intelligence tests are of marked value in the following fields:

(1) The classification of pupils in the schools - In addition to the uses in sorting pupils of the same school grade into different groups, these tests may show those who warrant immediate promotion or demotion, and are of assistance in rating the ability of children who transfer to a new school. The personnel director of the university or the teacher may watch the performance in classroom work and note whenever it falls below the standard which would be maintained according to the student's mental abilities. He may then interview the student at once in order to correct the factors which are interfering with the latter's optimum output. The intelligence score of a person is, accordingly, the best single measure of his ability, and forms a quick means of gaining an idea of his possible future development.

(2) Selection of college entrants — Particularly in the privately endowed colleges and universities intelligence tests have been

employed as a means of selecting the most alert applicants. When such educational institutions have two or three times the number of applicants for which they have available space and equipment, it becomes advisable to choose those high school graduates who hold the most promise of profiting richly by the college training. Other things being equal, the more intelligent men and women are of this type. Because of the lack of uniformity in standards of grading students from one school to another, a high school average of 93 from one institution may not mean the same as one of 93 from another. The intelligence test is usually a method by which inside of an hour the university director of admissions can gauge the intellectual capacity of all the applicants. Instead of using the numerical of letter grades which high school graduates cite, moreover, he is more interested in their relative standing within their graduating class, for the latter measure is now considered a more nearly accurate basis for comparison.

(3) Personnel administration - The vocational counsellor usually wishes to know first of all the intellectual capacity of his student. Although the public school system is a rough intelligence scale in itself, since most subnormals never are graduated from grammar school, and most normal children never matriculate at college, still a special mental test is even more nearly accurate. In employment, moreover, the intelligence score is also revealing, both as to the lower and upper critical limits. We have previously discussed this topic when we mentioned how Dr. Snow used to encounter Army Alpha scores like 45, 67, 83 , 56 and 175, among the taxicab drivers, and soon found that the 175 men were college students working their way through school.

The principal uses of intelligence tests, therefore, have to do with the sorting and classification of school children, the selection of college entrants, the guidance of young people into phases of industry in which they are intellectually capable, and the selection of employees who will be most satisfactory. In the following section we shall consider the intellectual strata in modern society.

Intellectual Levels of the Population

From the data procured by Army Alpha and Binet examinations Terman has presented the following apportionment of intelligence Quotients:

I. Q.	*Classification*
140 - up	"near" genius or genius
120 - 140	Very superior intelligence
110 - 120	Superior
90 - 110	Normal or average
80 - 90	Dull, rarely classifiable as feebleminded
70 - 80	Border-line deficiency, sometimes classifiable as dullness, often as feeble-mindedness
0 - 70	Definitely feeble-minded

Among the definitely feeble-minded, morons are usually considered to have Intelligence Quotients from 50 to 70, with imbeciles falling between 20 and 50, and idiots lying between 0 and 20. The adult idiot's mental age is under three, with the adult imebecile having the maturity of normal children of three to seven years, and the grown moron having a rating of from seven to twelve years. Terman presents the percentage of the population possessing various I. Q.'s in the following table:

Table 10.1

Of 1,000 Unselected School Children

The lowest	1 %	go to 70	or below; the highest 1	% reach 130	or above
The lowest	2 %	go to 73	or below; the highest 2	% reach 128	or above
The lowest	3 %	go to 76	or below; the highest 3	% reach 125	or above
The lowest	5 %	go to 78	or below; the highest 5	% reach 122	or above
The lowest	10 %	go to 85	or below; the highest 10	% reach 116	or above
The lowest	15 %	go to 88	or below; the highest 15	% reach 113	or above
The lowest	20 %	go to 91	or below; the highest 20	% reach 110	or above
The lowest	25 %	go to 92	or below; the highest 25	% reach 108	or above
The lowest	$33\frac{1}{3}$ %	go to 95	or below; the highest $33\frac{1}{3}$	% reach 106	or above

Since less than 8 per cent of students enter college and these are usually of the very superior type, it will be apparent that an I. Q. of about 115 is probably the lower level of college intelligence. Terman states that an I. Q. of 75 might even be considered the upper limit for the category of feeble-mindedness, in which case there would be almost 2,500,000 such persons in the United States. This figure is in fairly close agreement with Dr. Goddard's report of 2 per cent of feeble-minded among 2,000 public school children in New York City, and slightly in excess of the 1.5 per cent of feeble-minded found among the 12,000 pupils in the Toronto public schools in the survey under the direction of the Canadian National committee of Mental Hygience in 1919. Because in the latter survey a number of retarded children were absent from school during the time of the investigation, Professor W. G. Smith of the University of Toronto believes the total number of feeble-minded would also be about 2 per cent.

To illustrate an extreme case of intellectual brilliance in a child the reader's attention is called to the following comparison as given by Hollingworth *ct al*:

Table 10.2
Edward Rochie Hardy, Jr. Born: June 17, 1908.

November 4, 1916	*Edward*	*Norm**
Height	54.3 inches	49.5 inches
Weight	89.3 lbs.	54.2 lbs.
Intellectual status	I. Q. 187 (Stanford-Binet)	I. Q. 100 (Stanford-Binet)
School status	6th grade	3rd grade*
September 29, 1921		
Height	64.2 inches	58.2 inches
Weight	166 lbs. (light clothing)	89.5 lbs.
Intellectual status	194 points (Alpha, Form 5)	47 points (Alpha)
School status	4th semester college 8th grade*	

* Norms for height, weight, and school status are taken from Bird T. Baldwin, as established on children from Horace Mann School, Francis Parker School, and the high Schools of the University of Chicago, where the children are above average (for population at large) in intelligence.

In 1920 Edward took the Thorndike Mental Tests for freshmen for entrance to Columbia College and was second highest out of the 483 entering the college. Edward was then 12 years and 0 months of age, while the median age of the others was about 18 years. On the day cited in the table 10.2 Edward not only made 194 on Form 5 of Army Alpha, but a little later in the afternoon he took Form 6 and scored 201 thereon.

An I. Q. of 187 is obviously phenomenal. In our discussion of physical age, however, we mentioned that children mature at different rates, and as a consequence I. Q.'s would be more nearly accurate if we had norms for physical development so that we could insert physical age for chronological age in the formula by which I. Q.'s are obtained. From Edward's height and weight it would seem very likely that he is precocious in his physical maturity as well as in his mental alertness. His I. Q. would as a result be considerably less that 187 when he is matched with children of equal bone and muscular development. Even so, however, a score of 194 on Army Alpha puts him in the upper 1 per cent of Terman's classification, granting him a minimum I. Q. of 130.

In concluding our survey of the intellectual levels of the population, therefore, we may state that the average mental age of the adult is considered to be 16 years, although that of the principal sample of the white draft, when transmuted from Alpha and Beta examinations into terms of mental age, was placed at 13.08 years, a figure which is deemed a bit low. Hollingworth has placed the average mental age at 14 years, and includes 50 per cent of the American population in that category, with the other 50 per cent equally distributed above and below that point. The number of feeble-minded persons in the population is usually estimated at from 1 to 3 per cent. In the light of these intellectual differences in children, consequently, it is not difficult to imagine the struggles of the school teacher who has hitherto obtained her pupils chiefly on the basis of their chronological age alone.

The Relationship Between Health and Intelligence

The proverbial curiosity of youth is largely a function of an abundance of physical energy and vitality. As age advances, this surplus diminishes so that the average person curbs his desire for intellectual exploration in order to horde his strength. The parent has frequently noted the striking curtailment in his child's curiosity when the latter was suffering from sickness or was undergoing convalescence. Nature inhibits cortical activity when the vegetative functions of the body demand all the youngster's strength and energy. A partial measure of the child's return to health is accordingly his greater interest in his milieu.

Since a violent attack of disease will so markedly lower the curiosity of a youngster as to render him relatively oblivious to the stimuli in his environment, it is not difficult to understand the dulling effect of undernourishment and infection of a slower sort. The Army Alpha records from the war show a noticeable difference in the intelligence scores of white recruits infected by hookworm and a group of the same race not so infected.

In this connection the psychological examiners urge, "It is important, however, to guard against the assumption that data of this kind prove the existence of a causal relationship between hookworm disease and mental inferiority. Low native ability may induce such conditions of living as to induce hookworm infection, or poor environmental conditions may be responsible for both the disease and the low test record."

In this particular instance it may be granted that hookworm disease is not the sole cause of low native ability, but it is probably a safe conclusion *a priori* that hookworm disease and other long continued infections are causes of a mental dullness which may be as serious in its effect upon the behaviour adjustments of the individual as feeble-mindedness itself. Moreover, as Gault points out, "by way of social inheritance, the dulling effect of this and other diseases may be passed on to succeeding generations; for the dull head of a family, from whatever cause he may be dull, creates an atmosphere in his home in which his children live and grow . . . until fixed dispositions are built up in them."

It is quite probable that part of the greater altertness of children from better homes is to be explained on the basis of their greater energy and vitality with its attendant increase of the children's curiosity. We know, for example, that the onset of the menses in girls from poorer homes tends to be later than in those from better environments, and malnutrition is detrimental to scholarship; so anything which would lower the health reserve of a youngster should also begin to curb his curiosity.

It is consequently impetative for parents not only to remedy any visual and auditory defects of their children which can be corrected, but also to keep the youngsters in robust health, since the latter supplies the basis for intellectual activity. A listless child is likely to become an uninteresting and uninterested adult.

The Most Critical Stage in the Child's School Career

The first years of contact with the school system are the most important of all those spent in classrooms, for it is then that the youngster is likely to develop his liking for, or aversion to, education. After he grows older his experience with a teacher whom he dislikes is not so critical, for then he is more likely to realise that she is just the exception to the rule. At the ages of six or eight years, however, an antagonism for a certain teacher is often transferred to the whole educational system, after which the child loses interest and falls in scholarship. As his marks drop, his aversion to education tends to increase, and the youngster may dread coming to school.

Indeed, it is possible for a dyspeptic teacher of the early grades to alter the enthusiasm and delight of forty youngsters so that they become prejudiced against her and all that she stands for, namely, education. The fault in this kind of situation is not wholly the teacher's, for her ill health or increasing age may render her less patient and interested in youngsters, especially when they have not yet been fully "broken in" to the regulations of the classroom.

The advisability of having young teachers in the early grades is therefore apparent, for they are more inclined to have enough energy and patience to submit agreeably to the demands of a roomful of six-year-olds. It would probably be a good thing if teachers moved along toward the upper grades as they advanced in years. Instead of letting women 60 years of age deal beginners, it would probably be advantageous to both the youngsters and the teacher if she moved along toward the eighth grade, and let younger women take her place in the kindergarten. The average woman of 60 has not enough energy to keep up with the demands of 20 to 40 youngsters, so she is more inclined to resort to the ruler as a means of holding her young charges in check.

The more fatigued she becomes, the grater is her use of the stick, and therefore the less likely she will increase the children's fondness for school.

Because the young teacher is only a score of years removed from her own kindergarten age, and since she has the exuberance of health and vitality to cope with the demands of the early grades, she is much more likely to coax her youngsters into the desirable form of behaviour, and consequntly her influence is of lasting benefit. She is less inclined to be autocratic, and her recent graduation from normal college where she imbibed some of the idealism and social responsibilities entailed in teaching enables her to regard her youngsters as something more than just a monotonous method of earning her pay check. All too frequently old teachers lose sight of the ultimate goals of education, and they seldom grow tearful over their inability to deal successfully with a problem child. "Oh, you will get over that after you have been here as long as we have," they remark to the young teacher. Unfortunately, they are correct, which leads us to the opinion that young teachers should enter the educational system in the same manner as they first encountered it, namely, *via* the kindergarten and first grade.

The Nursery School and Its Future

Because of the diminishing size of the average American family, and the fact that apartment dwellers cannot let their youngsters run out to play as readily as used to be the case, there is a growing need for some means of enabling the only child to have social contacts with other youngsters of about his own age. In fact, at the present time many children of pre-kindergarten age seldom get outside except when with an adult.

In the previous chapter we explained the detrimental effect upon the child of a lack of siblings and playmates, yet many parents today seem little able to remedy matters owing to their limited financial resources. Except for his thirty minutes or so in Sunday school, their child is almost as closely confined to the apartment as the spinster's cat.

The nursery school offers an excellent partial remedy. By admitting tots who are old enough to walk, it socialises and extroverts these probably introverted children. In fact, it is frequently possible to pick out the nursery school child from others not so favoured simply by its greater cooperation in the play group. It seems not unreasonable to assume that a lowering of the entrance age for kindergarten would be a distinct advantage not only to children, but indirectly to the state itself through its tendency to lesson the divorce rate of these same youngsters. Since two-thirds of our population depart from under the tutelage of the school at the eighth grade, it behooves the state to prepare them for a happy adulthood, and the five idle years of the youngster prior to kindergarten offer a fertile field.

The church school might be impressed to offer such a service to the community, for there are churches in every village and city which stand more or less unused between Sundays. And there are many idle young women of good education and altruistic interests who would be rendering children and the state a great service by conducting daily nursery schools therein. Many city parents would be delighted to pay a nominal fee for an opportunity to place their youngsters in such a beneficial environment. As a method for the "ladies aid" and similar women's religious organisations to earn money for the church, nursery schools hold great promise. If necessary the women could alternate, or spend only half a day a week in the work, so it would not be burdensome to any and should, in fact, be almost as stimulating to these young matrons as to the tiny tots.

The future of the nursery school seems, therefore, to be very bright, although it appears that private organisations will be its chief sponsors, at least for several years to come. Eventually, however, the state may find it desirable to assume the instruction of children at a lower entrance age than the present five or six years.

The Qualifications of a Good Teacher

In discussing the factors which make a good teacher Dean Ashbaugh says, "The evidence of a great teacher is not that his students know the material he has taught but that they come from his courses with an insatiable desire to know more and more of his field."In order for this result to occur the teacher must usually possess enthusiasm. We have previously commented upon the salesman's need for enthusiasm if he wishes to be a success. After all, the teacher should also consider himself a salesman of education. Too many men and women, however, take the attitude that they are being paid their salaries simply to deliver a fifty minute lecture three times a week, and if the students do not get anything out of the address that is their bad luck. A good teacher, on the contrary, should be so interested in his own subject that, like the missionary, he cannot be content until he has converted his listeners.

In the second place, a good teacher should also possess intellectual perspective. He should be fairly well oriented in the field of education, so that he can relate the specific material within his own province to other fields, and his social intelligence should be such that he knows the current interests and humour of the group to which he speakes. Just because he is a member of *Phi Beta Kappa* and has held a fellowship for research is no positive indication that he is fitted for pedagogy. Indeed, it is this misconception concerning the cardinal purpose of teaching which explains in large part the students' ennui during lectures and the presence of Morpheus in so many classrooms. The fact that they wander "through courses in the Greek thought of the Fourth Century or the social institutions of Medieval Spain . . . somnolent and pathetic" cannot be gainsaid, for how can we expect a zestful interest on the part of youth in subjects which are often presented with a dyspeptic lack of enthusiasm by an instructor whose chief forensic virtue qualifies him for the degree Doctor of Somnolence?

Nor does it follow that because a professor spends years of research on the cultural significance of the castanet in medieval Spain and hopes to advance himself professionally through an article or two containing the results of his investigations, that his students will become enraptured listeners to the same subject. Since teaching is salesmanship, the instructor must remember the axioms of the salesman and strike at fundamental motive bases. As a public speaker, moreover, he should consider himself at fault if he cannot keep his students awake.

Aside from his enthusiasm and perspective, the teacher should bear in mind that his students also obtain ideas concerning politics and morality from him. They will go back to their respective communities and states with social attitudes coloured by their contacts with him. It is important for the instructor to remember that these same students may be sending their children to him a generation later if he has given them sound advice both as to his specific field and also as to morality, statesmanship, and religion. In the latter connection it should be evident that it does not become any young Ph. D. to ridicule the religious tenets of the 18-year-olds who sit in his classes and who lack the forensic training to defend themselves and their beliefs.

As regards the teacher's own scholastic and research back ground, Dr. Martin L. Reymert* has constructed with the cooperation of 42 psychologists a scale by which to evaluate such

Table 10.3

		points	
I.	Training		
	Ph. D.	4.9	
	Sc. D.	4.6	
	M. A.	1.8	
	M. S.	1.8	
	A. B.	.6	
	A. Degrees		4.9
	Professor	4.5	
	Associate Professor	3.1	
	Assistant Professor	1.8	
	Instructor	.8	
	Assistant	.3	
	B. Present Academic Position		4.5
	Fellowships	1.3	
	Scholarships	.3	
	Assistantships	.8	
	C. Appointments		2.4
	D. Amount and Quality of Labor-Atory Training		3.4
	E. Other Training is Psychology		2.6
	Other Science	1.9	
	Philosophy	.5	

*This survey is published in the Psychological Bulletin.

Mathematics	1.2		
Statistics	1.1		
F. Training in background subjects		4.7	
Attending University	.4		
Research	.9		
Travel	.3		
G. Training in vacation period	1.6		
Total		24.1	
II. Length of Experience in Years			
0 - 2	1.7		
3 - 4	2.9		
5 - 6	4.5		
7 - 9	5.9		
10 - 14	7.2		
15 - 19	7.0		
20 - 24	6.4		
25 - 29	5.6		
30 and over	5.1		
A. Years in psychology		7.2	
Under 5 years	.2		
Over 5 years	1.1		
B. No. of years in present position		1.3	
Total			8.5
III. Publications			
A. Books		8.6	
B. General articles (no experiment)		4.6	
C. Experimental studies		10.3	
D. Editorial Service		3.1	
E. Review and Abstract Service		2.5	
Total			29.1
IV. Recognized Contributions			
A. New Apparatus		3.9	
B. Improvement of Technique and Method		10.0	
C. Statistical devices (formulae)		4.9	
D. Contributions to Systematic Psychology		8.8	
Total			27.6
V. Membership Rank			
A. Associate		2.2	
B. Member		5.6	
C. Fellow		8.1	
D. Officer		10.7	
E. Promoter		7.5	
Total		10.7	

qualifications. Although it was intended primarily for rating psychologists, it may easily apply to teachers in other branches of knowledge. There are five general headings which are subdivided as in the preceding chart.

The training of teachers should also be such that their knowledge of statistics and grading methods is fairly uniform. Even at the present time there is considerable variation among teachers in the manner of scoring examination papers. Starch and Elliot, for example, took Question X from a final examination paper in geometry by a pupil in one of the largest high schools in Wisconsin. Plates of this answer paper were made and several hundred copies were printed upon foolscap, thus exactly reproducing the original in every detail.

A set of questions and a copy of the answer paper were sent to about 180 high schools in the North Central Association with the request that the principal teacher in mathematics grade this paper according to the practice and standards of the school. In the Figure 10.1 will be found the results. The teachers' marks varied from 39 to 88.

Figure 10.1

Passing grade 75. 75 schools Median 70. Probable 7.2.

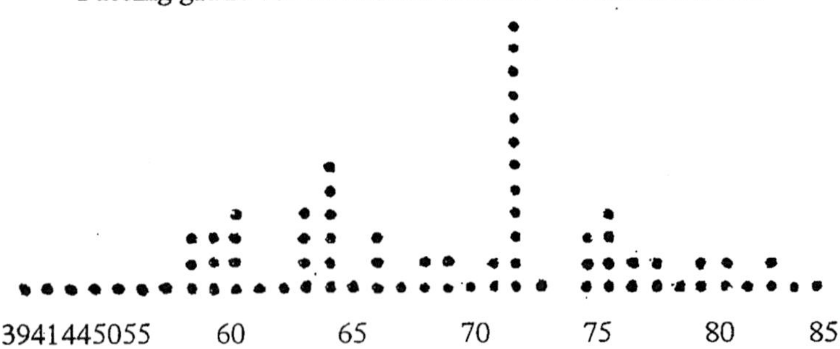

In the night schools of two large urban universities the following grade distribution shows a lack of uniformity somewhat comparable to that demonstrated in the grading of the mathematics paper mentioned above. The reader will note that a student in School B has a greater chance of making an "A" than in School A. It is this lack of uniformity among schools which has led the directors of admissions in American universities to place more reliance upon a high school graduate's relative position in his graduating class than upon his actual grades. The "Normal"

Table 10.4

	%A	%B	%C	%D	%E&F
School A	15	38	34	8	5
School B	21	46	23	7	3
"Normal"	5	20	50	20	5

has been included in the table 10.4 to show a distribution which would form what is called a normal distribution curve if plotted. The other two would form "skewed" curves, that is, there is an overloading of "A" and "B" grades for a five point scale, with a marked diminution in "D" and "E" percentages.

At this point it would be well to mention a few statistical terms. The *mean* or *average* is a measure of central tendency which is found by dividing the sum of all the individual scores by the number of cases. It is laborious to compute when there are a large number of cases, and when there are few cases it may give a distorted view of the data because of a few extreme scores. For example, let us assume that five persons contributed to a campaign fund the following amounts: $ 1,000,000, $100; $100; $100; and $100;. The mean contribution would, therefore, be $200, 080, which makes it appear that all the individuals gave large sums.

The *median* is the middle score in the series, and is not only easier to compute than the mean, but is not influenced by extreme cases. In the five contributions just mentioned the median is the third measure, or $100. In a normal distribution of scores based on a large number of cases the median, the mean, and the mode fall at the same place, which is the highest point on the distribution curve when plotted. In the event of an even number of cases, the median is the point above and below which 50 per cent of the scores fall.

The *mode* by common usage refers to the score or measure at which the most cases fall. In Exhibit 55 the mode is 75 while the median is 70.

The *inter-quartile range* is the spread of scores of the middle fifty per cent of the cases when the latter have been previously arranged in order from highest to lowest. Because it eliminates the highest and the lowest fourths of the group it is less influenced by extreme cases than is the total range.

The *average deviation* or *mean variation* is the average deviation from the mean or average score. The formula given below simply calls for the sum of the individual deviations from the mean score, divided by the number of cases. In this formulas

$$\text{A.D. (or M.V.)} = \frac{\Sigma d}{N}$$

Σ stands for the sum, while *d* represents the deviations from the mean, and N denotes the number of cases. An average deviation of 10 from a mean of 75 represents much less relative variability than an average deviation of 10 from a mean of 35.

The *standard deviation* is usually more useful and more frequently ençountered than the simpler average deviation, and is designated by σ as shown in the next formula, where the other symbols have already been defined above. If after the scores are

$$\sigma = \sqrt{\frac{\Sigma d^2}{N}}$$

arranged in ascending or descending order a distance equal to the standard deviation is laid off on each side of the mean score, then 68.26 per cènt of the scores or measures will be included in this range.

The *coefficient of correlation* is a statistical measure of the degree of similarity or dissimilarity existing between two series of scores from the same persons. There are several methods of obtaining it, but we shall illustrate only Spearman's rank-differences method. With any of the methods, however, the coefficient will range from + 1.00 to —1.00. If with a class of 40 children we compared their proficiency in spelling with their excellence in reading and found that the best speller was also the best reader, that the second best speller was also the second best reader, and so forth, the correlation would be +1.00. On the other hand, if the best speller was the poorest reader, the second best speller was the next poorest reader, and so on until the worst speller was the best reader, then we would have a perfect negative correlation which would result in a coefficient of —1.00. If some of the best spellers were the best readers, but some were also the poorest readers and so on, we would find a correlation in the neighborhood of 0.00, which denotes a chance and non-significant relationship.

In the rank-differences method the raw scores must first be changed into ranks, as will be evident from the following comparison between the Army Alpha scores and the final examination marks of 25 students selected from one of the writer's classes in applied psychology. In case of ties, the ranks involved are added, then divided by the number of identical scores. In Army Alpha, subjects "G. F." and "R. H." are tied for 6th place so we add 6 and 7, divide by 2, and award each a rank of 6.5. There will be no 6th or 7th ranks thereafter.

Table 10.5

Student	*Army Alpha*	*Exam.*	*Rank in Alpha*	*Rank in Exam.*	*Differe- Ence*	*Difference Squared*
J. A.	122	22	21	23	2	4
V. B.	133	89	18	6	12	144
N. B.	150	79	13	9	4	16
B. B.	156	67	11	15	4	16
E. B.	137	115	16	2	14	196
J. B.	194	91	1	4	3	9
J. C.	193	90	2	5	3	9
E. C.	143	118	15	1	14	196
L. C.	146	87	14	7	7	49
R. D.	127	45	20	19	1	1
E. F.	179	71	4	11.5	7.5	56.25
G. F.	164	68	6.5	14	7.5	56.25
F. G.	157	69	10	13	3	9
P. G.	109	19	25	25	0	0
C. G.	173	55	5	18	13	169
R. H.	164	66	6.5	16	9.5	90.25
W. H.	163	71	8	11.5	3.5	12.25
G. H.	135	56	17	17	0	0
J. K.	110	32	24	20	4	16
M. K.	162	84	9	8	1	1
J. L.	113	29	23	21	2	4
R. L.	129	21	19	24	5	25
R. M.	121	25	22	22	0	0
A. M.	180	93	3	3	0	0
L. S.	151	78	12	10	2	4
....						1083

The rank-differences formula is as follows:

$$Q = 1 - \frac{6\Sigma D^2}{N(N^2-1)}$$

in which Q stands for the coeffieient of correlation; D, the difference in rank in the two tests; and N, the number of paired measurements, which in this particular instance equals 25. After substitution, we find:

$$Q = \frac{6(1083)}{25(625-1)} = 1 - 0.416 = 0.584$$

The correlation is positive; therefore, it shows a definite tendency toward similarity in ranks between the two tests. Before we can rely fully on the correlation, however, it is wise to determine its probable error. Some mathematicians maintain that to be dependable the coefficient of correlation must be three times its probable error, while others say four times. By the formula below we are able to determine the probable error of Q.

$$\text{P. E.}q. = 0.706 \frac{1-Q^2}{\sqrt{N}} \doteq 0.706 \frac{1-(.584)^2}{\sqrt{25}} = 0.092$$

Our coefficient is accordingly six times its probable error, so we may state that the 25 college students showed a significant tendency to rank in examination grades according to their rank in Army Alpha.

In concluding our discussion of the various qualifications of a good teacher, therefore, we many repeat that they consist of an enthusiasm for the subject and its presentation to others, an intellectual perspective or orientation, the possession of social intelligence in order the better to understand the pupils, an adequate appreciation of moral values, and experience in the field of teaching, including as it does an elementary knowledge of statistical methods. The instructor who possesses these assets will find that pedagogy is intensely interesting, and will engender the gratitude of the alumni. In the following section we shall discuss one of the methods by which the teacher can improve his classroom effectiveness.

The case Method in Education

The case method in education is valuable, therefore, because it enables the student to apply some of the principles to which he has been listening and thereby find out if he has fully acquired a mastery of them. In medicine, law, and dentistry the case method has been used for generations, but other branches of learning have adopted it more slowly. In recent years economics has availed itself of the case book, and the project method is gaining favour in public school education. In abnormal and clinical psychology, too, the students encounter living cases. The writer has noted a difference in their interest even in psychology classes when personality cases of the following sort are a part of the weekly assignments.

PERSONALITY CASE No. 4

John Randall - aged 60; with the Blackburn Company 35 years fifteen of which he had been manager of a branch office; salary $ 75.00 a week; always on the job, even when so ill he could hardly stand; drank, smoked, and talked of his wilder youth but disapproved of his employees gambling, drinking, or running around nights - objected to letting his employees be promoted, saying, "I have a good office force together now and don't want it disturbed." Randall's immediate superior started with the Blackburn Company ten years after Randall did. Randall disliked him and said he got his promotion through lies and cheating. This superior placed Vernon Jenness in Randall's office. Jenness was a good worker, but drank a bit, and ran around nights. Jenness came up for promotions but Randall wouldn't let him go. Jenness had now spent five years in the office.

Jim Morton, department head in Randall's office but lacking initiative, often went to Jenness for advice. Randall once asked Jenness, "Doesn't he know anything? Do you have to do his work for him?"

Ed Wheaton, another employe, rather surly to customers and inefficient, continually pestered Morton with childish pranks, causing Morton to lose his temper on numerous occasions.

With the depression Randall laid off one of his employes. Was it Morton, Jenness, or Wheaton? Give full reasons for your judgment, assuming that all three had equal numbers of dependents.

From the psychological standpoint therefore the case method is valuable because it enables the student to apply his knowledge and find out what he does not know, thereby granting him the opportunity to concentrate further on the unknown. By working with actual cases the student is more vividly impressed with the practical value of his studies and his interest is accordingly heightened.

Education and Politics

The teacher should not attempt to inject bias and partisanship into his discussion of educational matters. He should, on the contrary, endeavour to encourage the scientific attitude regarding political questions, and minimise the employment of emotionalism in discussing international relations. Political impartiality is difficult to obtain, however, because so many politicians purposely stimulate the suprarenal glands of their hearers, and thereby incite them to emotional responses. Justice should be conceived of as emotionless, but even our law courts and juries are often led astray by propaganda, pretty complexions, and silk hosiery. Indeed, the peculiar nature of mankind makes individuals susceptible to appeals which short-circuit reason with emotion.

One of the functions of a good teacher, however, is the instruction of youth in the fallacies of reasoning until emotional appeals are so thoroughly understood that the commonly encountered ones are mentally tabulated by the student when ever he hears them. In so doing, he frees himself in part from their likelihood of inciting his own emotions, for a rational attitude is inimical to emotionalism, and renders its hearer partial immunity.

Public school teachers, therefore, by bringing before their students the commonly encountered emotional appeals, can condition the students to an intellectual process instead of an emotional one. The average adult not only never heard of *ad hominem* as a fallacy in reasoning, but he is not aware of the situation in real life to which that phrase belongs. After he has been taught the type of situation which warrants the *ad hominem* epithet, he is largely free of its dominace. This is the principle which is so commonly employed in psychoanalysis, namely, make the patient conscious of his previously unconscious slavery to a habit, and he thereafter becomes free. By using the case method and grading the student upon his recognition of emotional appeals, the teacher can build up in him a critical attitude whenever he encounters printed or oral speeches.

It is true that the average schoolboy and also the adult will be unable to ascertain the subtleties of much of the propaganda with which they are surrounded, but there is too much obvious emotionalism which could be nullified by the proper training of children. If a large fish by bumping into the glass partition separating him from minnows in an adjacent portion of the aquarium can be taught to ignore the minnows, even when the glass partition is removed and they are swimming around him, then it is not too much to hope for that intelligent human beings can be schooled to refrain from certain responses to which they now are addicted.

In fact, the writer has trained some teen age youths in the analysis of public speeches until they are quite adept in spotting the emotional appeals and fallacies of reasoning. When this habit becomes a part of the personality of the average citizen, then we can look for a more sensible and logical analysis of political problems by the politicians who stand before us, and political campaigns will be much freer of hatreds, "mud slinging", and emotional ranting.

From the teacher, therefore, must come the training in detecting fallacies and resisting emotional appeals. Until the educators of America point out these fallacies and stereotyped incentives to emotionalism, the graduates of our public schools should not be criticised severely for submitting thereto. Until an elementary course in logic and applied psychology is introduced into the public school system, two-thirds of the citizens will continue to graduate with little protection against the illogical reasoning of emotional demagogues.

The Teacher's Opportunity to Elevate Civilisation

Teachers should give their students not only a knowledge of spelling, arithmetic, reading, and geography, but also an appreciation of many virtues not specifically designated in the curriculum. Much of the child's spirit of fair play and honesty, his morality and confidence, his liking for education and music and art come from the teacher. These subjects are not designated when she is appointed to a definite classroom, but she finds them a part of her duties nevertheless, especially if she would be an excellent teacher.

The habits of brushing their teeth, of personal cleanliness, and of health are gained by many students almost wholly from their teachers. The latter even encourage the children to eat vegetables, and to retire at a certain hour each night. They also interpret literature and art and religion for their youngsters, and develop tenderness and kindliness in boys and girls who might be thoughtlessly cruel without such object lessons as are given to them. The teachers are chiefly responsible for the children's knowledge of American history and the relationships of this nation to foreign powers.

With ten years of contact with the children of America the public school teachers have almost unlimited opportunities for social, moral and intellecual improvement of the coming generations. Sometimes the entire future of a child is altered by the understanding sympathy of a good teacher. Foreign children are Americanised largely through the teacher's influence, and their home environments are often greatly improved because of her advice and interest.

The teachers in institutions of higher learning, of course, do not deal with more than 10 per cent of the youth of America, but these 10 per cent are destined to become the principal leaders in business, science, and the arts as well as in the civic and domestic affairs of their respective communities. It behooves the instructor who wishes to be most effective to remember the fundamental purpose for which he is teaching. Latin should not be taught for the sake of Latin, but for the sake of the student, and the same is true of all other branches of learning. Too often this mistake in emphasis reduces the effectiveness of the teacher as well as of his subject-matter. Pedagogy must never be looked upon as a parroting of information, but rather as an interpretation and evaluation of the mental heritage of mankind in the interest of more satisfactory adjustments of the student to his environment.

References

Anastasi, A., & Foley, J. P., Jr., *Differential Psychology* (Macmillan, 1949).

Ashbaugh, E. J., "Qualifications of Good Teachers" (*School and Society*, 30, 1929).

Bartley, S. H., *Beginning Experimental Psychology* (McGraw-Hill, 1950).

Bentley, J. E., *General Psychology* (Lippincott, 1947).

Boring, E. G., *History of Experimental Psychology* (Appleton, 1950).

Brandt, H. F., *The Psychology of Seeing* (Philosophical, 1945).

Brayfield, A. H., *Modern Methods of Counselling* (Appleton, 1950).

Brouwer, P. J., *Student Personnel Services in General Education* (Amer Council Educ., 1949).

Brown, W., & Cilhousen, H. C., *College Psychology* (Prentice-Hall, 1950).

Burgess, T. O., *Workbook in General Psychology* (Concordia, 1942).

Buros, O. K., *Third Mental Measurements Year Book* (Rutgers U. Press, 1949).

Carroll, H. A., *Mental Hygiene* (Prentice-Hall, 1947).

Cronbach, L. J., *Essentials of Psychological Testing* (Harper, 1949).

Crow, L. D., & Crow, A., *Educational Psychology* (American, 1950).

Cutler, T. H., *et al. Analysis of Teaching Load* (U. of Denver, 1949).

Dennis, W., *Readings, in General Psychology* (Rentice-Hall, 1949).

Dockery, F. C., & Lane, G. G., *Psychology* (Prentice-Hall, 1950).

Edwards, A. L., *Experimental Design in Psychological Research* (Rinehgart, 1950).

Ewing, J. H., *Understanding Yourself and Society* (Macmillan, 1946).

Feder, D. D., "An Evaluation of Some Problems in the Prediction of Achievement at the College Level" (*J. Educ. Psychol.*, 26, 1935).

Garret, H. E., *Psychology* (American Book, 1950).

Garrison, K. C., *Psychology of Exceptional Children* (Ronald, 1950).

Gates, A. I., *Educational Psychology* (Macmillan, 1948).

Gault, R. H., *Social Psychology* (Holt, 1932).

Goddard, H. H., *Feeblemindedness, Its Causes and Consequences* (Macmillan, 1926).

Goddard, H. H., *How to Rear Children in the Atomic Age* (Hopkins, 1948).

Goodenough, F. L., *Mental Testing* (Rinehart, 1949).

Guilford, J. P., *Fundamental Sialistics* (McGraw-Hill, 1950).

Guilford, J. P., *et al. Fields of Psychology* (Van Nostrand, 1950).

Hahn, M. E., & Maclean, M. S., *General Clinical Counselling* (McGraw-Hill, 1950).

Hearn, C.A., *What About Smoking* (Irwin, 1949).

Hess, L. W., Parents and Vocational Guidance (Ft. Wayne, 1950).

Hollingworth, Garrison, & Burke, "Subsequent History of E; -Five Years After the Inital Report" (J. Appl. Psychol., 6, 1922).

Hollingworth H. L., *Mental Growth and Decline* (Appleton, 1927).

Hopkins, P., *Gone Up in Smoke* (Highland Press, 1948).

Jeffreys, R. J., *God is My Landlord* (Van Kampen, 1947).

Jersild, A. T., *Child Psychology* (Prentice-Hall, 1947).
Katz, D. (Tr. by R. Tyson) *Gestalt Psychology* (Ronald, 1950).
Krathwohl, W. X., "Effects of Industrious and Indolent Work Habits on Grade Prediction in College Mathematics" (*J. Educ. Res.*, 43, 1949).
Krout, M. H., *Introduction to Social Psychology* (Harper, 1942).
Lauritsen, Marne, "And the Deaf Shall Speak" (*J. Expr.*, 2, 1928).
Lindesmith, A. R., & Strauss, A. L., *Social Psychology* (Dryden, 1949).
May, R., *The Meaning of Anxiety* (Ronald, 1950).
McNemar, Q., *Psychological Statistics* (Wiley, 1949).
Miller, J. G., *Experiments in Social Progress* (McGraw-Hill, 1950).
Olson, W. C., *Child Development* (Heath, 1949).
Ross, C. C., *Measurement in Today's School* (Prentice-Hall, 1947).
Sadler, W. S., *A Doctor Talks to Teen-Agers* (Mosby, 1948).
Schonell, F. J., *Psychology and Teaching of Reading* (Clark, 1945).
Segel, D., *Intellectual Abilities in the Adolescent Period* (Fed. Secur. Agency Bulletin No. 6, 1948).
Smith, G., *Psychological Studies in Twin Differences* (Gleerup, Sweden, 1949).
Soden, W. H., *Rehabilitation of the Handicapped* (Ronald, 1949).
Sorenson, H., *Psychology in Education* (McGraw-Hill, 1949).
Starch, D., & Elliot, E. C., "Reliability of Grading Work in Mathematics" (*School Review*, 21, 1913).
Stechle, L. C., *Problems of Human Adjustment* (Harper, 1949).
Stone, C. P., *Case Histories in Abnormal Psychology* (Stanford U. Press 1949).
Symonds, P. M., *Dynamic Psychology* (Appleton, 1949).
Terman, L. M., *The Measurement of Intelligence* (Houghton, 1916).
Thorndike, E. L., "Mental Discipline in High School Subjects" (*J. Educ. Psychol.* 15, 1924.
Tuttle, H. S., *Dynamic Psychology and Conduct* (Harper, 1949).
Tyler, L. E., *Psychology of Human Differences* (Appleton, 1947).
Wallin, J. E. W., *Children With Mental and Physical Handicaps* (Prentice-Hall, 1949).
Weitzman, E., & McNamara, W. J., *Constructive Classroom Examinations* (Sci. Res. Assoc., 1949).
Winn, R. B., *Encyclopaedia of Child Guidance* (Philosophical, 1943).
Woodruff, A. D., *The Psychology of Teaching* (Longman's, 1948).

11

PSYCHIATRY AND MENTAL HYGIENE

The importance of psychiatry and mental hygiene is seldom realised by the average person. At the present time there are more than 300,000 inmates of institutions for the insane, the feeble-minded, and epileptic, not counting the large number of such cases privately cared for in their own homes. Moss states that from one-third to one-sixth of every state's expenditures is consumed in the support of mental hospitals, while Dr. William J. Mayo is quoted as stating that mental ailments are the cause of more human misery than tuberculosis and cancer. The report from the Surgeon General's office relative to the second examination of the first million recruits drafted in 1917 indicated that 12 per cent of these were rejected on account of nervous or mental diseases. At the present time it is estimated that there are more hospital beds occupied by diseases and disorders of the central nervous system than by all other diseases combined.

Since the majority of these disorders could have been prevented by the timely application of knowledge, the great need for spreading the principles of mental hygiene becomes apparent. When parents and teachers are educated to recognise in their children the elements making for nervousness and to adopt the proper methods of training the neurotic liabilities of the children, they will be able to prevent a large percentage of future breakdowns.

In considering mental diseases from the historic viewpoint we find that abnormalities in behaviour were originally ascribed to demons. The insane were simply those persons afflicted with devils. This attitude regarding mental abnormality greatly retarded the advancement of its scientific study, so it has remained for the modern age to point out the organic bases for many types of anomalous mental functioning. Indeed, of the two groups of mental disorders now recognised, namely, the *organic* and the *functional*, the influence of the former seems to be advancing at the expense of the latter. With continued increase in scientific knowledge regarding infections of the brain and its membranes, the toxins in the body, and the functional interrelationship of the glands of internal secretion, it appears that several more of the present functional types of insanity may be shown to have an organic basis.

For example, before it was learned that paresis was caused from invasion of the brain tissues by the micro-organisms of syphilis, it was often ascribed to such social maladjustments as worry, emotional shock, and erotic frustration. In several instances, moreover, the diseased conditions underlying mental abnormalities are known, even though the specific causes for such pathological states are yet to be discovered.

Even when organic defects may be cited as the cause of many mental abnormalities, however, the psychiatrist today realises that the behaviour reactions of two persons having apparently identical organic defects, may be quite different. There are marked individual variations not only to drugs, but also to diseases. A moron, for instance, may be an honest, law-abiding citizen or he may be a chronic offender. His subnormal intelligence cannot be cited therefore as the sole basis of his atypical behaviour when we find him breaking the law. In a similar fashion, organic defects probably function along with social maladjustments to produce abnormality. Lacking a strain upon their adaptive capacity many persons are regarded as entirely normal, and lead useful lives until in times of stress, such as of war, death of loved ones, or sexual maladjustment, they "go to pieces", and may even require institutional treatment. These psychically unstable persons are more numerous in the population than are the feeble-minded.

Subconscious Learning and Maladjustment

Not only may habits like the pupillary reflex be conditioned to external stimuli, and operate entirely beyond the person's knowledge, but many other experiences of the individual may either have occurred in the margin of his attention-field, or else have been ostensibly forgotten, yet still continue to influence his adult behaviour.

The reader may already have observed this type of phenomenon in his neighbours or even himself, for almost every one has fears and compulsions which are difficult to explain but which are nevertheless potent determinants of behaviour. Bagby, for instance, cites the case of a man who was constantly fearful of being seized from behind. He always occupied a seat in the rear row, and even preferred sitting with his back to the wall. In his own home he was likewise nervous and fearful unless his chair was against a solid object, such as a partition or wall.

This peculiarity was so pronounced that the man's neighbours and acquaintances considered him queer as a consequence, and he himself was at a loss to explain what made him afraid. Even though he knew that there was nothing to fear, he could not escape this obsession. When he was middle-aged, he happened to return to the village of his birth and there met the old grocer past whose store he had always gone en route to school. The grocer laughingly reminded him of how he had always taken peanuts from a barrel in front of the store, and how the grocer finally hid in preparation for him. When the boy next reached for peanuts the grocer yelled and seized him from behind. The boy fainted from fright. Here was the origin of the strange fear which later dominated his adulthood. Lacking a knowledge of where it came from, the grown man was unable to escape its baneful influence.

The writer noticed that his older boy at the age of twenty-six months would go into a spasm and scream in terror when ever a stranger touched him or spoke to him. No verbal reassurance from his parents appeared to have the slightest influence upon the boy, nor did he seem to be wholly aware of his surroundings after he once launched upon his screaming. The writer was at a loss to comprehend what caused the attack. Spanking and reprimands had not the slightest effect, yet the emotional shock of the muscle spasm was too great to permit its continuance. Thereafter, of course, attempts were made to condition the child favourably to strangers, although he had never previously shown any fear of them.

For a period of nearly a month, however, the favourable conditioning was not sufficient to offset the boy's entering upon one of his attacks of screaming. By means of the favourable conditioning, however, the child was eventually led to a normal reaction to strangers. The writer then remembered that the boy had gone to the grocery with his mother about a month earlier, and had followed another woman out of the store. After walking for a block he suddenly realised that he was with a stranger, and lost from his mother. He began screaming in terror and sat down upon the sidewalk where he mechanically beat upon the cement with the doll which he had been carrying, although the stranger had attempted to lead him back. His mother found him a few minutes later still so terrified that he hardly recognised her, and with the doll's head crushed to bits. She finally quieted him, and thought no more about the incident, but it had apparently left a marked effect upon the child, for several weeks later the touch or speech of a stranger was sufficient to re-induce the terror response.

This case has been cited to show how indelibly a childhood experience may affect a youngster's nervous system, and how it might continue into adulthood if it were not treated early. The previous instance of the child and the peanut barrel shows the permanence of such influences when uncorrected. There are literally thousands of particular objects or situations that engender fears even in adulthood. Some people are terrified at the thought of being alone in a large open space (Agoraphobia), while others will not ride in subway trains and elevators or go into closed places, at least unless the windows are open (Claustrophobia). Some are afflicted with a fear of contagion and are incessantly washing their hands, while others are afraid of running water, and cannot endure the sound from a faucet which is turned on. Some are terrified by darkness while others feel frightened by crowds. A further cataloguing of such phobias and their explanations will be found in the references appended to this chapter.

Since Watson's research indicates that the only two ways by which fear can be demonstrated in the infant are by loss of support or falling and by loud noises, it is evident that the fear of the dark or of any other situation or object is acquired by an individual because of his contact with his environment. When the child is too young to recognise how he has acquired these fears, it becomes essential that his parents or teachers uncondition him so that he will not continue until adulthood a victim of injurious emotional habits.

When a young couple at Madison came home to their three-year-old son one evening they found that he was afraid of the wardrobe closet in the front hall. They later learned that the maid had told him about spook in this closet which would get him if he was not a good boy. The parents immediately played hide-and-seek with the child, the father hiding first in the living room, then in the hall with the light on, then in the closet with the light on, then in the closet with the light turned off. Soon the child wanted to hide and let his parents search for him. It was not long until the boy also hid in the closet. His fear had been overcome by a greater amount of pleasure which attached to the closet in consequence of the game.

In the conditioning of children it must be remembered that the greater of two rival influences will likely mask or cover the lesser. If the unpleasant is stronger than the good in its emotional effect, then it will make him dislike the good with which it is associated and conversely. In the above example the pleasure engendered by the game of hide-and-seek which he was playing with his parents, and his delight in discovering his Daddy in the closet, overcame the fear of the closet. If his parents had allowed the child to continue in his fear, he would have developed a habit of fright in connection with the cleset, which would later have been much more difficult to eradicate.

With adults it is usually sufficient simply to point out the original situation in which the fear reaction occurred, and they can free themselves from its dominance thereafter. In some cases their lifetime slavery to a fear may be destroyed in a few days. Until they can be shown how they obtained their fears, however, it is difficult for them to become free.

Freud's View of Repression and the Censor

Freud and the psychoanalysts look upon the mind as a stage upon which ideas are the actors. Some of the latter which violate our sense of justice, virtue, and modesty may be forbidden the right to perform upon the stage. The Censor who does this forbidding is the ego, which pushes the unpleasant ideas out of consciousness and submerges them in the realm of the unconscious. In explaining this process Freud speaks as follows:

> Suppose that here in this hall and in this audience . . . there is an individual who is creating a disturbance, and by his ill-bred laughing. Talking, by scraping his feet, distracts my attention from my task. I explain that I cannot go on with my lecture under these conditions, and thereupon several strong men among you get up and after a short struggle, eject the disturber of the peace from the hall. He is now "repressed" and I can continue my lecture. But in order that the disturbance may not be repeated, in case the man who has just been thrown out attempts to force his way back into the room, the gentlemen who have executed my suggestion take their chairs to the door and establish themselves there as a "resistance" to keep up the repression. Now if you transfer both locations to the psyche, calling this "consciousness" and the outside the "unconscious" you have a tolerably good illustration of the process of repression.

The quotation is typical of the attitude of the Freudians and confuses the student greatly, for the entire concept of repression intimates a repressor as a distinct entity or force which bodily "pushes" or "submerges" the so-called repressed idea. The analogy is fraught with connotations of special changes and muscular effort involved in the repressing. As a matter of fact, the entire idea of repression should be dispensed with. We do not "push" ideas out of our minds, but simply pursue trains of thought which keep away from the unpleasant ideas as the rat does not push the cat from his field of vision, but follows a course which will avoid his feline enemy.

Whenever a neural impulse leaves a sensory cell and enters the cortex, it seems to involve both an activation of specific conditioned reflex pathways as well as a partial arousal of many neural paths which function in associated habit. The course which it takes is the one of least resistance. If the person in question is hostile to ideas pertaining to sex and friendly to those having to do with virtue, this mental "set" facilitates an association process in the realm of honour and virtue because such associated habits are more active than the opposing ones.

During sleep, of course, the individual is less likely to try to facilitate one trains of thought in preference to another, so the neural impulse still follows the line of least resistance. Which now probably lies along the neural network of a fundamental motive base. Freud's view that during slumber the Censor no longer represses submerged ideas is a confusing analogy. If he must resort to analogies, however, it would be more in accordance with our present knowledge of neural action if he said simply that the "facilitator" was no longer operating. In the following section we shall discuss further the course of neural currents during sleep.

The Significance of Dreams

Dreams in olden times were looked upon as having prophetic value, as the reader will recall from the story of Joseph who rose from a prison cell to become ruler of Egypt because of his skill in interpreting the symbolism of Pharaoh's double dream. At the beginning of this century dreams had fallen into disrepute in the scientific world, although many rural families had a dictionary of dreams on the shelf and consulted it each morning to learn the significance of money, travel, death in the family, marriages, and other events about which they had dreamed the previous night.

With the development of psychoanalysis, dreams have been restored to a position of some scientific value, and are one of the chief data employed by the psychoanalyst. The origin of dreams is the same as the origin of any thought process, namely, the stimulation of some sense organ with the resulting entrance into the cortex of a nervous impulse. The dreamer's feet may be projecting from beneath the covers on a cold winter night, in which case the cold receptors are activated, and neural currents begin to bombard the cortex. The sleeper may in consequence dream that he is with Commander Byrd on a new polar expedition, or that he is wading through the snow barefooted.

Visceral discomfort resulting from indigestion, the sunlight upon his face, the sound of an alarm clock, and a host of other stimuli may cause the thought process to arise in the sleeper's cortex. The peculiar linkage of ideas which constitutes the dream will be a result of the previous habits of the slumberer, of his instincts and internal chemical environment, as well as of the external stimuli affecting him at the moment. If he has been without food for several meals, the internal chemical condition of his body will facilitate a train of thought pertaining to food. If he went to sleep thirsty, then his dream will probably have to do with cool springs of water. If his sexual appetite is whetted but unsatisfied, he will likely dream of the opposite sex. If he is obsessed by some constant fear, as of ill health or detection for having committed a crime, or if he has been puzzling over a problem of some sort, then these topics will probably be the center of his dream. If his feet are cold, or mosquitoes are biting him, he may construct dreams built around the stimuli of cold or pain.

Frued believes that dreams become expressions of unfulfilled wishes. They may commence in any one of the sense organs, but the free association chain of ideas ultimately leads to the subject of most interest to the sleeper. Freud admits that hunger is the chief motive force in life, but hunger does not present great difficulties to the average man and woman. They normally retire with no unsatisfied craving for food, so they consequently are not likely to dream of tempting viands. On the other hand, they may often go to bed at night with their sexual natures sensitised by romantic fiction and moving picture plays to which they have been exposed within a few hours before retiring, or by social contact with members of the opposite sex. This psychological sensitisation to ideas concerning sex may be further reinforced by the sleepers' physiological condition. If it is spring, or if for any other reason they possess an abundance of sexual energy, they are ready in mind and body for dreams of a sexual nature.

It will be obvious that this type of dream would occur more frequently in the unmarried than in the married. The latter no longer find sex of so much curiosity value, not are they likely to have the abundance of undissipated sexual energy. Since they are older and with interests centered more on their work, or the home and their children, the latter subjects are very likely to appear in their dreams. As a consequence, Freud's extreme emphasis upon the sexual basis for dreams may be valid for youths from fifteen to twenty-fivc ycars of age, and for mismated and sexually unsatisfied adults, but these two groups probably form a minority of human beings.

That dreams are generally with-fulfilling is probably true, for even little ones are prone to dream of the things which they desire. Very young children, moreover, do not always make a distinction between their dreams during sleep and their waking thoughts. When four-year-old Paul, had learned that he might become the owner of a kitten, he came downstairs the following morning and said, "Mother, there was a kitty in my room." His mother expressed surprise, for she realised that the doors had been locked and the windows were screened. "Yes it was," her son maintained. "It jumped up on my bed and said, "Hello, Paul," and then it jumped down and went out the door and that was all."

Before we conclude this section it would be well to state that many dreams are full of symbolism. If the sleeper has been reared in a moral environment where he has been taught not to think about sexual matters, and if in the dream world he dwells upon them nevertheless, he may attempt to avoid an emotional conflict by representing the sexual situation in a disguised form. There is nothing unusual is this performance, for it is converntional to avoid painful things, as in the representation of death by use of such euphemisms as: "He passed away"; "He went west"; "He crossed the great divide"; "He went to his rest". Freud has presented a long list of the conventional symbols which denote the two sexes, and cites numerous dreams to illustrate them. The writer, howerver, will offer two from his own files which are so evident in their symbolism as to warrant no explanation.

NUMBER ONE

Mary (eighteen and a stenographer): I dreamed about you last night.
Her Young Employer: That's interesting. What did you dream?
Mary : Oh, we were quarreling.

H. Y. E. : Quarreling? What about?
Mary: It was about a letter which I had just received. You wanted to open it and I wouldn't let you.
H. Y. E.: Well, how did we settle it?
Mary : Oh, I finally gave it to you and you opened it.

NUMBER TWO

A college girl dreamed that she and her male escort were riding in the rumble seat of an automobile with another couple inside the car and driving. In a park along the lake the car upset. Only she and her escort rolled out and down into a wooded ravine. She then discovered that she had a hole in her head and was trying to shake her escort into sensibility, but he seemed to remain unconscious of her attempts to awaken him.

In concluding our discussion of dreams, therefore, we may repeat that they are always initiated by some sensory process, but after they are started they tend to develop around the subject of greatest interest to the dreamer, whether it be appetitive, vocational recreational, or fearful. The dreams may be symbolic, and their parts may be illogical and impossible as viewed in the light of the next day. Persons long since deceased are present with the living and enjoying life with no intimation that they had ever departed from this world. This unreality of the dream is not evident to the dreamer, however, until after he wakens, for during sleep portions of his cortex are relatively inactive, thereby rendering inoperative many ideas which would inhibit the fantastic elements of the dream.

Emotional Conflicts

The reason why human beings are not coldly analytical persons reacting with the mechanical detachment of automatons is owing to their possession of an autonomic nervous system which innervates the visceral regions, producing thereby the emotional states of fear, love, rage, and the like. Human life accordingly does not proceed with mathematical monotony, but is made both pleasantly changing and often unpleasantly inefficient by means of emotional squalls.

In almost every phase of human affairs emotion creeps in, and complicates matters by producing conflicts. The mother, for example, finds that her child soon reaches the age where it is ready to transfer its interest to a sweetheart. In fact, at the time of its marriage both parents usually feel somewhat jealous of the newcomer who has been able to dominate the affection of their offspring. The average mother and father accept the situation, however, as one of the inevitable, and attempt to make a harmonious adjustment. Too many of them, though, inject bitterness and hatred into the situation, thereby definitely widening the breach to a point where it may never be remedied. Children are cut off in their parents' wills, or they are upbraided or else completely ignored simply because they wished to marry who they chose.

The reader is probably familiar with the innumerable emotional conflicts of human beings, so we shall forego a tabulation of them, and confine ourselves to a discussion of the Psychological Diagnostic Chart in Figure 11.1, which is a modification of Menninger's adjustment diagram. The "Personality" encounters a "Situation" such as the winning of a sweetheart, and goes through a period of attempted adjustment, ending possibly in success and marriage. On the other hand, if failure results, the Personality is still maladjusted, as represented by the circle and rectangle in juxtaposition. The Personality may be able to effect a successful compromise so that the emotional tension is reduced through sublimation, as in the case of the disappointed girl who goes into a convent, or becomes a settlement worker or missionary.

Again, the Situation may be too powerful for the Personality, in which case the Personality may crack. For instance, one of the writer's former students who had been a boyhood sweetheart and classmate of a girl who lived a few houses down the street, learned the week before their graduation from high school that she had betrothed herself to another senior and was to be married shortly. The disappointed youth fled the situation immediately after commencement by entraining for California where he remained so alcoholised for three months that he did not know when the date arrived for the marriage. The reverse of this response may take place where the disappointed person breaks the Situation by murdering his rival or even his sweetheart.

In the case of the student just cited, however, he did not remain permanently in the Broken Personality category, but

Figure 11.1
A diagnostic chart showing the various types of adjustments possible when emotional conflicts are encountered

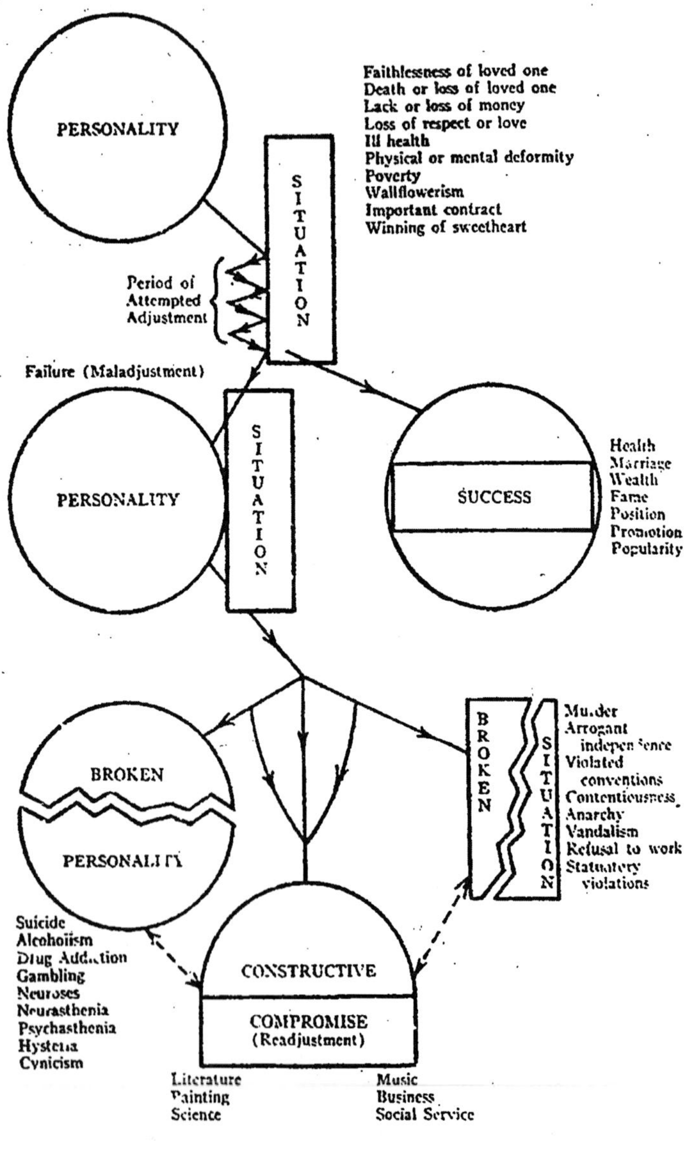

effected a Constructive Compromise, aided materially, of course, by the exuberance of youth. The reader's attention is called to the dashed lines running between the Constructive Compromise and both of the broken figures. The double arrows indicate that a Broken Personality, barring suicide, can often be salvaged and attain the Constructive Compromise category. On the other hand, an individual who has effected a Constructive Compromise may find that a change in his internal or external environments may cause him to slip into the Broken Personality or the Broken Sitation categories. A young man who flees his native town because of disappointment in love may settle down to constructive work in a neighbouring metropolis and be apparently readjusted until he encounters his former sweetheart on the street and learns that she and her husband have also moved to the same city.

The cases of Steinmetz and Stevenson are probably indicative of compensations and constructive compromises regarding childhood situations of physical deformity and ill health. Possibly the prevalence of slender pipe smokers among authors and newspaper reporters is similar in explanation. Napoleon, Byron, Kant, Demosthenes, and perhaps even Lincoln represent cases of constructive compromises to unfavourable physical and social elements in their childhood. Bernarr Macfadden, the sick little boy, and Theodore Roosevelt, Sr., demonstrate the category of successful adjustment to similar childhood frailty. In their cases they overcame the ill health itself, whereas in some of the former instances, notably Stevenson's, the health factor was unchanged but the individuals became powerful in other realms.

In concluding our discussion of emotional conflicts, therefore, we may state that they are a constant factor in human relationships. The child is jealous of his father's dominace of the mother, and to a greater or less extent the converse is true. The daughter likewise wants all of her father's affection and the mother may be somewhat jealous. When younger siblings arrive, new compromises must be made if wholesome personalities are to develop. As we shall point out in a later section, the secret of emotional stability and a wholesome personality lies in making a satisfactory adjustment to each situation as it arises. This response must not be the permanent or temporary assumption of oblivion through suicide, alcohol, or narcotics, nor the atypical behaviour of the radical or an archist, but a compromise which adequately dissipates the emotional tension through constructive activity. An intelligent person can steer his course of behaviour accordingly, and assist in the creation of stable personalities in his children by realising that emotional crises can be adjusted by intelligent action, not by sitting still.

The Normal vs. the Abnormal

There is no sharp line of demarcation between the normal and the abnormal. They both have probably the same traits but with a slightly different degree of synthesis thereof. The normal person possesses a social perspective and rapport which enables him to react with only a nominal amount of friction and emotional conflict, whereas the abnormal has lost much of his social perspective through organic or functional brain defects. Sometimes a paranoiac may discuss a subject quite intelligently so that at the moment the listener is unaware of his abnormal mental condition, but the conversation will soon veer around until he strikes his obsession, when it becomes apparent that he is not normal. The case of the guide at the asylum who took the visitors through the institution and explained the types of abnormality evident in the inmates is an example. When the guide came to the last inmate he said, "That poor fellow has a delusion of grandeur. He thinks he's Napoleon. But he isn't for I'm Napoleon."

The abnormal is usually considered as the individual who once was normal but has deviated therefrom, while the subnormal is looked upon as an individual who never fell heir to an Intelligence Quotient of 100. In fact the subnormal is now regarded as being the feeble-minded, with a maximum I.Q. of about 75. The abnormal may also have a low J. Q. because of the destruction of brain tissue, as in paresis, but he probably possessed a higher I. Q. at a former time. Feeble-minded persons, however, can become insane and abnormal. A destruction of brain tissue in a moron may render him insane and leave him an intelligence level of the idiot or imbecile.

One of the commonest methods determining abnormality is to find whether or not the patient can support himself in society, providing of course that he is not too aged for work. If he can maintain his economic existence without conflict with law and the policeman, he is usually deemed within the category of normality, despite his possible eccentricities and queerness. If, however, he persistently comes into conflict with his superiors or believes himself persecuted or is so deluded as to be a menace to society, then he becomes a fit subject for an institution. We shall quote cases 4 and 22 from the Presseys* to show instances of normality and abnormality, and to illustrate a common method of history taking.

CASE NO. 4

Name: Marion R. *Age:* 34. *Sex:* Female. *Race:* White. *Birthplace:* Massachusetts. Married, 3 children. *Sources of Information:* "patient," father, aunt, family doctor, husband.

1. History of the Family.
   - *A. Medical* - Mother's father and two uncles on mother's side chronic alcoholics, and several times in state hospital for the insane. Uncle on father's side a dementia praecox case, was brilliant but eccentric; an inventor whose inventions paid him enough to support him and his wife for the rest of their lives. Another uncle very eccentric. One cousin feeble-minded. Mother died at patient's birth. Father died of a shock.
   - *B. Social* - Harmonious family. Strict discipline.
   - *C. Educational* - Father and the two brothers all have college education.
   - *D. Economic* - Father was high school principal, one brother lawyer, the other a doctor.

II. History of the individual.
   - *A. Medical* - Sick from infancy with poor digestion. Had very mild attack of infantile paralysis when two years old. Suffered also probably from rickets. Had insomnia; subject to nightmares when able to get to sleep. Has had attacks of a somewhat undefined character when she had to be held down on the bed and fed forcibly. Was too sick to attend school regularly.

---

* Pressey, S. L., and L. C., *Mental Abnormality and Deficiency* (The Macmillan company, New York, 1926), pp. 102-103; 178-179. Reprinted by permission of and by arrangement with the publishers.

B. *Social* - Stole all sorts of small objects. Was almost never caught. Always played with boys. Began having sex experience at 7 years and continued until adolescence. Lied in preference to telling the truth, just to "fool people." Had terrific outbursts of temper in which she would break anything she could get her hands on. Was noisy, boisterous, and destructive. Once set fire to a barn. Was expelled from school for stealing.

C. *Educational* - Went through college although never very well. Graduated with honours.

D. *Economic* - Became successful professional woman. Has married and has three healthy children.

III. **History of the Present Crisis - None.**

IV. **Present Condition.**

A. *Physical.*

General Condition - In good condition, vigorous, but still has weak digestion.

Special Defects - None.

B. *Appearance and Behavior* — Somewhat overactive. Has several pronounced tics. Talks rapidly and a great deal. Gestures frequent and vivid.

C. *Intellectual Condition.*

General Level - Very high. Learns with great speed and retains remarkably. Once learned a three page poem in two readings and could repeat it eight years later.

Special Functional Disorders - Nothing.

D. *Emotional Condition.*

General Emotional Tone - Somewhat excitable and irritable; no marked pecularities.

Special Emotional Trends - Nothing.

Emotional Conflicts - Nothing.

V. **Summary and conclusion.**

A. *Summary* - A family containing many unusually capable and also many very eccentric individuals. Bad start physically in childhood. Many childhood delinquencies, possibly due to physical condition. Superior ability.

B. *Conclusion* - Normal woman, with considerable early physical handicap, probably due primarily to childhood diseases.

CASE NO. 22

Name: Charles M. *Age:* 60. *Sex:* Male Born in rural Indiana. Widower. *Sources of information:* the man himself, son, neighbors.

I. **History of the Family.**
   A. Medical - Normal.
   B. Social - Normal.
   C. Educational - Illiterate.
   D. Economic - Were modestly successful farmers.

II. **History of the individual.**
   A. Medical - Normal.
   B. Social - Has always been extremely religious. Is a Catholic. Has covered the walls of his house with "holy" portraits, crucifixes, etc. Had an altar built in his living-room. When he was about forty, he conceived the idea that he would be a great man, if he could only get to some city where he would be appreciated. He rented his farm, left his wife and boy with relatives and went to Chicago, feeling that he was fulfilling a "call". Five years later he returned, convinced that everyone in the city was plotting against him. He believes that the time will come when everyone will realise his greatness. For about the last ten years, has occasionally, after much praying and fasting, heard a voice calling him to become a follower of Christ. Since his wife's death, about five years ago, he has given his farm to his son and has moved into a near-by city to retire into a holy life. He spends most of his time in the Cathedral at prayers. He says that he has the power to communicate with any dead person, claims that he sits on the right hand of God and that the angels will do his bidding. Says he can hear angels sings and that he can see Christ on the cross. Spends most of his day in prayer and devotion.
   C. Educational - Had a grammar school education.
   D. Economic - Owned a large farm and became moderately wealthy. Before he retired he bought the house he now lives in, and is living on his income.

III. History of the Present Crisis - None.

IV. Present Condition.
   A. Physical.
   General Condition - He shows some signs of senility, white hair, tottering gait, and partial deafness, Is rather stooped and thin from constant fasting. Bears scars of self-inflicted torture.
   Special Defects - Partial deafness.
   B. Appearance and Behavior - Spends most of the time praying. Walks about with arms folded across his chest in the sign of the cross. Talks considerably, but always on religious matters. Has a pompous air and important manner. Talks as if he were giving commands. Is stiff and domineering.
   C. Intellectual Condition.
   General Level - Probably about average.
   Special Functional Disorders - Judgment - completely

dominated by religious ideas and delusions. Attention - excellent where anything religious is concerned, but impossible to distract from this channel. Memory - unimpaired. Association - normal. Intake - occasional experiences of an apparently hallucinatory nature.

D. *Emotional Condition.*

General Tone - Over - emotional and sentimental.

Special Emotional Trends - Dominated by religious fervour. Fanatic.

Emotional Conflicts - None determined.

V. **Summary and Conclusions.**

A. *Summary* - Approaching old age; underweight, gradual development (through "paranoid) of religious fanaticism. Now complete domination by religios ideas; religious delusions. Questionable hallucinations. Deports himself in a pompous manner that he thinks is fitting for one of his high position

B. *Diagnosis* - Paranoia.

In general, therefore, abnormality refers to a reduced abstract intelligence or a lowered social intelligence as a result of organic or functional disease. The abnormal person finds it difficult to make the social adjustments demonstrated by the majority of the population. In paranoia, however, the patient may show little if any reduction in abstract intelligence, although his delusions soon reveal his warped social perspective, as we shall discuss in a later section. In the following paragraphs we shall describe the methods by which the normal person avoids emotional conflicts.

Normal Ways Out of Emotional Conflicts

The normal person during the numerous emotional conflicts which he experiences endeavours to protect himself against defiation of his vanity or ego. We have previously mentioned the widespread tendency to think well of ourselves, and our constant efforts to avoid social pain, involving as it usually does a wounding of our vanity through some humiliating and therefore ego-deflating episode. The reader may note this basic tendency to guard the ego in the normal emotional outlets which we shall describe below.

(1) *Reveries* — When an individual finds himself in a difficult and unpleasant situation from which he cannot readily extricate

himself, he very often flees from his dilemma *via* his thoughts. He daydreams of the "good old days" when he was young and handsome, or affluent and popular, or a famous football hero or actor. He treasures his newspaper clippings and press notices to give tangible assistance to his reverie. He delights in recounting his war experiences, in part because then he wore a uniform which climinated many social distinctions between himself and his more sophisticated "buddies", and enabled him to gain attentions which he never could receive when dressed in civilian attire.

Ideas of heaven and a future reward for virtuous living sustain many persons who are having an unfortunate time of the present life. Indeed, reverie is an excellent means of maintaining morale providing it is used judiciously. The poor boy who dreams of the day when he will be a millionaire and return home to make life easier for his mother finds that his incentive is kept fresh before him by use of the imagination, and he is stimulated to renewed endeavour. However there are cases in which individual obtains so much pleasure out of the act of dreaming that he fails to work diligently in order to attain his goal.

As a general rule the more intelligent the person, the more capable he is of maintaining his morale by use of the imagination. The dullard finds it more difficult to deal in the rich ideas and complex memories which permit escape from present monotony and pain, so he flees the situation by alcohol and drugs or by the adoption of a nomadic life.

(2) *Inactivity* - In many emotional situations a person cannot make up his mind what to do, so he decides to wait for chance to settle the question for him, and thereafter remains passive. This attitude is well illustrated in Macbeth's conflict between his sense of loyalty to the kind and his desire for the throne, as shown in his worlds:

> "If chance will have me kind, why, chance may crown me
> Without my stir."

When this reaction occurs it becomes especially pernicious if the individual has a tendency to refrain from mingling with other persons. And since many unsolved problems have to do with people, it frequently happens that the passive individual remains aloof and dwells upon his own troubles. The etiology of functional insanity shows that such behaviour frequently precedes the onset of the disease. As a general procedure in mental hygiene, therefore, it is well to keep trying to make some sort of adjustment.

(3) *Flight* - A common characteristic of frustration in love is the desire of the jilted and disappointed suitor to get away from the region in which his sorrow occurred. He wishes to flee to the city, or travel afar. New scenes and experiences will help keep his mind occupied and also keep him away from people who are aware of his ego-deflation. Many workers, moreover, look to California, Chicago, or some other distant point as a place where they feel sure they can succeed. When they reach California, for example, they may then try to browbeat the natives and bolster their own self-esteem by taking the attitude that California is not what it is advertised to be, and that, conversely, the East or the Middle West is far superior. Failing in California, they return home with a rationalised explanation, and thereafter bemoan their fate in not being back in California, meanwhile minimising the good points of their home state and city.

(4) *Sour Grapes* - This category of responses is often resorted to in an effort to bolster one's hurt pride. When defeated or jilted, one is very likely to go through a psychological process in which one minimizes the talents and desirability of the previously sought object. "Oh, well, I would rather be popular with the crowd than win a *Phi Beta kappa key*," says one. In this procedure the individual attempts to render the stimulus inoperative upon himself so that he can thereafter meet it without so much suffering and social pain. In psychoanalysis, for example, it is necessary at the conclusion of the treatment to break the patient's attachment to the analyst. The patient ultimately finds himself dreaming the analyst is a repulsive individual when theretofore this dreams had always been most flattering to the latter.

(5) *Dissociation* - In this case the person refuses to acknowledge the incompatability of conflicting methods of response, and become a Dr. Jekyll and Mr. Hyde personality. He acts as if he had logic-tight compartments in which he segregates opposing habit systems. He may be the saint on Sunday and the

sinner on week days, or he may be gracious in company and a selfish brute inside his own domicile.

(6) *Compensation* - This is one of the most common emotional outlets, and takes various forms. As a rule, the compensator is an extremist. The physical weakling, for example, may become overly intellectual or develop into a health faddist. In fact, many fo the world's strong men have begun life as sickly children. Bernarr Macfadden is an excellent instance in point. Another illustration of compensation is the case of a certain newspaper editor, hunchbacked and weighing about 95 pounds, who is a reckless automobile driver. He made a parachute leap from an airplane which was passing over the center of the city and tried to alight on the top of a certain building on the main street. At another time when he learned that an automobile had swerved into a stone quarry in midwinter, and had sunk, he sprang into his automobile although attired only in his bath robe, drove out to the deserted quarry, and dived time and again into the icy water in an effort to locate the sunken automobile. He also spends far more money than he can afford on liquor, which he always indulges in, and is an inveterate pipe smoker. Although this editor is a Harvard graduate, he is so intent on trying to prove to the world that he is a regular "he-man", that he has lost perspective in his compensation.

Compensation is unfortunately often engaged in without the person's consciousness of his action, and is therefore frequently a detriment. If it is knowingly entered upon, and if the form which it takes is such that a creditable type of behaviour develops, then compensation is a desirable emotional outlet. The chief danger, therefore, comes when the person selects a form of compensation which is detrimental to his own best interests, or when he fails despite his utmost efforts. In the one event he creates antagonism, and in the other he falls into despair.

(7) *Projection* - A curious characteristic of human beings from infancy onward is their tendency to blame the environment for their errors, thereby avoiding deflation fo their self-esteem. The child bumps his shin against a chair and immediately blames the chair, often giving it a vicious retaliatory kick. In an automobile accident it is almost always the other fellow's fault.

The husband blames his wife because he cannot find his tie or collar, and the wife blames the husband and children because she cannot keep her home neat. There is occasionally a certain amount of truth in the accusation, at least enough to draw the critic's attention to the particular flaw which he thereupon magnifies.

A good instance of projection is demonstrated by the reaction of a slightly inebriated passenger whom the writer recently steered onto the right train, in which they later occupied the same seat. The drunken man was rather soiled in clothing. With trousers and coat which did not match, with patches on the knees of his trousers, and with a white shirt which was not very clean. He realised his unkempt condition and volubly explained that he had just come in from Detroit the night before, and was headed for Wilmette where he would be able to don other clothes. He apologized for his appearance for a period of ten minutes or so, while the writer meanwhile attempted to read. Receiving no attention, the drunken fellow finally surveyed the writer critically, then said: "Say, you look more near the end of your rope than I do! Gee, man, you look bad!" After this single resentful bit of projection, he lapsed into a different mood during which he said he would always be sympathetic whenever he met a fellow in the future who was drunk or down and out.

(8) *Identification* - This device explains our pleasure in fiction and movies, where we identify ourselves with the hero or heroine. Parents do the same regarding their children. Indeed, a person identifies himself to a greater or less extent with his possessions. A good example of identification is mentioned by Frink who tells of a young woman who came to him complaining of insomnia and a depression which had lasted for two years. During her second visit she mentioned that she had dreamed the previous night of Evelyn Nesbit Thaw. When asked what she thought of Mrs. Thaw, she began a vigorous and passionate defense of her. Because her emotion concerning Mrs. Thaw, whom she had never seen, was so excessive, Dr. Frink concluded that his patient must be identifying herself with that well known character, and inasmuch as her defense had pertained entirely to the question of sexual temptations to which Mrs. Thaw had been said to have

succumbed, he decided that his patient must have yielded to some temptations of that nature. This proved to be true. Her defense of Mrs. Thaw, therefore, was simply a defense of herself.

(9) *Rationalisation* - This is one of the most frequently employed methods of eliminating an emotional conflict. The person acts impulsively; then manufactures what appear to be very logical reasons why he has done so. His reasons are more often excuses, a distinction which it is well for every applied psychologist to recognise. A student confronted by a few hours of difficult study grows very sleepy, so he decides he really ought to get some sleep, arguing that one cannot profit very much from studying while in half a doze. Then the telephone rings, and he is invited to a party or to the theatre. Now he decides that it was not sleep which he needed so much as recreation, and falls back upon the adage that "all work and no play makes Jack a dull boy." His conscience does not trouble him, thanks to the adage, but the reader can readily see the fallacy in his reasoning.

As Robinson ably points out, thousands of argumentative works have been produced in order to vent a grudge, and despite the stateliness of the reasoning, it may be chiefly rationalisation. "A history of philosophy and theology could be written in terms of grouches, wounded pride, and aversions, and it would be far more instructive than the usual treatment of these themes." John Dewey has already reached the conclusion that philosophy is mainly rationalisation; Veblen and others have revealed a similar condition concerning many of the presuppositions of traditional political economy, and the Italian sociologist, Pareto, believes that the social sciences rest upon a bedrock of rationalised customs and beliefs which are the heritage of the middle ages.

(10) *Substitute responses* - In our description of the Psychological Diagnostic Chart (Figure 11.1) we showed the many possible responses to an emotional situation. *Sublimation* is one form, which on the chart was represented by the constructive compromise. A poet translates his sex cravings into beautiful verse, and his confrere in the field of music writes melodies. The artist paints portraits, and the average person labours in the industrial or commercial world. The sexual energy created by social contacts among young people also often finds a

legitimate outlet through dancing, hiking, picnics, swimming and the like.

As long as the emotional outlets lead into constructive compromises, the person is normal. When, however, they lead into the broken personality or the broken situation category, the person is approaching the abnormal type. Mental hygiene, therefore, consists of training the individual to sublimate, or substitute a legitimate and beneficial response for one which is injurious to his personality. In the following section we shall study the mentally unhealthful and abnormal responses to emotional difficulties.

Abnormal Ways Out of Emotional Conflicts

In discussing the atypical reactions of individuals to emotional conflicts we shall employ a two-fold category as follows:

(1) *Insanity* — There are various sub-divisions of insanity within the organic and functional types, and common characteristics are the presence of hallucinations, delusions, and a deterioration of intelligence. With the possible exception of paranoia the mental disorders show an impairment of memory and a lack of orientation on the part of the patient. On intelligence tests the scores tend to decrease when the patient is examined from time to time. Insane patients are frequently victims of hallucinations in which they hear voices advising or threatening them. They will carry on conversations with imaginary figures and often go to extreme lengths to free themselves from their visionary enemies, in many cases slaying friends and relatives who have been mistaken for evil spirits.

As for the delusions of the insane, they are false beliefs tenaciously held in the face of obvious evidence to the contrary. The patient is apparently impervious to logic or evidence, looking out upon the world with preconceptions which are unalterable. Of the commonly encountered delusions we shall briefly describe the following general classifications:

(a) *Delusions of Melancholia* — In this type of delusion the patient is usually characterised by an abnormal inhibition of mental and bodily activity, being relatively passive and unresistant. He monotonously repeats his delusion and makes no attempt to remedy his unfortunate condition. In this category falls the belief that one has committed the unforgivable sin. The patient may not be able to designate what this is, but he knows that he has committed it. Again, he may possess a delusion of negation in which he believes that his leg is missing or that he has no stomach, and the fact that his leg is not severed does not disturb his belief to the contrary. Furthermore, he may think that his arm is made of glass and caution attendants to take care lest they shatter it.

(b) *Delusions of Grandeur* —When afflicted with this type of delusion the patient identifies himself with some famous personage of the present or the past. He imagines that he is the King of England or the President of the United States. Again, his fancy runs to literature and he becomes Shakespeare or Goethe. The patients may often endeavour to dress the parts which they play. A General Grant constantly smoked cigars and discussed the campaigns around Richmond with the detail and familiarity, which would have surprised the original Grant himself. Patients may call themselves Mohammed or God, and seem undisturbed by the fact that their assumed omnipotence is oddly at variance with their present confinement in the institution.

(c) *Delusions of Persecution* — Unlike the patient who has a delusion of melancholia and admits that he has committed the unforgivable sin the patient who believes himself persecuted usually strikes back by actively declaring his innocence and frequently attacking his enemies. Here is a workman, for example, who lost his position because of his incompetence. To defend himself to his wife he demonstrated the common defense reaction of projection, and blamed his employer for having it in for him. His wife does not censure her husband, therefore, but vents her indignation upon the "boss". The husband gains sympathy and encouragement instead of reprimand. From subsequent positions he also is discharged, so he repeats his accusation and elaborates his story by telling that his former employers have blacklisted him, and are reporting against him to all the factory employment offices in the city. Later he begins to note hostile reactions from groups of citizens gathered on the street corners and overhears whispering which he knows is directed against him. Ultimately he may even link his wife and family with his foes, and when he comes to the asylum he fears to taste his food lest his enemies have slipped poison into it.

Delusions of persecution have a tendency to remain permanently and to grow worse with the passage of time. They are also the most dangerous from the point of view of the general public, for they are nearly always the basis of murders committed by the insane.

(2) *Subconscious Malingering* — There are many people who are afflicted with ailments which are apparently so critical as to thwart their remaining at work, yet which are entirely figments of the imagination. They are not conscious malingerers for they are not deliberately feigning illness. The whole process of developing the illness has occurred in the margin of the patient's attention-field so he is not consciously aware of what has happened even though the ailment relieves him from some very painful situation.

Shell shock was usually a physical illness which resulted when no other method seemed capable of preventing the emotional impasse resulting from the fear of battle and the fear of fleeing from it. In the "cannot fight cannot run" dilemma an imaginary ailment invalided the soldier to a base hospital where he seldom recovered until after the armistice. Many soldiers developed blindness, often in just one eye, which then happened to be the "sighting" eye for their rifles. Physical deafness and paralysis also were frequently resultants of shell shock.

It is not so difficult to realise how shell shock develops when one considers what happens when an individual is struck by an automobile. Let us suppose that he gets up immediately, brushes off his clothing, and goes on his way. When he gets home and his family or neighbours hear of the accident, they tell him he should have sued the motorist. How does he know, they argue, that he is not injured internally? They are sure to tell fo some case within their knowledge in which the effects of internal bruises and hemorrhages did not appear until months later. The accident victim begins to analyse his sensations, and also realises that if he fails to sue within a certain period of time, he will have difficulty convincing the jury that he actually suffered his injury from the automobile accident. He decides that he does feel a bit sore and pained in the visceral region, especially as the bruises of his muscles are more evident the following day.

"I told you so," his neighbours exclaim with emphatic nods, and he begins to feel worse. Two or three days later if he is not walking on crutches he may be bedridden, where he remains until the case is satisfactorily settled or else carried to the Supreme Court. It has been a common characteristic of railroad and automobile accident victims that the patient makes a remarkable improvement after his case is settled unequivocally. Even if he obtains no redress, he usually regains better health after he finds there is no further possibility of a financial settlement.

In subconscious malingering, therefore, it is evident that various "faith" cures are effective. A mental or functional ailment is often susceptible to mental treatment. And since specialists in internal medicine have stated that 60 to 70 per cent of all patients coming to them are simply mental cases, it is easy to understand why certain religious sects can cite thousands of records of faith cures.

We may conclude our discussion of the abnormal ways out of emotional conflicts by stating that they fall into two general classes, the inanities, and subconscious malingering. The latter classification is less dangerous inasmuch as patients therein can more frequently be restored to normal life by psychiatric treatment. Except for the strictly organic insanities, moreover, the application of the laws of mental hygience early in the career of the patient is of great prophylactic value, often thwarting the tendency toward an abnormal way out of emotional conflicts.

Stuttering and Stammering

Stuttering pertains to the repetition of a syllable in an endeavour to enunciate, as in "M-m-may I have some more cake?" and usually appears at the beginning of a sentence or clause, after which the stutterer proceeds fairly fluently to the end of the thought. In stammering, the speaker stops in the middle of a thought, as in "May I have . . . Some cake?" The two speech defects may appear in the same individual.

The etiology of the two varieties of defect is usually the same, although stuttering occasionally arises from a malformed denture, a tongue which is unwieldy, or incorrect habits of articulation. Stuttering may also be acquired by children through imitation of some confirmed stutterer in the home or the neighbourhood. In this case it may pass away when the child moves to a different milieu. Again, the child may be laughed at by his schoolmates and rendered so self-conscious concerning his imitative stuttering that the habit fastens itself upon him permanently. Brain injury may also be a factor explaining both kinds of disorder.

But the majority of cases of stuttering and stammering are a result of fear, and are therefore functional defects subject to correction. Shell shock may give rise to these speech abnormalities, but most of the functional instances of stuttering and stammering go back to instances of actual or threatened social humiliation and punishment. The child who masturbates, or who is in terror of a brutal parent, or who is introvertive and ill at ease among other people, or who has been ridiculed in a social situation like the classroom when he has attempted to speak — these youngsters often develop speech defects of the kind just mentioned. They usually suffer from a social inferiority complex.

Stuttering and stammering, therefore, result because the muscles of the larynx have been conditioned to abnormal reactions when their owner finds himself in a situation comparable to the one in which he developed his fear. Why the laryngeal muscles react atypically instead of the biceps is because they are the principle "social" muscles of the body and hence are likely to be affected by painful social conditioning. Because they are reacting overtly or implicitly all day long in the speech and thought of their owner and because they are therefore the chief functioning muscles in the situation where the fear originally arises, they become tied up with the fear reaction.

To show more clearly how this tie-up takes place, let us consider a somewhat similar situation in which the writer burned his tongue on some scalding hot coffee and spilled part of the contents of the cup because of the quick retractive jerk of his wrist. Thereafter whenever he brought a cup of coffee within three or four inches of his mouth his hand would immediately begin trembling to such an extent that some of the coffee was spilled. This reaction demonstrates a subconsciously acquired habit where the muscles functioning at the moment the pain was received became conditioned to trembling in the "sipping" situation. Had the writer not directed his conscious attention to this peculiar reaction, he might have become a slave to it, but by realising its origin and by deliberately going through the motions of raising a cup to his lips, he freed himself from it.

In the case of the stutterer and stammerer the laryngeal muscles have likewise become conditioned to "trembling" in the social situation of speaking, and their owners are victims of these subconsciously acquired muscle spasms. Their cures consist of their becoming cognisant of the origin of their trouble and of becoming the masters instead of the slaves of their laryngeal muscles.

Common characteristics of functional stuttering and stammering are an ability to converse normally with dogs and other infrahuman creatures, as well as the capacity to sing or read without trouble. The stutterer and stammerer can also pitch their voices higher or lower than normally and then speak without difficulty. A curious case which came to the writer's attention was that of an Englishman, a graduate of Oxford. His stuttering was so painful that he refused to talk over the telephone. But when his French sweetheart called him, he would converse with her in French with facility of the native Parisian. In short, he stuttered in his native tongue but was a fluent speaker in a foreign language.

The cure for stuttering and stammering consists of a realisation of the cause of the speech defect, plus a deliberate attempt to regain the mastery of the laryngeal muscles. In the public schools we often send the stutterers and stammerers to a special teacher, who encourages them to relax in all their musculature. Army cots may be at hand on which the children stretch out. Then they may be given a book from which to read aloud. In a modulated voice the teacher asks questions. As soon as the child's laryngeal muscles begin to tighten she again urges the youngster to relax. After half an hour or so the child is sent back to his own classroom with the injunction that whenever the regular room teacher calls upon him to recite he must first think of his relaxed condition in the speech room and try to regain the same kinesthetic sensations.

The advantages attaching to this advice are obvious. First, the child's tendency to focus his thought upon the speech room instantly renders him oblivious of his classmates and the social situation in which he stands. The chief stimulus for his laryngeal spasm is therefore inoperative. The attempt to regain the same muscle sensations which he felt while stretched upon the army cot also draws his attention away from his present audience. His resulting calmness is similar to that of the public-speaker who begins his address in a state of nervous tension and knee-trembling, but becomes poised as soon as he forgets his audience in his concentration upon the thoughts which he wishes to present. As soon as a stutterer or stammerer has demonstrated his ability to speak fluently in a group his inferiority complex is dissipated. The Oxford graduate just mentioned was completely cured of his stuttering inside of a fortnight.

In concluding our discussion of stuttering and stammering, therefore, we may repeat that the great majority of such cases are functional, and therefore can be cured, sometimes in a few weeks. The patient must be shown the psychological causes for his defect, and be given a means of forgetting his audience until his facile speech restores his confidence in himself. Until he understands the true nature of his defect he may go through life like the man who possessed the peculiar fear of being seized from behind, always a slave to a subconsciously acquired habit. Introverts and socially fearful youngsters are more likely to become addicted to these speech disorders than are extroverts.

Hypnosis and Its Significance

Hypnosis is characterised by a dissociation of the personality in which the normally adequate sensory stimuli operate only at the command of the hypnotist. Persons can seldom be hypnotised against their will, and they normally awaken from their trance in a few minutes even though the hypnotist forgets to rouse them. In case it is late at night and they are fatigued, they may sleep on throughout the night, if the hypnotist does not waken them, their temporary trance simply merging into normal slumber.

The hypnotic sleep is very similar to that of a young mother who goes to bed at night with the welfare of her baby upper-most in her mind. She remains constantly attuned to any whimper of the infant even though she may be oblivious to many other stimuli of a louder nature. She may even sleep through the ringing of the alarm clock. In a similar manner, the hypnotic patient must enter the trance with the idea in mind that he will be attentive to the hypnotist. During the trance which ensues he is alert to the commands of the hypnotist but does not heed other stimuli. He will perform the commands of the hypnotist but show no sign of hearing the shouted words of others who may order him about.

At the command of the hypnotist he may forget upon waking everything which occurred during the trance, but when re-hypnotised he regains functional control of the memories concerning his actions in the previous hypnotic state. By means of post hypnotic suggestions, the subject may perform duties the following day which the hypnotist ordered during his previous trance, yet be unable to account for his behaviour. He does not realise or remember that the hypnotist ordered him to carry out the idea now in mind, but he feels a compulsion to do so. The act, however, must not be at great variance with his normal behaviour. Even under hypnosis, moreover, the patient will not break his established habit systems. Unless he is a gangster, he will not attempt murder even at the command of the hypnotist.

Münsterberg employed post hypnotic suggestion in tapering off the dope friend's doses on successive days, and also cured chronic seasickness in this manner, Indeed, wherever functional disorders are encountered, hypnosis may be of aid, particularly in plumbing forgotten memories. Persons who are suffering from amnesia and cannot remember even their own names are often able to tell this information to the hypnotist.

Inasmuch as hypnosis is characterised by high degree of suggestibility on the part of the patient in respect to stimuli emanating from the hypnotist, and because the patient is freed from distracting stimuli, he is capable of focussing a greater degree of attention upon the problem before him. He may perform feats of strength which he cannot duplicate when in the normal waking state. We have previously contrasted the strength of handgrip of patients in the waking state with their strength when under hypnosis. In a similar manner he may concentrate his attention upon past events and resurrect memories which are too faint or too greatly inhibited by conflicting ideas to be available in the waking state.

In concluding our discussion of hypnosis, it is well to repeat that the patient's dissociation from extraneous sensory stimulation with its resulting increase in his utilisable attention, renders him able to bring forth memories and submerged fears which he has consciously forgotten. He accepts stimuli from the hypnotist uncritically, morever, and frankly recounts information which normally he could not or would not divulge. Feeling tones regarding certain objects may be implanted by the hypnotist and ideas for future action may be offered to the patient which in the later waking state he reacts to or carries out without knowing why he feels the compulsion to do so. His dissociation under hypnosis, moreover, may be so great that he fails to react to pain and can undergo a surgical operation without an additional anaesthetic. However, the principal use of hypnosis lies in the field of the psychoanalyst.

Psychoanalysis

The chief functions of psychoanalysis consist of an attempt to bring to the subject's conscious at tension the previous experiences which bear upon his emotional conflict, and then effect a constructive and conscious compromise through re-education and sublimation. We have already described several instances of childhood fears which fettered the adult life of the persons in question. The man who was always in dread of being seized from behind, the functional stutterer and stammerer, the patient addicted to phobias and compulsions are cases for the psychoanalyst.

In his endeavour to learn the disturbing causes for adult maladjustment the psychoanalyst tries to tap the experience of adolescence and the ostensibly forgotten wishes of childhood. In order to procure the information, which he desires he resorts to the following producers:

(1) *Free association of ideas* — When he comes to the office of the psychoanalyst the patient reclines upon a couch and begins thinking aloud. He talks in rambling fashion passing from one idea to another according to the laws of association. Despite the fact that he may be paying the psychoanalyst a high fee for discovering the etiology of the patient's emotional conflict, the latter usually avoids the very data which is most significant. His train of association will reach an impasse. This "blocking" as it is called is indicative of the fact that the patient is approaching the group of ideas which form his "complex" — a term employed to designate the related ideas and memories clustering around a central emotional situation often taboo. After hours and weeks of such rambling conversation the patient may finally exclaim, "I cannot think of another idea." Then the analyst will probably retort, "But you have not even begun to tell me about your trouble." The patient's speech has thus far been a camouflage to hide from the analyst as well as from himself the real cause of his conflict.

In explaining more clearly the significance of the conversational impasses or "blocking", we should recall that the normal individual who has a grave but unsolved problem relating to business or social life finds that he cannot refrain from thinking about it for any lengthy period of time. Wives know when their husbands are perturbed because of their repeated return to the same topic of conversation. In the realm of emotional conflicts the patients also tend to return to the complex which disturbs them, but they stop short at the threshold.

The psychoanalyst may stimulate them with a new word by asking, "What does "storm' make you think of ?" The patient pursues his train of thought until he will go no farther, at which point the analyst gives him a new starting word. Frequently these trains of thought leads, like the spokes from the tire of a wheel, into a central hub which is the complex. The patient may block out the thresholds of his complex by means of the ideas which ended each fresh thought sally. The skilful analyst soon guesses what is troubling his patient.

(2) *Controlled word association* — In this method the analyst asks his patient to reply with the first thought or word which

comes to mind as the analyst presents a series of verbal stimuli. The Pressey X-O test is also an attempt to plumb the emotional reactions of individuals by having them cross out from a list of words designating objects over which they have worried or which they dislike. By following the crossed out words, the analyst can make a fairly accurate guess concerning the complex or complexes of his patient.

(3) *The Interpretation of dreams* — The patient keeps a little notebook at the head of his bed and is instructed to write down every dream as soon as he awakens, whether it be in the middle of the night or in the morning. Psychoanalysts believe that chance neural currents soon lead to the complex and the tabooed thoughts. If these do not appear directly in the resulting dream, then they appear in symbolic guise.